The 9th Engineer Battalion,
First Marine Division,
in Vietnam

The 9th Engineer Battalion, First Marine Division, in Vietnam

35 Personal Accounts

by Jean Shellenbarger

McFarland & Company, Inc., Publishers
Jefferson, North Carolina, and London

The present work is a reprint of the illustrated casebound edition of The 9th Engineer Battalion, First Marine Division, in Vietnam: 35 Personal Accounts, *first published in 2000 by McFarland.*

Library of Congress Cataloguing-in-Publication Data

Shellenbarger, Jean, 1953–
The 9th Engineer Battalion, First Marine Division, in Vietnam :
35 personal accounts / by Jean Shellenbarger.
p.   cm.
Includes bibliographical references and index.

ISBN-13: 978-0-7864-3110-6
softcover : 50# alkaline paper ∞

1. Vietnamese Conflict, 1961–1975 — Personal narratives, American.
2. Vietnamese Conflict, 1961–1975 — Regimental histories — United States.   3. United States. Marine Corps. Marine Division, 1st Engineer Battalion, 9th — History.   I. Title: Ninth Engineer Battalion, First Marine Division, in Vietnam.   II. Title.
DS559.5.S48   2007   959.704'3'092 — dc21   99-55654

British Library cataloguing data are available

©2000 Jean Shellenbarger. All rights reserved

No part of this book may be reproduced or transmitted in any form or by any means, electronic or mechanical, including photocopying or recording, or by any information storage and retrieval system, without permission in writing from the publisher.

Front cover: (top) Helo Ops, in support of 5th Marines,
Operation Union II, April 1967 (courtesy of Jim O'Kelley);
(bottom) Christmas Day, 1968 — Joe Harran (left), Marty Brown.
and Thomas Costello (courtesy of Marty Brown).
Back cover: Route 1 repairs north of Tam Ky (courtesy of Jim O'Kelley)

Manufactured in the United States of America

*McFarland & Company, Inc., Publishers
Box 611, Jefferson, North Carolina 28640
www.mcfarlandpub.com*

This book is dedicated

to Bob Sperling for giving me the chance of a lifetime and for being my friend. I finished it without you, Bob, but I wish you were here to see it.

to Jim O'Kelley for taking up where Bob left off.

to my children, Jennifer and Joseph, for their patience, understanding and belief in this book during the countless hours it has taken me.

to authors Otto Lehrack, Catherine Hart and especially Jim Rayle for their encouragement along the way.

to Valerie, Becky, Eileen, Teresa, Cathy, Amy and especially Pat, who all shared my passion and enthusiasm, listened patiently when I was bursting with good news and enjoyed the journey with me.

to Jan, Bev, Jay, Dorothy and my Friday night friends, whose experience, strength and hope, love and friendship made it possible for me to fulfill my promise to these men.

to Tap, the man of my dreams and the answer to my prayers.

and most of all, to all the men and women who served their country in Vietnam, and especially the over 58,000 whose names cover the Wall. You are not forgotten.

TABLE OF CONTENTS

Introduction	1
List of Contributors	3
History of the Battalion	5
Formation of the Battalion	7
Why They Joined	9
Basic Training	13
Going Over	19
1966 May–July	27
1966 August–September	37
1966 October–December	45
1967 January–April	61
1967 May–August	75
1967 September–December	83
1968 January–April	91
1968 May–August	107
1968 September–December	119
1969 January–June	133
1969 July–December	143
1970 January–June	155
Homecomings	161
Yesterday and Today	171
Highway One to Heaven	185
Contributor Biographies	191
Appendix A: "Today I Went to Hear Dr. Graham"	215
Appendix B: Familygram	217
Appendix C: The Longest Bridge	219
Glossary	223
Bibliography	227
Index	229

INTRODUCTION

Early in 1993, a polite, soft-spoken mathematics teacher and former drill instructor came out of the closet about being a Vietnam veteran. Bob Sperling had come across a reunion notice in *Leatherneck* magazine for his old outfit, the 1st Marine Division, 9th Engineer Battalion. After many years of refusing to face his past, Bob jumped in with both feet and contacted Eric Kenney, who was in charge of the reunion. Bob found out that he and Eric had served together in Service Company, and he began to assist Eric in tracking down other 9th Engineers.

At some time over the next months, Bob and Eric discussed the fact that none of the numerous books written on Vietnam dealt with the engineer battalions. No one had ever told their story. In December of 1993, Bob walked into the bookstore I had at that time and introduced himself. We had met briefly at several meetings of a local Vietnam veterans group, of which I was an associate member. Bob assumed that I was interested in the Vietnam war and that because I had a bookstore I must want to write a book some day. His assumption in this case was correct.

We talked for over four hours that first of many visits, and he did a great job of capturing my interest in what the engineer battalions were responsible for in Vietnam. I learned that they were responsible for building the roads and bridges, installing and replacing culverts and clearing the roads of mines every morning, along with countless other jobs. In other words, they had a job to do in the middle of a war zone. Bob also told me about the first reunion that was being planned for the following August.

Before he left that day, Bob asked me if I would be interested in putting together this book. He had prepared the ground and planted the seed of this project, and I found I could not resist. To be able to talk at length with Vietnam veterans from around the country and put together a book at the same time was a dream come true.

Bob and I decided that the best oral history available for our reference was the book *No Shining Armor* by Otto Lehrack. We decided to follow the same procedure Lehrack used and send out letters to all the former engineers who had already been located for the reunion. I wanted to make it as easy as possible for the men to contribute to this project, so they were given different options. They could write, record a cassette, call and have me record our conversation, or be interviewed at the reunion.

By spring of the following year, I had sent out over 250 letters asking the men if they wished to contribute to this project. In my letter I told the men that it didn't matter how much or how little they contributed, whether it was one sentence or ten pages. Everyone who contacted me or sent me information is in this book. Some of their words were edited to eliminate repetitious stories, complete broken thoughts, or help the reader understand where the interview had led.

Any words or phrases in [ ] are mine. Some of these words represent editorial changes, and if they misinterpreted the original intent, I accept full responsibility. In other cases, bracketed words were used to convey the speaker's emotion. The historical notes at the beginning of every chapter are intended to help the reader understand what was going on in the world during the same time period.

Within days, I got my only negative response—a very angry voice on the other end of the phone demanding that if I wanted to know what being in Vietnam was like, I should have gone! Bob was afraid I would back out of the project, but I was not discouraged; I know that there is still a lot of anger and pain relating to Vietnam in this country. My second call came from Clyde Ricks in Idaho. He more than made up for the first call by telling me that receiving my letter was the best thing that had happened to him in years. Within two weeks I had heard from over ten men, either through calls, letters or cassettes and the project was off and running. At the reunion I was able to meet more former 9th Engineers and recorded several interviews at that time.

The men you will read about were willing to share their experiences with a complete stranger. They were honest and forthright in telling about what it was like for them in Vietnam and how it has affected them. They share why they joined and what their lives have been like since returning. Some share their views on Desert Storm and how they feel about Vietnam now.

All these soldiers "grew up" in Vietnam, changed forever from innocent boys to men, old beyond their years. I found that while they had lost their innocence, they had gained an appreciation for life and an awareness of what is really important. To me, these men and all Vietnam veterans are the heroes of my generation, even though many don't want to admit it.

There is no simple explanation for my interest in this subject. I lost no brother, no lover or father, no best friend to this conflict, but these men still trusted me to tell their stories and I have done that to the best of my ability. I have never met any more interesting people than these men. I hated that war, but never the warriors, and I am proud and honored to count them as friends.

Bob Sperling died from a brain tumor two years into this project. I will never know why he chose me to help him with the book, but he gave me one of the greatest gifts of my life by making it possible for me to meet these wonderful men. Now I give that gift to you, and I hope you are as touched and honored by their stories as I am.

LIST OF CONTRIBUTORS

Ranks throughout the book are those held by the individual during the time described. Dates given here represent time in-country.

Peter Allon, PFC, Service Company, November 1967–December 1968

Brian Althouse, PFC, A Company, March 1968–October 1969

George E. Ballard, Sgt., A Company, 1965–1967, SSgt., C Company, 1969–1970

Martin L. Brown, PFC, D Company, August 1968–August 1969

Thomas P. Carras, 2nd Lt., A Company, B Company, Hdqtrs. Company, December 1969–September 1970

Edward L. Casper, Cpl., Hdqtrs. Company, August 1967–August 1968

Mike Daly, PFC, Hdqtrs. Company, July 1967–April 1969

Dan Diridoni, LCpl., Service Company, December 1967–December 1968

Robert F. Goins, Captain, A Company, November 1965–May 1966

Robert Handley, LCpl., D Company, January 1968–February 1969

Wayne Hansen, PFC, A Company, May 1968–February 1969

Walter Hayes, Platoon Sgt., B Company, 1965–November 1967

Larry P. Howell, H & S Company, May 1966–November 1966

William C. Jung, Sgt., August 1969–July 1970

Eric Kenney, PFC, Service Company, November 1967–December 1968

Charles King, Sgt., B Company, September 1967–September 1968

Paul Kozak, PFC, D Company, September 1967–September 1968

Wayne McGinnis, LCpl., D Company, June 1966–July 1967

Dave Nichols, LCpl., B Company, January 1968–February 1969

Jim O'Kelley, 2 Lt.–1 Lt.–Capt, HQ & D Company, August 1966–May 1968

Ron Rainer, PFC, A Company, January 1967–October 1967

Edwin J. Raley, PFC, D Company, 1969–1970

Clyde Ricks, PFC, D Company, August 1969–February 1970

Lawrence Stephen Roberge, LCpl., Service Company, June 1966–January 1968

Robert A. Schaefer, Bn. Medical Officer, January 1965–January 1966

Fred H. Scheuter, PFC, B Company, May 1966–1967

Raymond Joseph Simonetti, LCpl., Service Company, May 1966–January 1967

Donald K. Snyder, LCpl., C Company, April 1967–May 1968

Bill Spadafora, Cpl., C Company, A Company, June 1968–July 1969

Robert Terry Sperling, LCpl., Service Company, December 1966–December 1967

Jim Tagye, PFC, D Company, August 1968–February 1969

Bill Turner, GSgt., D Company, May 1966–June 1967, November 1968–June 1969

John Vasarab, PFC, Service Company, 1967–1968

Paul E. Virtue, PFC, D Company, March 1967–March 1968

Ed Whitaker, PFC, Headquarters Company, December 1966–October 1967

Ted Zealley, Lt., D Company, November 1965–June 1967

HISTORY OF THE BATTALION

The 9th Engineer Battalion was activated 1 November 1965 at Marine Corps Base, Camp Pendleton, California. The nucleus was formed of experienced Marine engineers with many years of training and experience. First to form were Headquarters Company and Service Company with a total battalion strength numbering 30 officers and 93 enlisted Marines as the building program began. On 13 December the four remaining engineer companies, A, B, C and D, were activated, and by 31 December the number of personnel had increased to 43 officers and 790 enlisted Marines, reassigned from almost every station of the Marine Corps.

Operating without equipment for the first two months, the engineers spent most of their time training in general military subjects, physical training, Vietnamese language and orientation classes on Southeast Asia in preparation for deployment to the Republic of Vietnam.

With the arrival of equipment, long hours were spent in the inspection of each piece and the training of operators and mechanics.

On 1 April 1966 the battalion was redesignated to 9th Engineer Battalion, Force Troops, FMFPac, coming under operational control of the 29 Palms, California–based command, although continuing to be based at Camp Pendleton, California, where intensified training continued until an advance detail left the States on 2 May when one officer and eleven enlisted Marines embarked aboard the USS *Mathews* (AKA-96) and sailed from Long Beach, California, for the Republic of Vietnam.

On 15 May 1966 the battalion personnel embarked aboard the USS *Ogden* (LPD-5) at San Diego enroute to the Republic of Vietnam, and on the following day another group embarked aboard USS *Fort Marion* (LSD-22) at San Diego, California, enroute to their destination at Chu Lai, Republic of Vietnam. On 18 May an Advance Party departed MCAS, El Toro, California, by government air enroute to Vietnam, arriving 23 May to begin preparations for the arrival of the remainder of the battalion. Part of the Service Company arrived on board the USS *Mathews* (AKA-96) on 27 May 1966. The Battalion Headquarters, Headquarters Company, Company B plus other battalion elements arrived on 6 June 1966 abroad the USS *Ogden* (LPD-5).

Companies A and C arrived and disembarked 15 June with final personnel of Company D arriving in the battalion area on 17 June. On 25 June Company A departed Chu Lai for Da Nang aboard the USS *Summit County* (LST-1146) where it came under operational control of the 7th Engineer Battalion.

The 9th Engineers' new home in the Republic of Vietnam was a flat, sandy area stretching alongside Highway 1, one-quarter mile southeast of the Chu Lai "New Life" village. The engineers' first task was setting up camp in the sandy area and building a road network throughout so shops and living quarters could be set up.

Eleven days after its arrival the battalion made its first commitment in support of the 1st Marine Division. By the end of June the engineers were fully employed with the vast majority of their efforts being spent in support of the 1st Marine Division (Rein).

During its stay in the Republic of Vietnam, the battalion accomplished many varied tasks, including repairing and paving a segment of Highway 1, building and repairing bridges, building and operating cable-operated ferries, general camp construction, rock crushing, and installation and operation of water points. In addition to its many construction jobs the engineers were actively engaged in mine-clearing assignments, convoy security, and other general combat support operations. They also maintained their own perimeter and ran combat patrols in their own area of operation.

Although the battalion's main effort went to the 1st Marine Division, it also supported U.S. Army units and other Free World Forces, as well as local Vietnamese civilian and military projects near Chu Lai. Some of the operations that the battalion actively participated in were Colorado, Washington, Fresno, Napa and Golden Fleece.

In March 1970, though all operational commitments were continued, significant effort was placed on the relocation of the battalion to Da Nang. By 30 March, 475 personnel and 2,650 tons of equipment had been moved by convoy and sealift to the 1st Marine Division AO in the Da Nang area. During the remainder of its stay in Vietnam the battalion continued to stress its primary missions of minesweeps, upgrading and haul support, and keeping Highway 1 open to traffic in its area.

Company A completed its stay when on 2 March 1970 it was deployed out of the Republic of Vietnam. Its designation was changed to Company A (Rein), 9th Engineer Battalion, 1st Marine Brigade, FMF, as it departed for Hawaii, arriving there on 16 March and becoming an increment of the 1st Marine Brigade.

While a unit in Vietnam, its headquarters was Hill 10, south of Da Nang, with its primary mission being the maintenance of Highway QL-1 between Tam Ky and Thang Binh. In addition, it carried out such engineering assignments as minefield clearing, small bridge construction and bunker complex construction in and around various Marine elements located south of Da Nang.

During July 1970, Company C, 9th Engineer Battalion deployed from the Republic of Vietnam, arriving at Camp Pendleton, California on 1 August. While awaiting the arrival of its parent organization, it was attached to Provisional Service Battalion on 11 August and remained there until detached on 11 September to rejoin the 9th Engineer Battalion.

The battalion with Headquarters Company, Service Company and Company B departed Da Nang on 24 August 1970 aboard the USS *Juneau* (LPD-10), arriving at Long Beach, California, and joining the 5th Marine Amphibious brigade at Camp Pendleton on 11 September. Immediately operations began for deactivation of the 9th Engineer Battalion. On 6 October the battalion came under operational control and administrative control of the 7th Engineer Battalion. On 30 October 1970 the 9th Engineer Battalion was deactivated and its colors retired. Company A (Rein), 9th Engineer Battalion, 1st Marine Brigade FMF continued in existence at Kaneohe Bay, Hawaii.

FORMATION OF THE BATTALION

Operation Rolling Thunder, sustained American bombing of North Vietnam, begins on February 24, 1965.

Two Marine battalions land March 8 to defend Da Nang airfield, the first American combat troops in Vietnam.

President Johnson, April 7, offers Ho Chi Minh participation in a Southeast Asian development plan in exchange for peace. April 8, North Vietnam Prime Minister Pham Van Dong rejects Johnson's proposal.

American Command in Saigon reports on June 26 that Vietcong have put five South Vietnam combat regiments and nine battalions out of action in recent months. July 8, eighteen American combat battalions now in the country. Johnson approves Westmoreland's request, July 28, for forty-four additional combat battalions.

American forces defeat North Vietnam units in the Ia Drang valley in October, the first big conventional clash of the war. By December 1965 American troop strength in Vietnam reaches nearly 200,000.

Ted Zealley, Lt., D Company, 1 November 1965–June 1967

The story of the 9th Engineer Battalion does not begin in Vietnam. The 9th Engineer Battalion was unique in that I believe it was the first unit specifically formed and activated for the war. Up until its formation all units sent to Vietnam were already in existence prior to the war.

In late October 1965 Marines from about the U.S. were ordered to report to Camp Pendleton for duty with the 9th Engineer Battalion. A quick check on Marine Corps units indicated that no such unit existed. When we reported in to Camp Pendleton, those at the reception center didn't know of any such unit either and looked upon us and our orders with some suspicion.

Reporting in at Camp Pendleton in late October and early November 1965 was an unusual experience. Most of us know the base as one of bustling activity. Not so then. It was a virtual ghost town. Every FMF unit was gone. Most of the base units had been stripped of personnel to fill out units that had gone to Vietnam. When the 9th Engineer Battalion was activated on 1 November 1965, it was the only FMF unit on the base and remained that way except for the brief tenure of an MP battalion that formed and went overseas. It took us a lot longer to gather our personnel and gear than the MP's.

We were assigned barracks and office and shop spaces in the old 14 and 15 areas. When we opened them up, there was nothing inside. No racks, desks, chairs, phones, mops, brooms, pencils — not a thing. Our first quest was to obtain some of these necessary items. We were told that we needed to submit a DD1150 form to get them. We didn't even have a form. How to get the forms? One had to submit a DD1150 to get a DD1150. So we had to borrow a box of DD1150's from base headquarters just to get a supply of DD1150's.

I was the first battalion legal officer and battalion construction officer in the S-3 shop. As soon as another officer arrived that had been to Naval Justice School (Lt. Mac MacDonald), I shed myself of the legal officer duties.

Slowly we gathered personnel and equipment from all over the place. One memorable event occurred when we sent our order to have dump trucks shipped from Barstow for us. According to Marine Corps inventory, there were over 80 dump trucks there for us. When Barstow went to ship them, they found none. That did cause a bit of delay.

In the rush to get personnel properly qualified, several officers were sent to atomic demolitions school in San Diego. A month or so later there was a bit of a scare at headquarters because somewhere in the hierarchy of the Marine Corps there was concern about sending officers there [to Vietnam] that had such qualifications. We didn't escape the trip though.

Robert F. Goins, Captain, A Company, November 1965–May 1966

My name is Robert F. Goins and I entered the Marine Corps as a Second Lieutenant upon graduation from the Naval Academy in 1955. The engineer MOS was my choice. As a Captain with ten years' service in 1965, I was ordered to Camp Pendleton to become a member of the 9th Engineer Battalion, yet to be formed and trained for duty in Vietnam. My attitude was to fully commit myself and my unit to the assigned mission. My assignment was Company Commander, A Company. From November 1965 to May 1966 the company was organized and trained in the full range of subjects with emphasis on explosives and land mines under field conditions.

**George E. Ballard,
Sgt., A Company, 1965–1967,
SSgt., C Company, 1969–1970**

I was there when they first formed in 1965 with A Company, and I was about the twelfth or thirteenth person to report to A Company in '65.

WHY THEY JOINED

Fred H. Scheuter, PFC, B Company, May 1966–1967

When I joined the Marines, I was only nineteen and I volunteered to fight in the Vietnam War. I almost didn't get in. I am completely deaf in my left ear from a childhood illness.

Larry P. Howell, PFC, H & S Company, May 1966–November 1966

I joined the Marines 7 April 1965 'cause I wanted to be a Marine and wanted to go to Vietnam. I volunteered. I thought it was something we had to do and I wanted to do my part.

Raymond Joseph Simonetti, LCpl., Service Company, May 1966–January 1967

The reason why I joined the Marines was in search of fulfillment of my military obligation. I wanted to get that out of the way and then I wouldn't have to be fooling around with the draft. Back in those days I was a kid in need of some direction and possibly some self discipline and things of that nature. I originally tried to join the Navy and due to the fact that I was in trouble and on probation before a verdict, the Navy wanted me to wait an additional three months. The Marine recruiter said they could take me right now. So I signed up with the Marines in '64 for a three year tour.

At that time in my life there was no war, per se, in Vietnam. I guess we were some of the first guys when that thing started cranking up in '66. I served with a few guys that were advisors or had served in 'Nam but in an advisory capacity and certainly their roles in combat were limited.

Lawrence Stephen Roberge, LCpl., Service Company, June 1966–January 1968

I joined the Marines in the spring of 1965 while still in high school. I joined under the 120 day delay plan and went to Parris Island on Sept. 13, 1965. When I enlisted my recruiter told us "I can guarantee you that you will go to Vietnam." I was young, foolish and maybe gung-ho. I didn't have the grades for college and I had no idea what to do with my life. I knew that I wanted the Marines and there was no changing my mind. Many friends and relatives tried to talk me out of it, but they did not succeed. The idea of Vietnam did scare me, but it did not stop me. I knew that boys were dying there every day, but it wouldn't happen to me. Now, to this day, I would not change a thing. Like the flag that hangs in front of my home that says "Our cause was just," our country asked us to do a job and we did the best we knew how.

Jim O'Kelley, 2 Lt.–1 Lt.–Capt., HQ & D Company, August 1966–May 1968

My fraternity at Duke University had an unusual number of Marine ROTC candidates and Marine Corps officers' sons in it at the time I was there—1959 to 1964. I roomed with Skip Chapman my Junior year — his father, at that time, was CG at Camp Lejeune and later became Commandant. So I had that influence. Also, I think many of the WWII movies affected me — especially *Sands of Iwo Jima*. Thirdly, I was very patriotic and felt a need to serve my country.

I graduated from Duke in 1964 and took a job with IBM Corporation in Winston-Salem, North Carolina. I got bored very quickly, so when the Marines landed in Vietnam in March 1965, I went down and signed up the day after my 24th birthday, 25 March 1965. Ironically, the officer who swore me in was Capt. Carl Mundy from Waynesville, North Carolina, which is just a bit west of my home in Asheville, North Carolina. Capt. Mundy later became General Mundy, Commandant of the Marine Corps; he also retired me at a ceremony at the Iwo Jima Memorial in June 1996 after 31 years of service.

**Ed Whitaker, PFC,
Headquarters Company,
December 1966–October 1967**

I was drafted. The day we went down to be inducted into the service I had every indication that I was going to go into the Army. They did not tell us that day, but for each branch of the service they had to have so many. They were going to wait and let everybody choose as to which branch they wanted. If they only need ten for the Marines, and they got fifteen, that would be fine … but they couldn't come up short. They had a quota of at least ten for the Marines, and only one person volunteered ahead of time. So then they come back and said, "Okay, this is how many we need for each branch. You can either volunteer, and if you don't, we're going to volunteer for you." Not anybody said a word. So when we came along the line, guess what, I'm going to the Marines.

**Robert Terry Sperling, LCpl.,
Service Company, December 1966–
December 1967**

I joined the Marine Corps in early March 1965 and left for Parris Island. We were watching the news on TV and heard about two Marine Infantry Battalions landing in Vietnam. One of us said, "Where is Vietnam?" When I got to Boot Camp, my D.I.'s told all of us in Platoon 219 that we were going to die in Vietnam.

A few weeks later they said that they wanted to apologize because they did not know whether we were going to die in Vietnam or Santo Domingo, but we were going to die…

**Ron Rainer, PFC, A Company,
January 1967–October 1967**

In 1966 I volunteered for the Marine Corps and I also volunteered for Vietnam. In that particular period of time in 1966 we were pretty hawkish on Vietnam in this country. One of the main reasons I joined the Marine Corps was that I knew if I wanted to get a college education that I would be able to do that after three years. I wouldn't have to worry about depending on my family so much. There was a war on, people were dying and it was a cause that pretty much everyone was in positive agreement with at that time.

**Mike Daly, PFC, Hdqtrs. Company,
July 1967–April 1969**

I was born in Alpena, Michigan, December 19, 1947. I graduated from Cherry Hill High School in June of 1966. I realized that I had my fill of school and sought the adventure that the Marines promised me for signing my name to four years. I enlisted in September 1966, completed boot camp, ITR, Heavy Equipment school and jungle training, to be placed upon the boat USS *John Pope* and sent to Vietnam in June of 1967.

Charles King, Sgt., B Company, September 1967–September 1968

The rebel in me lead me to join the Marines. Everybody in my family, both sides, either went in the Air Force or the Navy, and I just wanted to be different.

John Vasarab, PFC, Service Company, 1967–1968

You are the first person who is asking about my experiences and not about the government's policy. First, I am not anybody special. I was eighteen years old when I enlisted in the Corps. I went from high school to Parris Island within one week of graduation. I joined the Marines because I figured they were the best choice of all the armed services. I had no idea they were going to make me a heavy equipment mechanic. We called it "heavy junk" when I was in.

When I joined the Corps, it was in June of 1966 right out of high school. I had no idea what it would be like, but I figured that they were special and that was for me. I thought that my father would be proud of me also for becoming a Marine. I went to Vietnam with no preconceived notions about what would happen to me when I arrived. I arrived there as a PFC and picked up the ranks of lance corporal and corporal during my tour. I was in-country during 1967 and 1968. There is nothing that would change my mind about the opportunity that was presented me. Our government was playing a serious game with our lives. They did not go there to win a war as far as I am concerned. We could have cleaned that place out if left alone to do our thing. Wasn't that what they trained us for?

Dan Diridoni, LCpl., Service Company, December 1967–December 1968

John Wayne movies had a lot to do with it. I'm not being facetious. I joined in 1966. I graduated from high school in 1965 and didn't really know what I wanted to do with myself, so I went to junior college for a semester. Unfortunately, I moved out with a couple of buddies. [laughs] I found out what the word "party" meant. As a result, my grades suffered and I got my draft status changed from 2F to 1A. So I decided that I had better take a long hard look at things. If I was going to go into the service, I would like to decide what it was instead of being drafted in the Army. My dad and I didn't get along too well at that time and so he wanted me to go in the Air Force and try to learn a trade. Of course I did the complete opposite of what he said to do. I went down and signed up for the Marine Corps for three years. I guess I got my point across, 'cause he was pissed. He was smarter than me. He knew what was going on. I didn't know. I didn't care. I was aware of Vietnam, but I wasn't aware of the severity of what really was going on. My head was in the closet at that time.

Robert Handley, LCpl., D Company, January 1968–February 1969

Why did I join the Marines? [laughs] Nothing else to do. I was nineteen. I didn't have a job. I was with some friends, a couple buddies of mine, and we walked into the Marine Recruiter in Milwaukee and listened to him and all of us signed up for four years. I think we knew in the back of our minds about Vietnam, but you're a kid out of school.

Dave Nichols, LCpl., B Company, January 1968–February 1969

My name is Dave Nichols. I was raised outside of Grand Rapids, Michigan. I joined the Marines in May 1967 on the delayed entry program. I reported for active duty on July 27, 1967. As crazy as this sounds, I joined the Marines because I wanted to kill "Commies." I figured the Marine Corps would get me to Vietnam the quickest, with the best training. I felt that we belonged in Vietnam to stop the spread of Communism through Southeast Asia. I still feel that we had a good cause over there. Even though the government of South Vietnam was not the most honest, it was better than Communism. We saw this after North Vietnam took over and thousands of people were killed or put in re-education camps.

Brian Althouse, PFC, A Company, March 1968–October 1969

I wanted to get away from home. I came from a split family and I knew from the time I was in the sixth grade I liked the Marines. I thought that they were the greatest. I went and signed up for the Marine Corps and then I went home and told my mother. She was upset. She didn't believe me at first.

Bill Spadafora, Cpl., C Company, A Company, June 1968–July 1969

I was born June 14, 1948, Flag Day. Until I was the age of 12 I believed that everybody put a flag up just for my birthday. But I guess that wasn't true.

Why did I want to become a Marine? I guess I watched too many John Wayne movies. When war broke out, I was in high school and I went to college for a year, but I really wasn't satisfied. Once I finished that first year of college, my dad said to me, "If you're not going back to school, you're going to get drafted into the Army, so you better go look and see what you want to do. Look at the different branches of the service." So what I did is, I went out and I looked at the Army. I looked at the Navy. I looked at the Coast Guard. I looked at the Air Force. Then I looked at the Marines. And that was it. I enlisted in the Marine Corps.

Jim Tagye, PFC, D Company, August 1968–February 1969

I had a family tradition of the Marine Corps. My uncle and aunt were both in the Marine Corps. My uncle Bob was one of the original members of First Marine Division when it was at Guantanamo Bay. I had a cousin who was a Marine and fought in the Korean War. I had two brothers who were Marines. So I more or less just followed suit.

Martin L. Brown, PFC, D Company, August 1968–August 1969

I had to stay back my junior year in high school because I started skipping school. So when I was a senior, I went about a half year and dropped out. Basically I enlisted because I think I wanted to overcompensate. I had a lot of low self-esteem back then. [laughs] Marines are tough, so I went in there. I was going to do the service anyway, but I just went Marines.

Clyde Ricks, PFC, D Company, August 1969–February 1970

I joined the Marines in 1968 and I'd say it was just because I love this country and I wanted to protect the Vietnamese from communism. I mean, I was just a kid. I went with that rationale that we couldn't fight Russia and China at the same time so we had to keep it in South Vietnam.

I could have beat it, the draft. I'm Mormon, LDS. My folks wanted me to serve in LDS mission. I'm a believer now, but at that time, I really wasn't that strong of one. I had some real spiritual experiences at the time 'Nam fell to the communists. I think that was a hard thing for me at first. I thought Ford would send them back in. I really did.

BASIC TRAINING

**Walter Hayes, Platoon Sgt.,
B Company, 1965–November 1967**

I was the third one to check into Bravo company out there in California. I was twenty-three then, and I was classified as one of the old guys. All we got was a bunch of young kids right out of schools or out of boot camp. They may have gone to Engineer school, which teaches you very little except the basics. It was really interesting forming up the whole Battalion. We went in there and the only thing we had was pencil and paper to do the paperwork at first.

Out there [at Camp Pendleton] we went through staging, which is nothing more than going through your mine fields out there, and mines and booby trap trails. There were three Sergeants really set that thing up. I helped out. It was to show the basic booby traps we would encounter. Your head-knockers and Malaysian whips and pungee pits and pungee traps and different things.

Jim O'Kelley, 2 Lt.–1 Lt.–Capt., HQ & D Company, August 1966–May 1968

As an officer candidate, I was sent to OCS at Quantico, Virginia, for eleven weeks. I completed that in December 1965 and reported to The Basic School (TBS) for six months of basic officer training. I did well and enjoyed that time, especially the physical training and combat training. (One sortie away from TBS occurred in April 1966 when I was selected to be an escort at the National Cherry Blossom Festival in Washington, D.C. I ended up being paired off with Miss Kentucky, whom I later came back and married in August 1968.) After TBS, I was assigned MOS (Military Occupational Specialty) 1301—basic engineer officer because I had a degree from Duke in Civil Engineering. I had asked for Infantry, Tanks or Artillery! But I got my first choice for duty station—Vietnam! Good 'ole Marine Corps! Anyway, I then reported to Courthouse Bay at Camp Lejeune, North Carolina (CLNC), for six more weeks of the Basic Combat Engineer Officers Course. I ended up being the course leader and Honor Graduate which helped me immensely later on. I left CLNC in July, took a few day's leave, and left for Vietnam via San Francisco (the song "I Left My Heart in San Francisco" still hails me emotionally) and Camp Hansen, Okinawa.

**Ed Whitaker, PFC,
Headquarters Company,
December 1966–October 1967**

It was very dramatic at first. Because of the Vietnam conflict, the Marine Corps was pushing us through in eight weeks rather than twelve weeks. We got up there on the 10th of March 1966. We graduated May 12. We had like two hours of on base R&R. First thing you do is eat all the candy bars you have, because you can't have them ahead of time. The Marine Corps is very strict versus the other branches of the service. At least that is my opinion. Then, of course, we could call home and so forth. From there we went to Camp Pendleton for advanced training and that was also the same year the airplanes were on strike. When we were finally allowed to come home, we had to take the slowest train that was in existence to come to Michigan. It took us forty-nine hours to come from California to Michigan. My next duty was going to be in Camp Lejeune in North Carolina. So now we take twenty-nine hours by bus and we stopped at every little, small town from Michigan to North Carolina. When we were at Camp Pendleton we got assigned our MOS. As far as I know it was random. It must have been. I did not sign up for it.

I knew more than likely I would end up in Vietnam. What was devastating to me was when we were in boot camp and how mean they treat people. Of course, I know a lot of it is respect and I understand now... Of course I've got this image now of being a Marine. At the time I thought I was going to die. I'm proud of the fact that I was a Marine, but it was just a whole different atmosphere than what I was used to here on the farm. No comparison. The drill instructors would yell at you for dumb things.

We had one drill instructor that was extremely mean. The person that was the head of our company, he was a very nice gentleman. The guys respected him. I understand the point of the discipline. As years went by, even after I was out of the military, it meant more to me than it did at the time. At the time I thought it was somewhat wrong because it was such a change to my life.

Ron Rainer, PFC,
A Company, January 1967–October 1967
I went to staging out in California, at Camp Pendleton. When I left there, I got my orders cut for A Company, 9th Engineers, First Marine Division in the heavy equipment platoon. I wasn't what you would call an engineer, but I was with the heavy equipment platoon with engineers.

Paul E. Virtue, PFC,
D Company, March 1967–March 1968
P. E. Virtue, 2303059, USMC, 9th Engr. Btn., Chu Lai

Paul E. Virtue, born January 24, 1947, in Cambridge, New York. After enlisting in June, I was activated on September 21, 1966, to Parris Island, South Carolina, for basic training. Appointed as a 1371 (Combat Engineer), I completed my Engineer schooling on January 26, 1967, at Camp Lejeune, North Carolina.

Donald K. Snyder, LCpl.,
C Company, April 1967–May 1968
I came out to Camp Pendleton, California, went through staging battalion, left US through MCAS, El Toro, California. I reported to Camp Pendleton, 5th Bridge Company.

Edward L. Casper, Cpl.,
Headquarters Company,
August 1967–August 1968
At the time of Vietnam, I was a corporal with Com Platoon, Headquarters Company, 9th Engineer Battalion, 1st Marine Division, U.S. Marine Corps, located at Chu Lai, Vietnam, August 1967 to August 1968.

My career began February 22, 1966, when I reported to boot camp at San Diego, California, after being drafted into the United States Marine Corps. It was the first time the Marine Corps drafted since World War II, and they needed 13 to fill the quota and my name was first. Then there was advanced infantry training and wire communications school. Then I reported to A Communication Battalion, Camp Lejeune, North Carolina, where I completed teletype communications school.

It was here that I received orders for Vietnam, went on 20 days leave and left for Vietnam in August 1967.

**John Vasarab, PFC,
Service Company, 1967–1968**

The drill instructors would give us some insight into the war, but that only goes as far as your imagination can take it. During this time there was a couple of "Boots" who were told that a brother they had was killed over there, and this kind of gave us food for thought. I mean, we were not even there yet and the hand of death was already touching our lives. We just tried to learn what they were trying to teach us a little better.

**Dan Diridoni, LCpl.,
Service Company,
December 1967–December 1968**

I played a lot of sports in high school and I considered myself in good shape, but mentally it was really tough. At that age nobody is used to that kind of mental discipline. They really poured it on you. They are masters at it.

The head games were absolutely worth it. To this day it has benefited me no matter what I have endeavored to do. As far as having my own business and as far as going to college after I got out of the service. It's really helped me in my life. A lot of guys, and I mean, I guess you could classify me as one of those guys that was aimless. I didn't know what the hell was going on and I could care less. I shortly found out later that you have to have some direction if you are going to survive. So, that's how I ended up.

I got out of boot camp in October 1966, and then went to infantry training at Camp Pendleton in November, which is four weeks. At Camp Lejeune the job or MOS that I was assigned was water purification. It boggled everybody's mind when I got my order. What the hell was that? I didn't know what the hell they were talking about. So, I went back to this school and it was three months. It was very intensive training in how to use different equipment and how to purify water in all situations, whether you were in the jungle or whether you would be purifying salt water. I know how to do that.

The training was excellent. I graduated from that school and got my orders to go back to Camp Pendleton. I was stationed with the 13th Engineers there at main side. I got there in March of 1967. I was there for one month and the Fifth Marine Division was forming there at Camp Pendleton because the First Marine Division and Third Marine Division were in Vietnam, so they needed somebody to take their place at Pendleton. So they pulled cooks, truck drivers, engineers, radio guys, anything you can imagine.

**Robert Handley, LCpl.,
D Company, January 1968–February 1969**

If you had a driver's license, you had half of the schooling for motor transport licked. There was a lot of classroom, a lot of driving. Convoy driving, nomenclatures, principles of convoy traffic laws in a combat zone and types of vehicles. You were qualified with up to five tons coming out of school which was then an M54 cargo truck, troop transport. Anything after that you had to get additional training. I eventually was certified up to tankers, ten ton tractors. Those are the ones that haul the tank trucks for liquid fuel.

**Brian Althouse, PFC,
A Company, March 1968–October 1969**

I was in Parris Island for twelve weeks. One week of reforming where you get your shots and they test you. A whole bunch of written tests and stuff like that. Then you had eight weeks of training. But I was there for twelve because the third or fourth week I had strained knees and I got bursitis in my heels. I couldn't keep up with the platoon so they sent me back to the hospital platoon and I was there for ten days. After I was okay, they sent me back to another platoon and I graduated in December. That's when you found out where you were going and what your MOS was.

I was a 1371 which was a combat engineer. They just assigned it to you. When I enlisted, I enlisted for four years because I wanted to go in the air wing. I didn't care if I was just putting bombs on planes or whatever. I wanted to have something to do with aviation, so I enlisted for four years. The recruiter said if you enlist for this amount of years, this amount of time, you can do this. But my IQ wasn't high enough for that, so I wound up being an engineer, which is okay because I'm still alive and proud of it. At that time, I figured we'd win. I figured we'll go in there and we'll kick butt and it'll be like Korea. Because America always wins because we carry the flag.

That's what was disappointing in 1975, and that was long after I was out.

**Bill Spadafora, Cpl.,
C Company, A Company,
June 1968–July 1969**

I went to boot camp October 22nd, 1966. After boot camp I was stationed at Camp Lejeune and Camp Geiger. Then I was transferred to Marine barracks in San Francisco, and from that point I went to Westpak.

**Martin L. Brown, PFC,
D Company, August 1968–August 1969**

Boot camp for me was hell. I got picked on a lot by the DI's mainly because I was insecure and I used to watch them all the time. My eyeballs used to follow them around and they knew it. There was a guy from New York there that I used to stand directly across from, and that's about as close as you got to anybody. So I guess he considered me his best friend. He got in trouble one day and he said that him and I were going to kick anybody's ass that made PFC out of there. At that point, I was up for PFC, so I didn't make it. They gave me hell after that and I didn't know why either, until the day we graduated. Then they told me.

**Jim Tagye, PFC,
D Company, August 1968–February 1969**

I thought boot camp was very controlled. I was a squad leader and I was up for PFC, just like Marty here. I lost that on the rifle range when we were trying to qualify to shoot the .45 caliber. I had my finger on the trigger and you weren't supposed to do that. After that they said, "Okay, you just lost what you were going to get." And the assumption among the other guys was that I was going to get a PFC stripe out of boot camp. I also lost being a squad leader that day just because I had my finger on the trigger by mistake. I just unconsciously had it on there. I wasn't doing it on purpose or anything. It was supposed to be right next to the barrel. When you're at the range, you had to keep it that way. Your finger had to be next to the barrel, not on the trigger, until you pointed at the target. I thought it was difficult but I was a jock coming out of high school and I was pretty well fit. I could do most of the things they wanted us to do. I was in very good shape at that time.

PFC Martin L. Brown

At Engineer school they covered mine warfare, demolition, explosives, bridge and construction. How to lay bolt bridges, put up combat bridges, pontoon bridges, ropes. We did ropes. Outside of the barracks I used to stay in there used to be a tower with a three strand rope bridge across it, then another tower. I would go down to the area two club every night and get shit faced. It was a ritual for me when I came back through to climb up that thing and go across the bridge and down the other side. I used to do it every night. [laughs] Drunk. [laughs] And I'm scared of heights.

PFC Jim Tagye

We went through a VC village training. Then they told you, just give your name, rank and serial number. Don't divulge any information. But what do you do if you're being tortured? Let's face it, most guys are going to tell them what they want. But we were PFCs and Corporals, we didn't know much. I was a PFC. What did I know? I didn't have any intelligent information. What they would have done with us was just kill us. They wouldn't take us. We would be of no value to them.

PFC Martin L. Brown

I remember making a decision if I ever got to the point where I thought I was going to get captured, I'd probably just fight until they killed me. I read a lot about the POW-MIA issue. My personal opinion is lifting the embargo is a mistake. There's a little part of me that says maybe it might work, but I don't think so. I think if anybody is alive, they probably aren't anymore. I really believe they are in Laos. I read a lot of stuff that indicates that they moved them up there in '85 and kept them in caves.

PFC Jim Tagye

POW camp. We went through a survival camp and training for three days. Most of it was spent in the mountains. Everyone going to Vietnam went to the same place for training, no matter what your MOS was. As a Marine you're still an infantryman. We were combat engineers. Which meant that we could have been put in an infantry battalion with like the 1st Marines or the 5th Marines. 1371. That's an MOS for a demolition person who takes out mines and really acts as an infantryman on the side.

GOING OVER

Ted Zealley, Lt.,
D Company, November 1965–June 1967

Our departure to Vietnam was staggered mainly due to the scarcity of shipping necessary to get such a large unit with all its gear over there. The Navy and Marine Corps were quite used to thinking about one or two ships to get a battalion overseas. As I recall, we took six. The first to leave, I think, was D Company, who went aboard an old style LST. They were also the last to arrive in Vietnam, having the joy of several breakdowns along the way.

I was part of the advanced party of about six, three officers and three enlisted, as I recall. We were the last to leave and first to arrive. We flew out of El Toro on a C-130 loaded with aircraft tires and lubricants. We had stops in Kaneohe Bay, Wake and Okinawa on the way. Four days on a C-130 left quite an impression on us, at least our rear ends. Those canvas seats do get hard. By the way, there was no one at Kaneohe Bay, either. We finally managed to find a hamburger at the bowling alley at night, but breakfast and lunch consisted of what we could get out of the snack machines at the hanger the next morning.

The six of us arrived and were unceremoniously deposited on a pile of sand outside the Chu Lai airfield perimeter. At night we stayed at the 1st Marine Division CP, but the rest of the time we laid out what was to be home for 9th Engineers for some time to come. We were actually fortunate to be stuck in the sand, though we didn't think so that May 1966. We could have been swamped in laterite mud by winter had we been elsewhere.

Walter Hayes, Platoon Sgt.,
B Company, 1965–November 1967

That day when we were loading on ship, we had already sent our seabags to be loaded and everything and the commanding officer was going through inspecting our barracks to make sure when we left everything was spotless. That's how Marines are. Everything's got to be white glove clean and everything in its place and all that. When we finished inspecting the barracks, he went in to the shower and the bathrooms and there was a PFC in there. He had cut his wrists. He cut both of them real good. He was married just a short time and he came at us with a razor blade. Well, we stopped him. The CO made us take him to sick bay and tell them to patch him up and get his butt down on that ship. We went down to sick bay and they wrapped his wrists in gauze and we took him on the ship and put him in the brig. A couple of days out to sea they let him out and gave him his seabag and his rifle and gave him a rack. That night he takes his seabag and rifle and throws it over the rail of the ship. [laughs] Back into the brig he went. This time they gave him bread and water for a couple days then let him out, but they wouldn't give him no more rifle. I guess it was about a week after we were in-country before he accepted it. He turned out good. He went home the same time as I did, but he sure didn't want to go. He was the only one. I think he did it because he was just immature. I guess we all were. [laughs] That was the only incident that I could think of where somebody was not wanting to be where he was.

When we pulled into Chu Lai, it was just too late in the afternoon to unload. They just held us all aboard ship and set up a perimeter on the ship in case anybody came too close to it. That night was really interesting because there wasn't one person, Navy or Marine, went to sleep that night because we just watched firefights. You could tell the difference by the tracer, the color of the tracer rounds. You'd see green and red. You could tell the good guys and the bad guys. We have red. Green ones were from other countries. You could just sit there and watch them. Then you'd watch rockets and mortars from a distance. Everyone knew they were going into that the next day.

Then they took us to where we were going to be forming the 9th Engineer Battalion. They took us by trucks and it was an overgrown beach. There was nothing. No bushes, no trees, no nothing, just one gigantic beach. It looked like it was just pure sand. Right from the time we got off the trucks, till about two and a half, three weeks later, we just humped and humped and busted it twenty-four hours a day. Taking breaks when you could. Trying to work in shifts which didn't work out very well. It just seemed like you just worked around the clock. Slept when you could and ate when you could and it was in pure sand.

Fred H. Scheuter, PFC,
B Company, May 1966–1967

This is my story, as much as I can remember. I started for Vietnam in 1966 right after Staging Battalion in Camp Pendleton, California, on a ship called the USNS *General Weigel*. There were mostly Marines and some Army on board. The first day on the ship the water was rough and it seemed like about three quarters of the men were seasick. I was all right. Maybe because I was brought up on Staten Island, New York, and I always rode the Staten Island Ferry. We stopped for a couple of hours near Hawaii and then at Okinawa for a day where we had a good time.

Thirteen days later we arrived at Chu Lai. It was early in the morning, a couple of hours before daybreak. My first impression of the area was how it was lit up with flares. The first day I was flown to Da Nang with about a hundred other Marines. The next day I was to go up North for a couple of days. I was flown up North in a small plane to somewhere south of Hue. I was with the 3rd Engineers. I was finally issued an M-14 rifle. I was sent up to near the DMZ on top of a dump truck filled with large wooden planks in a convoy. On the way up I remember going through Hue. After Hue we were in Phu Bai. We had a little problem getting through Phu Bai. The Viet Cong had blown up one of the bridges and we had to go on a temporary type of ferry, a couple of trucks at a time, over a river. On the way up it was bumpy and slow going until snipers started firing on us. The wood on the truck which I was on was bouncing up and down. It was hard for me to hold on with a rifle in one hand. My right trigger finger got caught between two pieces of wooden planks. It looked like my finger was squashed one inch longer. The medic didn't put stitches, just a large bandage. My finger never healed right.

Raymond Joseph Simonetti, LCpl.,
Service Company, May 1966–January 1967

My name is Raymond Joseph Simonetti, Jr. My rank at the time was E4 and my company was C Company. I left

California temporarily attached to Service Company where we had 11 guys and one officer. We were the advance party going by ship to Vietnam. Once the companies got to Vietnam I went back into C Company and then later transferred or started working out of the heavy equipment platoon.

My thoughts were just rampant. You name it you were thinking about it. You didn't know if it was going to be like the John Wayne movies, Iwo Jima, hitting the beach and all that kind of stuff. It was sort of like, "What the hell. I ain't going to make it back, so just do my thing." When you first arrive in-country, it was different. It was relatively quiet and that's where your concern came in. Why is it so quiet? This is supposed to be a war going on here? How come people aren't shooting at me right now? So you had mixed emotions. I think my thoughts before and after I got there was basically the place was just definitely bad for your health record... I don't know what more you say. It wasn't like the thing that you see in the WWII movies and all that stuff.

Wayne McGinnis, LCpl.,
D Company, June 1966–July 1967

They had us on an LST, and that's the damn thing that broke down for a couple of days out in the middle of the ocean and the other group damn near caught up to us. The people on the LST were all in D company.

When we first got there it was just pure white sand that looked like snow and it hurt your eyes. They had us for three or four days just going around and we had to put the barbed wire up. We had to build wooden floors to put our tents on and stuff like that and you got to sleep for a couple two or three hours early in the morning when it was a little bit cooler. Then it was up and at it and you did all you could during the day. It was so doggone hot and walking in that sand, it hurt.

Lawrence Stephen Roberge, LCpl.,
Service Company, June 1966–January 1968

I can't say that anything was very humorous unless you can picture a marine sitting in his military pick up on the beach in Chu Lai with his hands tightly gripped on his M-14. I sat there all night the first night we landed. I can't say that I was scared, but I think that you could see my fingerprints in the stock of my clean and fresh M-14. I didn't close my eyes all night. Seeing the Vietnamese civilians walking around the next morning had me wondering. I guess I expected the beach landing I had always seen in the movies. Things soon changed and fear was gone.

The next day when we arrived at Battalion Compound, I couldn't believe how little we had. Large tent [sleeps 10], canvas cot, and that was it. I couldn't imagine how I would survive 13 months like this. But being an Engineer Battalion, we soon grew and had more comforts. No matter how little we had at first, it was like living in a mansion compared to the "life of the grunt" in the field. I thanked God many times for the privilege of being an Engineer, and not a grunt.

One of my first showers at the newly constructed 9th engineer compound was outside, of course. As I was showering, I looked over to the fence area and there was a bunch of Vietnamese kids watching. At first, a slight shyness, but it didn't last. I still remember the kids saying we "look like fish." We had no tans yet.

Jim O'Kelley, 2 Lt.–1 Lt.–Capt., HQ &
D Company, August 1966–May 1968

I flew from Asheville, North Carolina., (my home) to San Francisco, then from Travis AFB, California, to Kadena, Okinawa and Camp Hansan — this was all by 707 jet. Then I left Okinawa after three days and flew to Da Nang on a C-130 prop USMC Cargo aircraft. Spent one night in Da Nang at Transient Officer's Quarters and then took a DC3 to Chu Lai. I checked in there and was sent to the 9th Engineer Battalion "across the airfield headed towards the mountains."

**Ed Whitaker, PFC,
Headquarters Company,
December 1966–October 1967**

We flew to Okinawa and when we got there we had to leave all our extra stuff there that we would not normally need. Before we got on the plane to leave, we had to unload the ... whatever the extra clothing was of anybody that was killed in Vietnam.

Let's say some person was killed in Vietnam, all their clothing and so forth was put into a sack and so forth, and put on this plane and went to Okinawa. The first thing I had to do was help unload this stuff. This is the way to get to Vietnam? This is really cute. I come from a very religious background. I don't believe in predestination ... but I think God has a plan for everybody on this earth. And I thought, "God, why did you put me here? What is my mission here?" I think I could do better elsewhere.

**Robert Terry Sperling, LCpl.,
Service Company,
December 1966–December 1967**

It was early December 1966. The plane ride in a C-130 from Okinawa to Da Nang was very rough. I vomited just a few minutes before we landed. The mud, the smells and the people all seemed very strange.

The first night hundreds of us were packed into a huge airplane hangar. The runway was right next to us and the sounds of the Phantoms taking off was unbelievably loud. I thought I would be clever and go to the back of the hangar to escape the noise and get some sleep, we only had our seabags. Around midnight I was awakened by a Marine Captain talking as loud as he possibly could about three feet from me on a field phone. Myself nor anyone else in the hangar said anything at all. I was a Lance Corporal with one day in Vietnam and thirteen months to go, hopefully.

**Ron Rainer, PFC,
A Company, January 1967–October 1967**

My first impression of Vietnam was very hot, very muggy, but a very beautiful country. I thought the people were quite friendly at first. But I think I was like everybody else. I had a big old knot in my stomach. Eyeballing everybody [laughing], taking one step at a time. A little frightened, too.

**Donald K. Snyder, LCpl.,
C Company, April 1967–May 1968**

My father died in Feb. 1964 and he was a United States Marine from 1920 to 1924. He died thinking I could not make it through the schooling, but I did.

**Mike Daly, PFC,
Hdqtrs. Company, July 1967–April 1969**

Arriving in Vietnam in July, it was extremely hot. The platoon policy was to climatize the troops before being sent to the field.

**Edward L. Casper, Cpl.,
Headquarters Company,
August 1967–August 1968**

The first thing that hit me as I stepped off the plane was the heat as it engulfed you with the humidity and you broke out into sweat immediately. I was trucked to Chu Lai on a deuce and a half, which bounced you around all over the road, and the 9th Engineering Battalion was situated on sand. This was on a beach. The huts that were living quarters were made out of plywood half way up with the rest being screened with a tin roof and sitting on stilts. I always wondered why the huts sat up above the ground until the monsoons came and the rain could not soak in the sand and the water rises to the bottom of the floor and you have to use pallets to walk on.

Charles King, Sgt., B Company, September 1967–September 1968

I was older than a lot of the guys, and I knew what to expect, to a certain extent. When you landed and they opened the doors of the airplane and the smell hit you, you knew where you were. It was the smell of 'Nam I guess you'd say. A distinct odor you'll never forget. And the heat and humidity, and when the planes come in and they opened the doors there was a distinct odor Vietnam had like nowhere else in the world I've ever been.

Eric Kenney, PFC, Service Company, November 1967–December 1968

We got off the plane there in Da Nang and every day we'd have to go over to a little building where they'd call out names. They'd call your name, then they would give you orders and tell you where you were going. You just sat there all day waiting on them to call your name. There were a lot of people coming and going in this place, people rotating back to the states. The first day I was there I observed this dog handler. He had to be one of the grubbiest looking, dirtiest looking bums you ever saw. He had a German shepherd dog on a chain and he was laying on the ground, asleep, and his dog was next to him, tied to a chain link fence. Jets and planes and everything are going up and down the runway and here he's dead asleep, laying on the concrete in the hot sun with this dog right beside him. So as I laid there and watched him and observed him, I could see that he had scalps … from his belt. And as I looked a little closer … he had ears … on a key ring and they were also hanging off of his belt. So that was my first impression and the first thing that I saw when I came in-country. And I can remember thinking to myself, "Oh shit! What have you got yourself involved in here, buddy."

John Vasarab, PFC, Service Company, 1967–1968

When I arrived, the first thing they did was put me in a hut and gave me a rifle. Then it was perimeter guard duty for a few days until they assigned me to the heavy junk repair company. At first, I said to myself, they don't even know me and here I am on guard duty. This is a little too fast as far as I was concerned. After settling in it seemed like an everyday job. The only difference was that you did not go anywhere without your rifle. Your weapon was part of you every day you were in-country. It was strange at first, but later on you felt like something was missing when you were without it, like on your way back to the world.

Dan Diridoni, LCpl., Service Company, December 1967–December 1968

I got down to Chu Lai and they said you're going with B Company. You are going north to build roads up near Hue City. Of course I had never heard of Hue City. I didn't know where it was. I met up with B Company in Tam Ky, which is halfway between Da Nang and Chu Lai. The next day we took off and went to Da Nang and stayed there. We stayed with the 7th Engineers there for a night. The next morning we took off and went up over the Hai Van Pass and down on the other side of it, and that's where I had my first experience with war.

Robert Handley, LCpl., D Company, January 1968–February 1969

When I first arrived in-country, it was at the end of the Tet offensive. The jetliner in front of us had taken fire. We had heard that there were casualties. I remember getting in-country with no flak jacket, no helmet, no rifle and you could hear

9th Engineer Battalion compound at Chu Lai. Courtesy of Jim O'Kelley.

explosions. You could see smoke. Nobody was there to tell you what was going on. It wasn't heavy activity but you could tell there was some shooting going on.

**Dave Nichols, LCpl.,
B Company, January 1968–February 1969**

I guess I must have been real naive because I couldn't believe we flew into Vietnam in a Continental Airlines Boeing 707. I expected to land on a muddy dirt runway. I was sure we would be under attack. Was I surprised to land in this huge airport (Da Nang) with concrete runways and big buildings all around. I later found out that at the time Da Nang airport was the second busiest airport in the world.

**Bill Spadafora, Cpl.,
C Company, A Company,
June 1968–July 1969**

As we're flying into Southeast Asia and

I'm looking out the window of the plane, I see this beautiful countryside. I see these beautiful mountains, these beautiful green hills, rivers and streams, and a bustling, hustling city below us. When I get off the plane it's about 7:00 in the morning and the heat hasn't really come up yet. It feels like a Florida day. It wasn't so bad until about 8:00 in the morning when the sun came full out, we started to sweat to death and the stateside utilities I had were completely drenched.

Jim Tagye, PFC,
D Company, August 1968–February 1969

When I first stepped off the plane, I can remember we went to a staging area and we had no weapons at all. I can remember looking out at the B-52's. They were the most eerie looking creatures, they were like creatures to me. They were scary looking. That was my first impression.

Martin L. Brown, PFC,
D Company, August 1968–August 1969

I remember coming in for a landing, it just turned dark, and it was like 7:30 at night. We were looking out the window and could see tracers flying all over the place. Looked like a wicked firefight going on. I'm thinking Jesus! Everybody was getting nervous because we could see it from up above.

Edwin J. Raley, PFC,
D Company, 1969–1970

The first thing I remember was when I stepped outside the plane and two fully loaded F4 phantom jets were taking off. My thoughts were just like boot camp, serious fear for my life. At that point life got very precious to me and every day I spent there was spent in fear of being killed.

Thomas P. Carras, 2nd Lt.,
A Company, B Company, Hdqtrs. Co.,
December 1969–September 1970

It was December 9, 1969, and after OCS, TBS and the Engineer Officer Orientation Course at Courthouse Bay, Camp Lejeune, I was finally in-country. The one thought that kept nagging at me as we headed for final approach was that I didn't have a weapon. What was I going to do if we came under attack? My naivete became apparent as soon as we taxied to the gate. I observed hundreds of GI's drinking, eating and just lined up along the fence. Everyone seemed to be quite at ease and relaxed. Of course it didn't register with me that these guys were waiting for me to deplane so they could catch their "freedom bird" back to the world. Their thirteen months in Vietnam were over and mine was only beginning.

Clyde Ricks, PFC,
D Company, August 1969–February 1970

The thing I remember on the way over is when the Beach Boys' song "Wouldn't It Be Nice" came on. I just remember a kind of lonesome feeling, thinking you could very well die before you've ever lived.

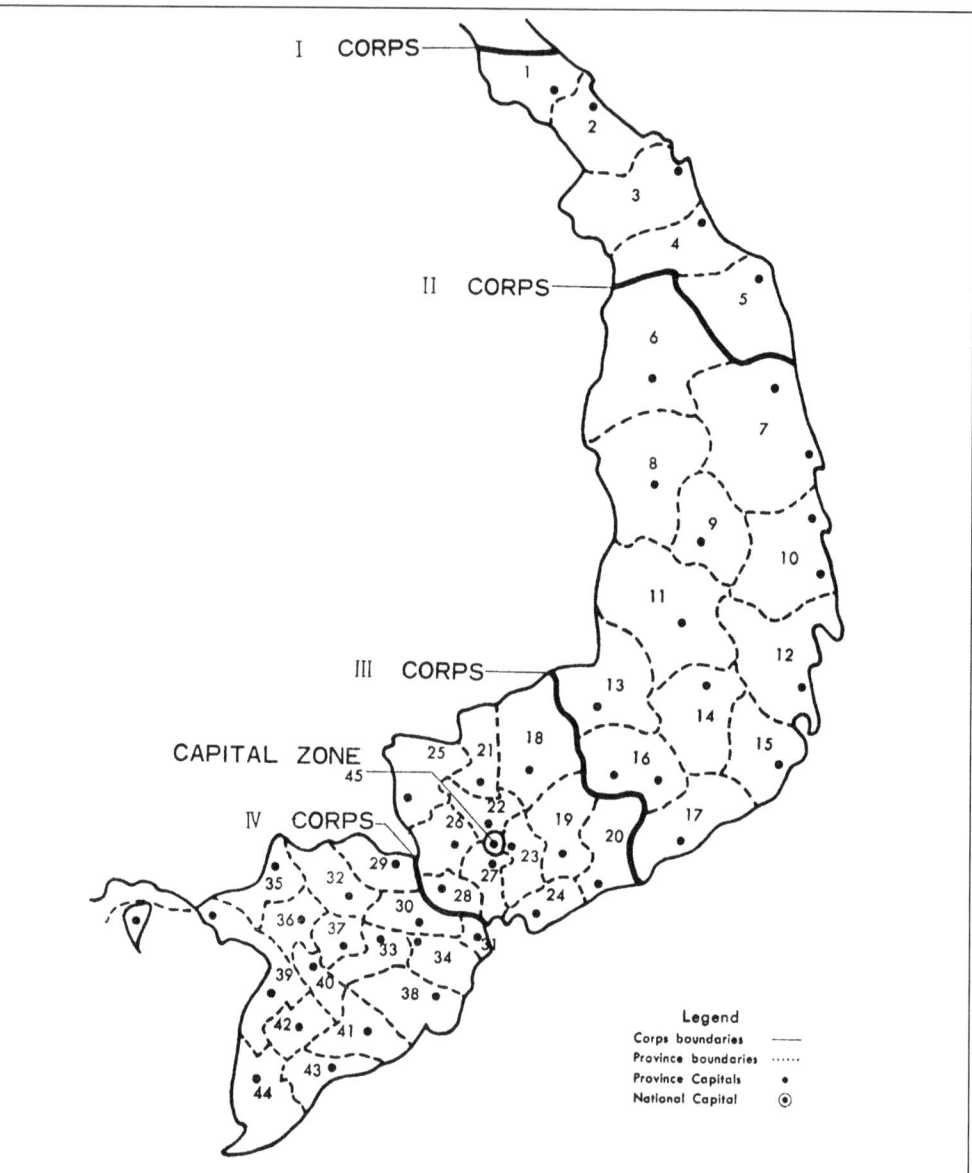

Tactical zones in Vietnam. 1. QUANG TRI, *Quang Tri.* 2. THUA THIEN, *Hue.* 3. QUANG NAM, *Hoi An.* 4. QUANG TIN, *Tam Ky.* 5. QUANG NGAI. 6. KONTUM, *Kontum.* 7. BINH DINH, *Bong Son, Qui Nhon.* 8. PLEIKU, *Pleiku.* 9. PHU BON, *Hau Bon.* 10. PHU YEN, *Song Cau, Tuy Hoa.* 11. DARLAC, *Ban Me Thuot.* 12. KHAN HOA, *Nha Trang.* 13. QUANG DUC, *Gia Nghia.* 14. TUYEN DUC, *Dalat.* 15. NINH THUAN, *Phan Rang.* 16. LAM DONG, *Bao Loc, Di Linh.* 17. BINH THUAN, *Phan Thiet.* 18. PHUOC LONG, *Phuoc Binh.* 19. LONG KHANH, *Xuan Loc.* 20. BINH TUY, *Ham Tan.* 21. BINH LONG, *An Loc.* 22. BINH DUONG, *Phu Cuong.* 23. BINH HOA, *Bien Hoa.* 24. PHUOC TUY, *Ba Ria.* 25. TAY NINH, *Tay Ninh.* 26. HAU NGHIA, *Khien Cuong.* 27. GIA DINH, *Gia Dinh, Saigon.* 28. LONG AN, *Tan An.* 29. KIEN TUONG, *Moc Hoa.* 30. DINH TUONG, *My Tho.* 31. GO CONG, *Go Cong.* 32. KIEN PHONG, *Cao Lanh.* 33. VINH LONG, *Vinh Long.* 34. KIEN HOA, *Truc Giang.* 35. CHAU DOC, *Chau Doc.* 36. AN GIANG, *Long Xuyen.* 37. SA DEC, *Sa Dec.* 38. BINH BINH, *Phu Vinh.* 39. KIEN GIANG, *Ha Tien.* 40. PHONG DINH, *Can Tho.* 41. BA XUYEN, *Khanh Hung.* 42. CHUONG THIEN, *Vi Thanh.* 43. BAC LIEU, *Bac Lieu.* 44. AN XUYEN, *Quang Long.* 45. SPECIAL CAPITAL ZONE, *Saigon.* (*U.S. Dept. of Defense map.*)

MAY–JULY 1966

Buddhist demonstrators against Saigon regime in Hue and Da Nang, March 10. Government troops take over Da Nang, May 23. Government troops take over Hue, June 16.

American aircraft bomb oil depots near Hanoi and Haiphong, June 29. President de Gaulle of France visits Cambodia in September; calls for American withdrawal from Vietnam. American troop strength in Vietnam reaches nearly 400,000 by year-end.

MAY

**Wayne McGinnis, LCpl.,
D Company, June 1966–July 1967**

When we first got there, Highway One was a cowpath. It was just like an old back country dirt road, and when it rained it turned into mud. It was just in terrible shape, terrible. I found it very hard to believe that that was the main artery between north and south Vietnam. It was a cowpath full of holes. When it rained, it turned into total mud and was impassable in a lot of places.

JUNE

**Walter Hayes, Platoon Sgt.,
B Company, 1965–November 1967**

We were real fortunate. We had a couple of rocket attacks the first week we were there but not on us. They were going for the air wing and we'd watch the rockets go overhead. It was just amazing to see. We built a berm around the camp, to start off, then set up our perimeter watches. Then we just started building the Battalion from scratch. When I say scratch, I mean scratch scratch. We had a few unique incidents

Building water tower. Courtesy of Jim O'Kelley.

where they brought in teak wood from the Philippines which there wasn't a nail in this world could go through. We had to go back and get different lumber. It was just a real good experience. I've never worked with such great people in my life. The men

KEY LOCATIONS IN I CORPS
(U.S. Dept. of Defense map.)

we had there, they weren't all young and they weren't scared to get out and hump it.

Our water came from water buffaloes. A water buffalo is a big tank type trailer that holds a couple hundred gallons of water. It gets warm after awhile, but at least it was clean. We'd go over to the air station and fill our water buffaloes up until we got our own water. Eventually we built our own purification tanks. After it was purified, we'd pump it into our water tower. It was just an ongoing constant thing. We had six, eight tanks purifying at all times.

We didn't supply water to other people, not at first. We just did it for our own battalion. Eventually we had our own water purification plant. We had our own laundry. You name it, we could do it. Eventually we were totally equipped to handle anything electrical. We never did get a sewer system. [laughs] We still burned it, to the day I left. If you were a turd bird, you got the privilege of going out there and burning it in the morning. Keep your nose clean and you didn't have to bother. You couldn't get no volunteers for it.

On my first tour, we disarmed the mines and booby traps to find out what they were all about and what type of mines they were using against us. I got a picture of a raincoat mine that I dug up. It was made by a Viet Cong with a raincoat, bamboo strip beams and a Chinese blasting cap and a Russian detonator on it. So it was a combination of three countries, really, right there. We turned that stuff in so they'd know what the enemy were using in our area.

We basically knew that other countries were supplying parts for mines. We basically knew what we were going to encounter, or could encounter from what other companies had bumped into and other people had found. They passed it on through our S-2 and everything. We were not surprised at all. You didn't hear that much about it. You knew that they used anything they could get their hands on. Homemade or foreign devices, like the mine made up in the raincoat. They used anything.

Ted Zealley, Lt., D Company, November 1965–June 1967

When the battalion arrived, we concentrated on setting up our own house. I think we were somewhat criticized for that, but as a result, once we were done with that, we were able to do our job better. We started out with strongback tents and slowly converted to frame sides and tin roofs. Of the compound construction projects, the two most celebrated were the completion of the showers and the completion of the mess hall in time for Thanksgiving dinner in 1966.

When we first arrived, our power was supplied by GM diesel generators that "screamed" at 1800 rpm. Later they were replaced by Cummings diesel plants that hummed at 1200 rpm. We couldn't get to sleep for the first week because the new units were too quiet.

Raymond Joseph Simonetti, LCpl., Service Company, May 1966–January 1967

I was partial to the Vietnamese children. I felt sorry for them. There was a little Vietnamese kid that would come and pick up our laundry and stuff. They were entertainment. They were nice kids and they made you feel you were doing something right there. There were times in-country where you would begin to question … just what the heck it was we were doing. We tried to help the civilians in any way we could. The bad part about it was, those guys that we were helping in the daytime were probably Victor Charlie in the nighttime. And that was the problem…

I never had any R&R. I was approaching R&R and I was notified by the Red Cross I had to go home because my mother was dying. So, I guess my R&R was being sent back to the States for an emergency leave for my Mom.

Lawrence Stephen Roberge, LCpl., Service Company, June 1966–January 1968

Our company gunny used to drink a lot and give us a lot of grief, but after somebody left a .50 cal. round on his desk with his name on it, he quieted down some. When I first got there, we had a motor pool C.O., what an ass. His main concern was landscaping. We spent countless hours planting trees, moving rocks, and putting mortar tubes between the trucks, so everything would look pretty I guess. The Captain was more concerned with what the motor pool looked like than how it operated. I soon got transferred to five-ton driver. Happy days! Out of the office and on the road. Like I said, the Sgt. Major and I never got along. I was always on his shit list. For me it was a learning process, screw around and pay the price (fill sandbags, guard duty). Never had any problem with the other men. We were a family. We got along, and we worked and played and drank and fucked and drank and survived. We weren't grunts. We weren't getting shot at every minute. We had a job to do and we did it. Drinking water was a problem, but everybody had that. Fresh bread, fresh fruit, steak, those were all luxuries. And boy, did I miss them.

Wayne McGinnis, LCpl., D Company, June 1966–July 1967

I can remember the very first time I ever got shot at. I'd been there about two weeks and a Lieutenant come down and he said, "Does anyone here have any artistic ability?" Well, I always knew in the Army you never volunteer for anything, and I asked him what do you have in mind. He said, "They blew up a bridge down south of here. What we want you to do is just go down there and maybe give an artist's rendition of what it looked like before." So I slung my rifle over my shoulder and they're sitting up in a jeep on the road. I waded out into this rice paddy which is maybe only halfway up to my knees. I get a pad and my rifle's over here and I'm looking, "Yeah, I can almost see. It would have been this way."

I'm drawing it, pretty soon I hear like, "pling." I didn't know what it was. I'm looking around and they're screaming, "Get down, get down!" Well, here there were a couple snipers over on the treeline. They've taken a couple of shots at me. When it dawned on me what it was, pad, pencil and everything was gone and I'm in the water going through there like an alligator. I'm heading over to that damn bridge and that's the first time that I had ever been shot at for real.

The constant threat was sometimes enough to drive you crazy, 'cause you would hear an air strike going on over the hill or you would hear machine gun fire off in a distance. You were thinking how very vulnerable you are, just out there, although your rifle is laying right there. You don't have it in your hand, you're not just sitting there looking for an enemy, you are busy working.

First mess hall. Courtesy of Jim O'Kelley.

JULY

Walter Hayes, Platoon Sgt., B Company, 1965–November 1967

We built our own water towers, shower units, and we built wash racks outside. We had a platform where you could walk from one end of the camp to the other so you wouldn't have to walk through sand all the time. We were completely self-sustaining.

We had to build all of our own bunkers. A lot of them we just built out of 55-gal. drums, filled them full of sand and then sandbagged around them. We had one 1st Sergeant, just come in-country, and we got rocketed that night. He got in a bunker. Then they sound "all clear" and all we could hear was "help, help." We thought somebody got shot. It was him. He couldn't get out. He was too short and fat. It was pitch black out there and nobody knew where he was.

It was a regular thing teaching new guys about mines, especially when you knew you were going out on an operation and you were going to have to take six, eight guys out. You'd sit them down and explain the type of mine they'd been finding in that particular area, raincoat mines, box mines, or just what type of booby traps they were using. You'd give them the best class you could give the day before you would go out as a refresher.

With 1st Engr. Battalion we made it mandatory that everybody who came in went to mine warfare school, again. A two week course before they would be assigned to a Battalion or anything. At 9th Engineer Battalion we didn't have that luxury because it was just constant work. There was

Large rock crusher. Courtesy of Ted Zealley.

never a time when you could say everything was done.

It's just one man trying to outsmart the other man. You take your bayonet and get down on your hands and knees then insert it two to three inches into the ground as you go. Back and forth, left to right. Then, just move real slowly. Hopefully you can just find the mine that way. After you find it, you have to check for booby traps, which is a matter of digging around it and under it, through sand and dirt depending on the area you were in. A lot of times our detectors would miss them because there was so little metal on them, they were easily overlooked. And the guys running the mine detectors would literally just miss them. I found some of them visually. I knew a little bit more what I was looking for. I was looking for some terrain broken. We had one where it looked like a tank tread had gone down the road. Well, there was a jeep track within the tank track. All of a sudden the jeep track disappeared, yet the tank track was still there. I said, what did the jeep just get up in the air? They put a mine in there and then used their fingers to simulate the tractor track for the tank but they couldn't simulate the wheel track for a vehicle. I spotted that. In that little break, there was a mine.

Trip wires got a lot of guys. One place we used to go they would set the trip wire about six and a half feet up in the air. That was to get the radio antenna on the man carrying the radio. People would just walk under it but they wanted to get the radio man because usually it's near the officer in charge. They'd use that once in awhile.

Ted Zealley, Lt., D Company, November 1965–June 1967

The roads in the vicinity of Chu Lai and the village of An Tan were in bad shape. The heavy military traffic had beaten through the thin asphalt and into the sand. Our leaders decided to place a layer of laterite on the roads, because it was firm and would hold up better than the sand. We spent the summer of 1966 spreading laterite on the roads. When the rains came, the laterite turned to brown soup and we spent the winter of 1966-1967 scraping the laterite off the roads (often into the nearby rice paddies, which did not endear us to the local residents) and capping the roads with stone.

One of the most precious pieces of equipment that we had was our rock crusher. We had a small single stage crusher that ran but didn't produce much. The real "prize" was the multistage roller crusher. When it came ashore, Lt. Mike Lundy, battalion embark officer, had to come ashore with it. If it went down in the surf, he was to go with it. We spent a great deal of effort getting a retaining wall and "grizzly" built for our rock crusher. Unfortunately, neither the retaining wall, grizzly or crusher ever worked very well. When we could, we'd beg stone from the Seabees, but were more successful in buying stone from the Vietnamese who made little ones out of big ones the hard way, with hand-held hammers.

Most of our rolling stock suffered from being in storage for so many years. Tires fell apart very quickly. Our lowboy trailers were usually down because we had to steal tires from them to put on the dump trucks.

We had no water trucks to provide water for compaction. Somewhere we came up with a large water trailer that had to be mounted on a dolly and pulled, being a fifth wheel truck tractor. But there were few, if any, places we could turn it around and we didn't have much equipment available to fill it. When the civilian contractors that were building the concrete strip at Chu Lai were done, they buried their equipment rather than ship it back to the States. One day they drove the equipment into a pit they had dug. Before they returned the next day to cover it all up, enterprising 9th Engineer supply scouts extracted two identical water trucks of a reasonable size and delivered them to our compound. We kept one running (#007) with the parts from the other. Of course, when IG inspectors came around, they had to be hidden.

Later in our first year the Americal Division (Army) moved into Chu Lai. They had next to no engineer support, so they were glad to have us around. We were glad to have them around, too, because we could swap a load of fill dirt for a tire. Good trading going on. I'll bet the Army supply folks were wondering why the Americal Division was going through so many large truck tires when they didn't have many such trucks themselves.

When the winds blew crosswise on the concrete strip at Chu Lai, the planes leaving on early bombing runs north of the DMZ had to use the old "tin strip," which unfortunately was in a direct line with our CP. I don't know if anyone slept through those F-4 Phantoms taking off one hundred feet or so above our heads with full afterburners on to get them on their way after launching from the short tin strip. Those days were long ones because the planes usually took off between 0400 and 0430.

Other activities in which we were involved included the design and erection of watch towers around the Chu Lai perimeter. The colonel in charge of the security force had me fly up to Da Nang to see the towers that had been put up around Marble Mountain. He wanted some "just like those" put up around the Chu Lai perimeter. I went to Da Nang and discovered that they mounted 106mm recoilless rifles on the top of their towers. The "rifles" normally had a crew of three — gunner, loader and ammo bearer. The ones at Marble Mountain had a crew of four — the usual three plus a "hammer man." After each round, the hammer man had to scurry all

Watch tower with .50 caliber gun. Courtesy of Jim O'Kelley.

over the platform and tower and renail the tower back together before the next round could be fired. I respectfully reported to the colonel in Chu Lai that he really didn't want towers "just like the ones" at Marble Mountain. I designed the towers and they were built as designed. We didn't put recoilless rifles in them — just .50 cal machine guns. When Jim O'Kelley arrived in-country, it was just before the monsoon season. The Battalion C.O. got "cold feet" about the towers and had Jim check the design to see that they would stay up in the anticipated winds. They withstood not only Jim's checking, but also the winds and a direct hit from a mortar shell on one of the four legs. The tower still stood strong.

Floating bridge at Da Nang. Courtesy of Ted Zealley.

There were other interesting problems with materials. After we ran out of lumber and nails that we brought with us from CONUS, we were supplied with Philippine mahogany 2 × 4's and Okinawa nails. We had to predrill the nail holes if we ever expected to make more than ten percent of them get through the first 2 × 4.

When the Americal Division came in and most of the Marines left, except for air wing, comm battalion and 9th Engineers, we few Marines took great pleasure in deriding the Army, although we were a bit outnumbered. We noted with some disgust that one of the first projects we had to do for the Army was to enlarge and improve the morgue over by the hospital.

In the early days in Vietnam we used to send the HQ Company survey crew out to survey routes and other things. There were times when the crew found themselves a long way from help, sometimes miles from the nearest Marines. After a couple of shots being sent their way, they decided to go prepared. I think their old 3/4 ton "PC" was among the best armed in Vietnam. Everyone had automatic weapons, a machine gun was mounted on the hood, and grenade and rocket launchers were in the back. But best of all, the crew became very proficient at collapsing the survey gear and loading it into the truck and moving out mighty fast.

Robert F. Goins, Captain, A Company, November 1965–May 1966

Landing in Chu Lai, our battalion established security in an encampment and carried out mission assignments in the general vicinity. Within two weeks, A

Company was assigned to the operational control of the 7th Engineer Battalion located in the vicinity of Da Nang. Upon relocation to that TAOR, A Company was assigned mine sweeping and other missions while preparing for a classic road, bridge and mine sweeping operation from the Song Cai Do [River] to the village of An Hoa. This was in the Third Marines' TAOR, and A Company was assigned a position on a hill between Hill 22 and Hill 41 with artillery support. The mission was to sweep, clear and improve Route 5 in a five kilometer sector to complete the surface link between Da Nang and the industrial area south of An Hoa. This was expected to require about six weeks.

To accomplish this mission A Company was reinforced with earth moving equipment and personnel from the 7th Engineer Battalion, an interpreter, corpsman and communicator. Also, additional crew-served weapons were assigned. Artillery support and patrol coordination was accomplished with 2nd Battalion, 3rd Marines. Resupply was provided by 7th Engineer Battalion with hot meals brought out every three days.

The normal routine was to sweep the entire sector of road for mines early each day and then to move the heavy equipment out of the company position to the assigned work sector. Engineer platoons provided security for the equipment by establishing listening and observation posts and patrolling. Borrow dirt was available in close proximity to each sector, and bulldozer and grader equipment shaped the road surface as required. Over 80,000 cubic yards of dirt were emplaced on Route 5 during this operation. Upon completion of the dirt emplacement and surface preparation, Sea Bee units sprayed liquid asphalt on the road to suppress dust and provide some water shedding capability.

Another major task of this mission was the construction of a Class 60 timber trestle bridge to replace a floating bridge. Again, A Company, reinforced, constructed the 116' bridge while providing security at the construction site. Friendly patrols were available during the construction period and no hostile fire adversely affected the project.

Fred H. Scheuter, PFC, B Company, May 1966–1967

When we got up near the DMZ, we made camp and I stayed there for about a whole month. Two other engineers and I would support the Marines out on Operation Hastings. We did a lot of things, from blowing up Charlie's ammunition, mine sweeping and bringing back water to camp while snipers fired at us all the time.

I remember one night the Viet Cong tried to hit us with mortars but missed and hit the village next to us and killed and wounded some Vietnamese people. Another night I woke up in the tent the three of us had made and were sleeping in. The guy in the middle (I can't remember his name) was bitten by a water moccasin. He was evacuated after he was vomiting. I never knew what happened to him.

After a whole month there, I started to smell and my clothes to rot, with a big hole in my pants (knee). I didn't take any extra clothes because I thought I would only be there for a few days. To make things worse, I got dysentery and the pills I was given didn't work. The Medic in charge ordered me back to the main camp. I left on a small pickup truck back to somewhere north of Da Nang.

Raymond Joseph Simonetti, LCpl., Service Company, May 1966–January 1967

On the Fourth of July we were on alert all that night. I guess the gooks was trying to get to us. An infantry unit was out in front of us. They sure did a hell of a job because there was green tracers and red tracers going everyplace. Those fellows did a hell of a job. We never saw a gook or anything, but we were certainly on alert. I guess they were trying to get through to us and those guys, out there in front of us, [pause] I'm sure some of them didn't make it. They had a hell of a battle all night long. God bless them fellows. They kept my butt safe.

I guess the best day I had in Vietnam was the day that I requested to see my Captain and he allowed me to switch over and go into heavy equipment. That's been the start of my career and certainly had to be a pretty good day because I've been able to provide a living for myself and my family. So that was a good day for me.

Lawrence Stephen Roberge, LCpl., Service Company, June 1966–January 1968

A letter from home was like gold. My mom used to write regularly and send me all the news from home. I felt mail was so important, I used to write to everyone. Relatives, friends, I even picked up names and addresses of girls from other Marines and wrote to them. I even wrote to my father a few times. (I hadn't seen him in 19 years or so.) I used to write to my dear aunt in French. She liked that. One time the PX was offering tiny cassettes, reel to reel, to mail home as letters. I sent a couple home. I still have them, but I don't have any way of playing them.

It was a real downer not getting any mail for a few days. My mom, bless her heart, used to send me care packages. Gum, candy, canned fruit, you know the good "junk food." She used to pack it with popcorn to fill the box. No matter how stale that popcorn was we always ate it. I always shared. My aunt sent me some homemade cupcakes once. They took so long coming they had mold on them, but we still ate them. Mom always sent me family pictures. One Christmas she sent me a picture of the Christmas cake and it was enough to make our mouths water. I used to get teary eyed when I got family pictures, wondering if I'd ever see them again. It's amazing how a letter from a loved one or a friend can mean so much.

Wayne McGinnis, LCpl., D Company, June 1966–July 1967

Most of my work consisted of rebuilding Highway One. We had to build it up and build it out. And I mean up because a lot of low lying areas in monsoon it just became water-logged and mud. We put culverts in, rebuilt the road and rebuilt three bridges. One they had blown up, so we set up a ferry system, what you call a floating bridge. We put a new decking on an old bridge that was there. One looked like it was an old railroad trestle. There used to be a railroad that ran parallel with Highway One. We took the old railroad bridge and we put wooden treadway down and we made a nice bridge that way for the vehicles. The other one we just tore down.

AUGUST–SEPTEMBER 1966

AUGUST

Walter Hayes, Platoon Sgt., B Company, 1965–July 1967

I saw a lot of good things and a lot of scary things. I've seen grunts shoot at other grunts across the river. They would think it was VC patrols and it would turn out to be us. I saw a lot of stupid things, things that I still can't believe happened. You'd be on an operation and they'd pass the word 'no rounds in the chamber' until you got shot at. Now here we are in a combat zone and they're telling you, you can't load your rifle. That happened to me twice and I think both of them were probably in 9th Engineer Battalion. You'd be going along and they'd tell you to unload your rifle until you were shot at. Now that doesn't make any sense. They said it was for safety. If you're going to get shot, you're going to get shot. They say it just takes a fraction of a second to throw a round in a chamber and return fire, but still it's a fraction of a second more than you needed to use.

We went out and sat on the air strip one time for two weeks waiting to build a bridge. They sent an Army battalion of tanks across this one bridge and they were afraid the VC would blow it. They had us there because it was their only way back. They had us stay on this air strip close by so we could go repair the bridge if needed. In the meantime, a couple of the Army Majors and Captains volunteered to take our guys up in Piper Cub airplanes. I went up just once and saw the light. There was no future in that. These were little spotter planes and if I kicked too hard I'd fall through the bottom. We were there about five days and finally convinced them to let us go to the Army club in town. They didn't want us to come. We promised there wouldn't be any fighting or anything like that. Well, twenty minutes after we got in, they threw us out and told us to go back out on the runway. [laughs] Stupid, hardheaded kids. They just wanted to get in a fight.

I've never seen so many people want to get killed. I mean, it was great. You never had to ask twice for volunteers for operations. I had young boys bribing me with beer to let them go out on patrols and on operations. They'd shine my boots for me. They'd beg for it constantly. It was funny. I guess I did it myself a couple times. Go out on an operation, just wish you'd get hit, that you'd get attacked. Then, when it would happen, it would probably last five or six minutes and the whole time you're praying that it gets over with. When it's over with, you're the baddest thing on the face of this earth.

You've seen "Rat Patrol" on TV with the jeeps going across country. 1/1 had two jeeps. One had a .50 caliber machine gun on it and the other had dual 60's on it. They had a waiting list of over a year of people wanting to go out at night and ride the roads in them things. I wouldn't even go on that road at night. You'd have to be a blooming idiot. And they had over a year waiting list. My guys would beg me to let them go out on those.

The hardest experience was that it didn't bother me to see the VC or Viet Cong shot or mutilated. It did when I saw Americans. You couldn't help from being bothered. You could even see the civilians while you were on a road sweep go down the road and they would pass you while you were looking for mines. Then they would get to a certain part of the road and actually drive around it, and you knew there was a mine there. They knew it was there. They'd just go around you like, "well, good luck guys." Even the ARVN soldiers would do that. I found two mines that way, watching a soldier on a motorcycle go up to a place and then actually just swerve and continue to go on. They wouldn't stop and let us know or anything. Some of them were sympathizers, I'm sure.

Ted Zealley, Lt., D Company, November 1, 1965–June 1967

Bridges were a real problem. None were in good shape and few designed to carry heavy tanks or guns. The bridges were favorite targets for the VC. The VC that dropped the spans on the bridge over the Song Tra Bong was a real expert. The bridge was reinforced concrete with precast concrete spans. He and his crew just dropped one pier and the two adjacent spans so cleanly ... a real work of destructive art. 9th Engineers built a temporary raft to keep traffic going. The RVN engineers had the task of putting a "Bailey Bridge" back in place of the old spans. Every time they got a piece of bridge in place, they had to take time out to cheer and celebrate. It was almost like watching a sporting event.

The bridges that the VC didn't take out, we Marines did. One bridge north of An Ton was quite weak, but could carry self-propelled guns if the drivers crept across in low gear and didn't shift. Of course, one driver couldn't be bothered to follow instructions and shifted from first to second at mid span, the worst place. He and his vehicle became instant submarines.

There was usually a railroad bridge fairly close to the highway bridges. Since the railroad was totally out of commission, we'd just reroute the road over to the railroad, tear out the tracks, and convert the railroad bridge to highway use. The load rating of the railroad bridges was no problem, it's just that the supporting beams were too close together for highway loads. It took a little doing and lots of timber to rework those bridges, but we became fairly proficient at it. To my knowledge, none of our converted bridges ever collapsed.

I often thought that we avoided major damage to Route 1 in our area because the VC was using it for resupply at night. We used the same route during the day.

The engineers were always welcome additions to infantry outposts. Soon after our arrival the infantry started getting the new M-16's which were plagued by jamming problems early in their use. The engineers still had the more reliable M-14's and typically came along with a couple of M-60 machine guns and often .50 cal's, too.

Raymond Joseph Simonetti, LCpl., Service Company, May 1966–January 1967

We were repairing a bridge up around Tam Ky, and one of the fellows ran a chain saw through his leg. Daggone, he ran it right through his leg and the chainsaw just kept on going. Up north, I backed a bulldozer right in an area that we suspected of being a mine field after we got off the truck. We got the dozer out of there. There was mines in the area. We marked it off and went back the next day to blow the area up. A Papasan came over to me at the time. Papasan said VC came through the area that night. Papasan picked up a can which happened to be a grenade and the white phosphorus went all over his face when it exploded. White phosphorus in the air just eats away at anything as long as it is composed in the air, [pause] and by golly, that old Papasan was in pretty bad shape.

I learned that right and wrong doesn't necessarily apply in Vietnam. I put the old man in the back of the PC truck, put a cover over the back and ran him back to the Battalion area looking for more medical attention than what we could do for him in the field. So, my compassion was to help the Papasan and get this stuff eating away on his face. When I got back, I was denied access. He didn't know I had an old man with his face being eaten away as we looked at it, but I was denied access. Of course, I raised a little hell. I thought that's what the hell we were here for was to help these people. And, following orders, I took the old man back, dropped him off, and got him some medical attention from a corpsman in the field. That was the best we could do for him. Who the hell knows whatever happened to him. The gooks probably wasted him that night anyway.

I was informed by our officers that this was a common tactic/ploy put on by the VC to take an old guy, screw him up, guy like myself takes him back to the area, he gets in the area and he maps out your hootch. Come that night, Victor Charlie comes around and pops you with some mortars and he has everything clocked out. So, live and learn horrifying things. I never seen a face being eaten away, [pause] while you were watching it.

Lawrence Stephen Roberge, LCpl., Service Company, June 1966–January 1968

We loved music in 'Nam. It was as important to me as eating. The music seemed to keep me in touch with the world. We had small radios to get local stations and armed forces radio. Then the reel to reel tape players came into the picture. Those were great because we could choose our music. I loved it. Some songs, when I hear them today, I get chills and tears in my eyes. I hear the songs and I instantly go back to the days of 'Nam. Some of my favorites are "California Dreamin'" by the Mamas and the Papas, and "These Boots Are Made for Walking" by my girl Nancy Sinatra. I used to be in love with her. I even had her autographed picture on the wall by my bunk.

When I left home at 18 I didn't drink. I had never tried it. I didn't fool around with girls. I had never tried that either. After a few months in Nam I couldn't get enough of either one. I remember my first two cold beers. The Battalion had a giant fridge in the center of the compound and you got two cold beers. I got mine, sat in the sand with some buddies, drank one and that's the last thing I remember until I woke up in my bunk the next morning. Wow. Great stuff. Give me more. Then I started drinking 45 whiskey that I'd buy from the kids in the village. I found the more I'd drink, the easier the days and nights were. I never drank on guard duty, and I never drank while I was sleeping.

Jim O'Kelley, 2 Lt.–1 Lt.–Capt., HQ & D Company, August 1966–May 1968

I can remember arriving in Chu Lai aboard a KC-130 from Da Nang. We were told that Chu Lai was "Indian Country" and to "hit the ground running." Well, it was hot, white hot sand, humid and extremely picturesque. I remember going from the airstrip (old Marston matting) on which was parked a DC-3 Marine Corps aircraft of WWII vintage to the reception area—a GP tent that had been strongbacked. They called to 1st Marine wards. Then the new S3 arrived — Major Fred Paige, who I think was an outstanding officer — very knowledgeable, Mustang (up through the ranks), kick-ass and take-names, get it done, get out of the office, highly skilled, hard driving, hard working, hard drinking, a Marine's Marine. He got the most out of me by using my school skills and teaching me field skills. He also probably kept me from getting killed on numerous occasions when I would want to do "Combat Kelly" things like volunteer to go to the grunts, etc.

Wayne McGinnis, LCpl., D Company, June 1966–July 1967

We used to cut three by twelve timbers with a two-man chainsaw. I remember this big D handle on the one end where the engine was at, and at the other end of that bar was another handle. We'd do that for a couple hours a day and it wears your butt out.

Bridge over Son Tra Bong river after the enemy blew it. Pontoon bridge erected for middle spans, with 9th Engineer in foreground at ferry site used for military traffic. Courtesy of Jim O'Kelley.

Division HQ and they sent a jeep to get me. I spent the night in transient officer quarters. Then down to 1st Engineer Bn where I was assigned to 9th Engineer Bn. I checked in with Lt. Col. Crispen, the CO, and Major Wayne Floyd, the XO. The XO used to have a habit of calling all of us junior officers — "you asshole!" It was a joke and only done to humble us rookies before folks like him who had served in two or three wars. It worked!

They assigned me to the S3 (Operations) section when they found out I was a graduate Civil Engineer. I reported in to a Major J. C. Floyd who left shortly after-

SEPTEMBER

Ted Zealley, Lt., D Company, November 1, 1965–June 1967

Before there was an official "officers' country" with tin roofed huts, we had to locate ourselves as best we could around the compound. We had quite a conglomeration of folks in Headquarters Company. I found myself sharing two tents with Capt. Bill Hocart, WO Steve (Seabags) Johnson, and WO's Love and Wright. I must admit I was probably the misfit in that particular crowd. But I was most appreciative of being among real veteran scroungers. We did fairly well. I do remember in the fall of '66, that we started feeling cold at night. Our bodies had become acclimated to 110 to 120 degrees each day. We even were having to resort to using two blankets on those "cold" nights. Someone came up with a "max-min" thermometer.

No wonder we were feeling so cold. It was getting down to 78 degrees at night!

The S-3 Construction Section consisted of Lt. Ted Zealley as Battalion Construction Officer, MGySgt. Daniels as construction chief, GySgt. Lelansky as survey chief, Sgt. Kono as chief draftsman and three to four surveyors and draftsmen whose names regretfully I have forgotten. They were a good and cheerful crew. I do recall their one casualty. When we were resurfacing Route 1 with gravel, they had their level set up to check grades and cross-slopes. Alas an MRS 100 and compactor made the level into part of the roadbed. It was a sore loss because levels were very hard to come by over there.

After being Bn Construction officer in the S-3 shop for a few months, I was anxious to move on to be a company commander, especially once I was promoted to Captain. But, since I was one of two or three graduate civil engineers in the battalion, the CO let it be known that I would stay in the "3" shop until another graduate engineer arrived. I sure was glad when Jim O'Kelley showed up. As soon as I found out he was a "real" engineer, I introduced him to the CO right away. True to his word, Lt. Col. Crispen reassigned me shortly thereafter.

But we all came to appreciate Jim (Combat) O'Kelley for another reason. Jim was a real "gung-ho" battlefield Marine, or so he wanted to be. Jim volunteered to take the patrols out on any night we would let him. Not that we were chicken, but us married guys didn't mind "Combat" taking the nighttime strolls at all.

Wetting down parties got to be quite hazardous at 9th Engr Bn. When Capt. Austin and I were promoted, 9th Engr Bn had no club. So, as many as were allowed to leave the compound, went to the 1st Engr Bn Club. Just as our crowd walked in the club, someone at the bar rolled all aces. That took care of round #1. Then Lt. Mizerak

9th Engineer base camp, September, 1966. Courtesy of Jim O'Kelley.

forgot to take off his cover when he entered the bar. Round #2. Then another poor Lieutenant (who was about to become poorer) walked in and forgot to take off his pistol. Round #3. So that took care of all the drinks for all the heavy drinkers. Dare I admit that Austin and I got off for about $5 each for our combined wetting down party?

But when 9th Engrs got their own club, things got really "nasty." The game was to see how much of a bill could be run up at the bar. Remember these were the days when lieutenants were still making $222.50 or just a little more when they got their promotion to "first." Bills over $100 were not unusual. Champagne and the like were often ordered. It was helpful to be on good terms with the barkeeper (GySgt. Lelansky) and restrict what was available on the night of the wetting down party. Those who did not take that precaution paid dearly.

**Fred H. Scheuter, PFC, B Company,
May 1966–1967**

I was farmed out the next couple of months to different Marine Infantry outfits. I was always in the field on patrols and operations. Lots of times I had to carry a mine detector, crate and all, on my back while on patrol.

I remember going on one patrol to the Laos border. I was the senior PFC among the other two engineers with three tanks and a platoon of grunts. The Lieutenant in charge was new and I was new. I had to mine sweep in front of the tanks. The terrain was hilly with no jungle at first. I got the Lieutenant real mad at me because I was slow and careful, blowing up everything that looked like a bomb. Instead of taking us a couple of hours to get to our destination, it took us all day! That night, at the border with Laos, was the worst night for mosquitoes. Even with protection net over our faces and repellent, they bit like hell. The next day the Lieutenant took a different way back instead of me mine sweeping. We rode some of the way on the tanks. One of the tanks got stuck in mud and they had to call for a tow tank.

After a while they sent me to south of Da Nang where the fighting was more intense. I went on an Operation one time with the South Vietnamese Army. They needed an engineer and I was elected to go. I was in an armed vehicle with a couple of US Army men and a company of South Vietnam Army. One shot was fired and the whole company of ARVN's ran. The US Army guys were mad.

**Raymond Joseph Simonetti, LCpl.,
Service Company,
May 1966–January 1967**

It was pretty horrifying seeing little kids have grenades tied to them looking to blow away the Americans. I think it's a damn shame that before you drink a beer out of a village you pull out a handkerchief or your shirt or whatever, and pour the beer through it. Then you could pick up any shavings of glass because some of our people got crushed glass in their beer.

I was attached to the South Korean Marines on a project down south, and them boys didn't bullshit around. We had a slope shoot one evening ... having a beer, seeing a chopper fly over, and a guy in black pajamas fly out. I asked what the hell was going on. I was told they didn't have the right information. There were all kind of neat things just happening all the time.

**Lawrence Stephen Roberge, LCpl.,
Service Company,
June 1966–January 1968**

Guard duty wasn't bad at all. You got to know the other guy in your bunker real good. Talking kept us awake and alert. The worst part was the last shift when you got stuck with the early morning hours. I hated those. First you had to wake up, then you had to stay awake, and then it was day already and back to work. I remember sharing those cigarettes. Passing it back and forth, it would get so hot. One of us would sink down, inhale and pop up, pass it to the other while he sank down. There was always one of us keeping watch, both out and in. We didn't want the officer of the day sneaking in on us without challenging him. "Halt who goes there" "What's the password" "Advance to be recognized" I don't think I'll ever forget that, but I always forgot my general orders. That got me in trouble a few times by some gung-ho staff N.C.O.

The other thing about guard duty I hated were the huge rats running around at night and the snakes. I hate snakes. They worried me more than the gooks.

Cold fruit was a real luxury in 'Nam.

My mom used to send me canned fruit and I would buy some ice from the vil. That was the greatest. Today when I have fruit I wonder how something that small could be missed so much.

Jim O'Kelley, 2 Lt.–1 Lt.–Capt., HQ & D Company, August 1966–May 1968

1 September 1966 Got up at 0630. Is very muggy, overcast & very damp here. Hang on bronchitis! Went to 1st Div Engrs. Capt. took me to briefing. There was assigned to 9th Engineers. Jeep picked me up brought to 9th HQ. Lt. Col. Crispen & Major Floyd — was assigned to S-3 with Maj. J. C. Floyd. Went on road recon up to "BoBo" Bridge at edge of Chu Lai TAOR. Got set up in tent with netting & air mattress. Took shower in portable shower unit.

2 September 1966 Got up at 0600 & ate chow at Cols Table. Been squaring away gear all day — oiled deck of the tent, drew 782 gear. Went to Division PX for odds & ends. Drew a locker box. Wrote home. Was with Lt. Zealley afternoon for briefing on S-3 jobs. Malaria pill!! (Big Orange — 1 per week)

6 September 1966 Went out on patrol/convoy 30 miles below Quang Ngai. Couldn't proceed to mission — VC MGing (Machine Gunning) the road. Air strike in progress. Returned to Chu Lai. Slept in afternoon. Read about Steve Synder KIA. Cleaned pistol. Have cramps & diarrhea. Showered in portable unit.

7 September 1966 Morning — nothing to do so read Strong Men Armed. Went to Division & picked up travel pay & mold preventive. Submitted drainage project for roadway & camp area. Rained like hell at chowtime. We ate on picnic tables outside. Put up screen on half tent. Wrote letters. Sent for Army Engineering Course.

8 September 1966 Went on road recon with Lt. from III MAF and Lt. Zealley. All over TAOR & outside it. Saw Ted Rathbern at 3/7. Heard that our convoy for bridge this morning was ambushed. One Lt. injured. Got drivers license.

9 September 1966 Read Death of a Citizen. Went to Chu Lai Defense Command (CLDC) to see Col. Curtis about 45' OP towers — said go to Da Nang & see there. Ran differential levels on RMK road for drainage problem. Cut hand on nail — got tetanus shot. MacAllister left — got his gear — fixed up tent. Pete Allen came in today. Lots of gunfire. Malaria pill.

10 September 1966 Went on recon of Op towers with Col. Curtis. Read Strong Man Armed. Wrote home again. Over to Div. Engr about Maintenance sheds. Planned drainage, recon on intersection, designed culvert, read again, no letters, no nothing.

11 September 1966 Wrote 3 letters. VC blew the Son Tra Bong River Bridge — 3 VC routed a CO (Company) of ARVN. Ordered glasses (plastic combat lenses) — checked on mail problem.

12 September 1966 Bn 00D — flare bombardment, 4 men asleep on posts, heavy storm damage, inspected drainage, Sandy Kempner 3/7 came by for help (2/Lt. Marion L. Kempner, Duke buddy, KIA later, Movie The Face of War is dedicated to him), no sleep yet since Saturday nite. Got letter from home — had steak tonight. Read Assignment Budapest.

14 September 1966 Went to LAAM Bn, went to 2/5, got caught in firefight on way home — had to hit dirt. 2 rounds over jeep from right — 1 from left — big firefight all over — got out OK though. Finished film & sent home — owe for stamps.

15 September 1966 Went to Song Tra Bong River Road recon & surveying — I carried radio & 2 M-26 grenades & shotgun (12G-Rem sportsman — full choke) & .45 with 5 loaded clips. Assigned investigation, assigned pay officer for tomorrow. took some pictures — new roll of film, got

letters from home. John Stuart gave me jungle trousers!

16 September 1966 Pay officer — picked up $15,547.00, went from office to Rock Crusher to Ferry at Bin Sohn to KMC-CP to KMC jobsite to 3rd Ferry, 2nd Ferry, 1st Ferry, Utilities DIV CP, and back. Received letters. Read Never Leave Me by Harold Robbins. Killed viper (snake) on RMK road. Appointed Asst. S-2/Military Geologist — Capt.'s billet. 60 mm mortars dropped near us on south trip.

19 September 1966 Went to KMC about airfield, went to 3rd Amtracs about Maintenance shed & parking pad. Had to redesign shed. Sent Mom check plus 2 letters. Mailed film. Received letters. Had VC attack on An Tan about 9 P.M.

21 September 1966 VC attacked Airfield & camp at 0130 — 8 planes damaged, 12 Marines injured, big firefight, UHIE's illuminated TAOR. Began investigation. Received cholera, plague flu shots. Letters from home. Checked amtrac job site. Designed weight room.

26 September 1966 Finished investigation. Very sore all over from football yesterday. Investigation accepted. No mail. Checked CLDC (Chu Lai Defense Command) tower sites. Beginning to get cold.

27 September 1966 Received Soils, Drainage, Pavements courses from Army Engineer School. Letter and package from home. Checked road to 2nd bridge N and 3/8H (3rd 8 inch Howitzer) tower site & 50 mount (.50 caliber Machine Gun). Studied S-2 material. Wrote home.

28 September 1966 No letters today. Wrote 3 letters. Checked on towers with Col. Curtis. Litwin (1/Lt. Mike Litwin) moved to Charlie Co. Went to wreckage & salvage for steel plates, LAAM Bn & An Tan to check jobs. Received fudge and letters from home.

Wayne McGinnis, LCpl., D Company, June 1966–July 1967

It was always a treat to go on our patrols at night, out around our own area, because we weren't the grunts. We'd go out there and see movement or somebody would shoot a flare over our heads. There'd be eight or ten of us out there and that would get to be a little hairy.

We were supposed to know where other friendly forces were when we were out on patrols. We knew what hills they were on. If they were out on an ambush, we didn't go over that way, but they knew we were going through a certain area, so that we didn't receive friendly fire. Our people along the fence and at the different bunkers were notified that we were out there, but we never had any problems with D company. We were at the outer most edge of the battalion, in the corner, and we had our one big main bunker and we always knew when there was a patrol out. Heaven forbid you start firing on your own people.

I remember on patrol at night you'd sit there. Just the sound of that country, you really understand how far you were from home. Just how small and insignificant you are. It's just a weird feeling, almost like an empty feeling. The moon would shine down through there. We always got through them pretty good. Sometimes you received enemy fire, most times you didn't. To tell you the truth, I don't even know why they had us do it.

OCTOBER–DECEMBER 1966

OCTOBER

Walter Hayes, Platoon Sgt., B Company, 1965–November 1967

I seen a lot of dumb things typical kids would do. Like I say, you blow things in place. You set your time fuse. We always left a big safety factor in there, for time, and they would cut short fuses ... and run like hell. Sometimes we would be on a road sweep and I'd go out and check them out. I'd see them set the charge and they'd take off running. They'd tell me to run. Once they'd tell me, I knew what they did. Little hardheaded rascals would short fuse it, it would blow up. They'd just be tickled pink they outran it. [laughs]

I came around one time and they had found three or four five-hundred pound bombs that didn't go off. So they wanted us to go out and put charges on them and blow them. They came from aircraft. I set my charge and went around and I heard a clicking noise. I came around the corner and here's one guy sitting on the doggone thing, while the other's taking his picture on it. I got on them and chewed them out. The one taking the picture says, "he's dumb, sitting on it. I wouldn't." Well, if it exploded, it wouldn't have made no difference because he was so close. Yet he was swearing to God how dumb the other guy was.

Ted Zealley, Lt., D Company, 1 November 1965–June 1967

I cannot claim to taking part in any great battles or firefights. The closest I came was when Jim O'Kelley and I left the 5th Marines CP and were returning to our own CP. Before we reached Route 1 we crossed through a clearing behind a 6 × 6 truck. When we got to the middle of the clearing, firing commenced from both sides of the clearing. Both vehicles stopped and we crawled under the 6 × 6 with its occupants. It soon became apparent that whoever was firing at whom, they weren't firing at us. Jim and I decided that it might be best to leave before someone decided that the truck was a good target. So we jumped back in our jeep and took off out of there.

I often said that my view of the war was very narrow. Our area of responsibility was from An Tan (Chu Lai) north to Tam Ky. Sometimes we went south to Quang Nai where the Korean Marines had a camp. But we didn't seem to care much what went on outside about 500 yards either side of our long strip of road.

There was excitement enough, I'd guess. Twice I lead convoys (one north and one south) to repair major collapses of roads. We had almost 100 dump trucks loaded with rock to try to fill the holes when the roads literally gave way into the rice paddies. Both times I had a truck slide off the side of the road and into the rice paddies. Of course, such incidents happened just as it was getting dark, and we had the uncomfortable task of extricating trucks out of the rice paddies with the

9th Engineer Battalion, Chu Lai Command Post. Courtesy of Jim O'Kelley.

wrecker lights on full beam so we could see what was going on.

Trucks weren't the only thing to get stuck in rice paddies. Tractors were a real joy. They'd sink in right up to the top of the engine housing. We had sort of a game with the Seabees taking pictures of each other's tractors that got stuck. Other tractors could not get them out. We had to call on tank retrievers to break the suction and get them out.

Fred H. Scheuter, PFC, B Company, May 1966–1967

After about three months in Vietnam, I was south of Da Nang getting shot at just about every day. Then I was told I was in the wrong outfit. I returned my M-14 rifle which was all rusted and left on a windowless cargo plane back to Chu Lai. When I got there, I was in the 9th Engineer Battalion, B Company, 1st Platoon, and got another M-14. I met some of the guys I was on ship with. When I got to the 9th Engineers in Chu Lai, it was still being built. The Seabees had shown them how to build the huts we lived in. I remember building many of them. I also remember helping pour cement in the heavy rain for the Mess Hall with the Gunnery Sergeant working with us. I can't remember his name but I remember his smile while he worked in the rain. After it dried, that floor looked like (you know what). We were always working (six and a half days a week). We worked in the heavy rain, in the village, on the road, in the mud two to three feet deep with a poncho, rifle and shovel. We built a bridge going west with cement and rocks. I was young and a gung-ho hard worker.

Raymond Joseph Simonetti, LCpl., Service Company, May 1966–January 1967

We came back in off of a road patrol and the guy says, "Hey, who wants to go to a firefight? Some people have our guys pinned down, and we have some trucks and whatever stuck." Just like coming in and saying, "You want to go to a drive-in movie?" Everybody grabs their shit, hop in the back of the truck and off we went. And no orders or anything, you know. Who wants to go? Bingo. Everybody is gone. I get down there, right away you deploy your people and make a hasty perimeter and stuff. Of course, I never thought the Marines would ever retreat, but as it turned dark and we had our perimeters set, then everything but a few shots were fired here and there. The next thing you know our guys said that's enough, let's get the hell out of here, so I kind of thought that was kind of humorous. Right then, you know, the gooks were there. I believe they had left and we left too, just get back into the safety net of the network of the compound, so to say.

Lawrence Stephen Roberge, LCpl., Service Company, June 1966–January 1968

Horrifying? The worst part of 'Nam was having to see the "hell" the children had to live through every single day. I could sympathize with what the adults were going through, but not the kids. No child should have to go through war. What was so amazing is most of these kids were happy and quite content. One day, during the monsoon season, it was raining hard and cold. I was driving my dump truck and I noticed a young girl standing in the rice paddy tending her water buffalo. She was shivering and looked cold. I stopped and gave her my utility shirt, trying to help her. She didn't wear it. She brought it in the hootch and gave it to mamasan. It was real hard for me to understand but I guess when you never had anything, you don't miss it. When your whole life has been in misery and you don't know anything else, it just doesn't matter. To this day, I can still see that little girl standing in the water, in the rain, near that huge water buffalo with a big smile on her face. So many great kids and no way to help them, makes you feel kind of useless. I don't know what ever happened to the shirt, but I learned a most valuable lesson that day. No matter how bad we think we have it, we just have to look around. We had a way out of that misery, they didn't.

Jim O'Kelley, 2 Lt.–1 Lt.–Capt., HQ & D Company, August 1966–May 1968

I remember my first patrol I took out from the Battalion through the boonies to An Tan and back. It was 2 October 1966 — a day patrol — to familiarize us with the area in daylight before starting the night patrols that I took out most every night through the summer of 1967. Anyway, we were moving along fine through our radio checkpoints, we came to the river west of An Tan and I called a halt. I moved over near the river to some higher ground and stood near a tree with my binoculars, looking around — especially across the river. All of a sudden — whack, whack — rounds started impacting on the tree and around me — and my Marines opened up with their M-14's and M-60's and M-79 grenade launchers. Well, we got into a pretty good firefight but they wouldn't let us cross the river to go after the gooks. We (or they) broke contact after awhile and we assessed our situation (no casualties) and then we continued on and returned to base. When I got to the wire, I had a radio message for me to report directly to the S3. Major Paige was waiting. I walked in and stood at attention before his desk. He looked up at me and said in his most stern voice, "Lootenant O'Kelley — read what it says on that sign on my desk!" I looked down and read "The Seven P's — Prior Proper Planning Prevents Piss Poor Performance — sir!" He then said, "We've had a nice quiet war over here, suddenly we get this wild Irishman in here and you start raising hell, getting into firefights and throwing rocks into a bees nest! What in the hell happened?" Well, we talked for a long time and at the end I left with a better understanding of the do's and don'ts on patrol, etc. And I think Major Paige realized I handled the situation okay because he assigned me to take out those night patrols and to be Battalion Security Officer as well as Battalion Construction Officer.

The fall of 1966 was very busy. Chu Lai had been "pacified" during Operation Starlight in late 1965, so we were in a building frenzy. It ultimately became the second busiest and biggest airstrip in I Corps ("eye corps"). Much of the construction was done by the 9th Engineer

Battalion and the Seabees—with the First Engineer Battalion handling much of the pioneer/combat engineer effort with the Division units. I remember working with 1/Lt. and later Captain Ted Zealley on the 50 foot high guard towers that ringed the airfield. Ted, who was the only other school-trained civil engineer, designed the towers and I checked his design and calculations. It wasn't really necessary to ever check Ted's work; he was and continues to be an outstanding engineer—very thorough, precise, and conscientious. I had the privilege of working for and with Ted for a few months in 1966 before he was promoted and took over Delta Company. It seemed like I followed in Ted's footsteps until I retired in 1996. I took over Delta Company in 1967, met Ted again in 1978 at CLNC Combat Engineer Officers Refresher Course, worked with him from 1989 to 1995 at Quantico and in my final tour relieved him as CO of the DCS/I&L Reserve Augmentation Unit at HQMC.

2 October 1966 Recon patrol 0445–1200. Hit by sniper fire 0800—returned 85 rounds across river at fleeing snipers. Charged by water buffalo—everyone scattered off trail.

4 October 1966 Five letters from home. Worked at drainage site. Drew up retaining wall for Bridge Plt for 1st Ferry. Finished 2nd lesson of Drainage course and mailed. Okie trip canceled today. (Was going to Okinawa to be trained in Atomic Demolitions (ADM).)

8 October 1966 Carried ops to drainage site. Washed clothes. 2 WIA–1 KIA (SSgt. Friddle) at KMC—Chu Lai road. Worked on lesson 4 Drainage—prepared for inspection. 2 letters from home.

10 October 1966 Finished lesson 5 Drainage & mailed. Major J. C. Floyd transferred to 1st Engineers. Took a picture of jeep & truck (hit by ambush). Washed clothes for 1½ hours—no lunch. Checked drainage project in afternoon. Went to SSgt. Friddle's memorial service. Division wants five—1302's to go to Infantry—taking 40 from Division—I volunteered!

11 October 1966 Raining all day. Staked out chapel and EM club. Sent Sea Tiger home (Vietnam USMC newspaper similar to Stars and Stripes US Forces newspaper). Checked grizzly & Rock Crusher & drainage site. Letters from home.

13 October 1966 What a day! Started off with early comshaw run to 2/5—got 2 jackets, 1 boots. Gave 1 jacket to SSgt. Lelansky. Next went on mine sweep recon. When returned had pair of boots waiting via 3/7. Took tools to Heavy Equip Hq Co. Letter from home. Patrol warning order at 2000. Mailed box home—bermudas, glasses, papers, doll. Wrote 2 letters.

Ammo dump at Chu Lai, blown during Tet, 1968. Courtesy of Jim O'Kelley.

14 October 1966 Studied Lesson 1—Soils Engineering. Got AR (M-14 Automatic Rifle) with 6 magazines for tomorrow. 60 VC hit us last night — also VC Rgt coming this way from old 3/7 at Song Tra Bong. 6 WIA Shore Party PC 2 miles south. Drove our PC to DIV CP. Recon at 1300. Scrounge to 3/5, Hill 69 and 3/7 for boots — gave to Zealley, Duncan & Knowlton (Cpl. Bill Knowlton). Letters from home.

18 October 1966 Rain all morning. Tried to work in afternoon. Received letters from home. Ate chow at Army Radio Station (Army MARS radio site). Got books from Army soldiers.

23 October 1966 Rained all day. Washed out our campsite. My CP under 2 feet of water.

24 October 1966 Returned to 9th CP from ROKMC. Letters from home. Saw VC victims this morning (hanging on wire where they were killed while attacking our camp).

26 October 1966 Commander for convoy 83 vehicles to Quang Ngai — 175mm guns. No mail. Fire mission on "B" Co– 10–12 VC, 6 Rds — was BN OOD. (4–175 mm guns, 4 Ontos, 12 Low Boys, 1 MRS 200, 1 APC, 25 jeeps, 30 6×6–5 ton, 1 Wrecker and 5 AN/MRC 83)

27 October 1966 Wrote home, sent film. Can't hear due to concussion from firing yesterday. (Had to get "combat earplugs" from 3/7 Battalion Surgeon.)

28 October 1966 Malaria pill. Recon to 1/5–2 rds SA (Small Arms fire) from sniper at jeep while going thru fishing village N of 2nd Ferry (Caused by event: Marines in trucks were riding through village — young girl ran out of hootch and threw a grenade in truck & grenade was a dud but Marines killed girl. Villagers were pissed off at us for killing her!?). New chow hall opened up. Wrote 2 letters. Finished hot locker & moved into tent. Procured tin for 3/7.

NOVEMBER

Ted Zealley, Lt., D Company, 1 November 1965–June 1967

On the way over to Vietnam, D Company was aboard an old LST. The Marines apparently did a lot of work fixing things up on the ship, and the ship gave D Company a pretty good supply of .50 caliber ammo which was not Marine Corps issue … like it wasn't supposed to be used by ground troops against ground targets according to the Geneva Convention, or something like that. It was kept in the D Company ammo bunker. Just before I went on R&R we heard that there would be an IG inspection, so we had the ammo buried alongside the row of our tents. While I was gone, new tin huts were constructed, with one or two being placed right on top of our ammo stash. No one could tell the construction crew not to build them there for fear that the ammo would be discovered. It could be there to this day.

I suppose much of what we built has long been destroyed or rotted away. One structure I could hope was still there is a hospital (clinic) that we built for the people of An Tan. It was a memorial to Dickie Chappelle, a woman war correspondent killed near Chu Lai. The materials for the hospital were donated by her friends.

Speaking of women, there were none in our units in those days. It was a big deal when the USO shows came around. Bob Hope never came to Chu Lai, but a few others did. The most memorable for me was the visit by Martha Raye. She made no pretense at being a beauty queen, but she remarked that "at least they're round," referring to her eyes. She had drinks with the officers and then toured the area hollering and hooting at Marines as they left the showers as she rode atop an MRS 200. She was quite a kick. But there was a lot more to Martha Raye than the showmanship.

Reconnaissance of road, bridges and culverts on Route #1. PC (¾ ton truck) with security up ahead. Left to right: Cpl. William Knowlton, S/Sgt. LeLansky, 2/Lt. Jim O'Kelley. Driving jeep: Farley. Note: radio, machine gunner in jeep, motor running all the time — road usually heavily mined. November, 1966. Courtesy of Jim O'Kelley.

Her traveling companion told us she was a nurse in the Army Reserves. When things got really bad somewhere near the DMZ, and casualties came flooding into Da Nang, she canceled her performances and reported to duty at the hospital, working there for 72 hours without a break. And when Martha came to Chu Lai, she went to every unit she could find. When a company was pulled out for action before she could reach them, she came back later that month and put on a show for that company alone.

Larry P. Howell, PFC, H & S Company, May 1966–November 1966

The weather was hot and a lot of rain. The food sucked, supplies weren't easy to get, as some of the supplies were being sold or traded on the black market. Some of the Vietnamese were okay and friendly, but you still had to watch them 'cause you never knew what they would do. R&R was good but not long enough, a week not much time. Goods in the PX was okay when it wasn't being sold or traded on the black market. Out of 18 months in Vietnam, I saw Martha Raye once. I knew the entertainers were there but couldn't get to them to see them.

We listened to AFARTS Radio Golden Oldies. Favorite songs — "We Got to Get Out of This Place" and "I'm a Believer." Mail was pretty important and a good feeling.

Rear, left to right: *Fred Brown, Larry Howell, John Broomes, J. L. Hillard.* Front, left to right: *Hanson, Hanigian. Courtesy of Larry Howell.*

Raymond Joseph Simonetti, LCpl., Service Company, May 1966–January 1967

Talking about respect for the Marine Corps, I was deployed on a TAD team, during monsoon season, keeping the Route One open. In a certain section gooks would come down there with a bus and load it up with just people all over the thing. My job was to keep the road open, even if I had to push them off the sides, do that so our troops could move at will. You should have seen that gook. I hooked on to the dozer, hooked onto the front end of his bus. I guess I had a poor sense of humor. I went to pull that bus out of the mud and all those people wouldn't get off and lighten up the load. I pulled the whole damn front end out of that bus. Them guys had to walk down. We ended up shoving the thing off the side of the road. Them guys were pissed. It was kind of funny.

Wayne McGinnis, L/Cpl., D Company, June 1966–July 1967

They had a company meeting one morning and said that Martha Raye was gonna come to 9th Engineer Battalion at Chu Lai. They were looking for two fellows to be her bodyguards. The only reason Martha Raye came into that area, I don't know if it's the only reason, but they said she came because it was considered a "hot" area at that time in early '66. Whereas Bob Hope, John Wayne, etc., they wouldn't come into that area because it wasn't secure enough. They would go into Da Nang.

Civilian bus. Courtesy of Jim O'Kelley.

Billy Graham came as far in as Da Nang in December of 1966 and we went up to see him. So he wouldn't even come down there.

Martha Raye was a people person. She really related to the guys. She had a little bit of a foul mouth, I don't want to use that word "foul mouth," but she made the guys feel real relaxed. I remember having dinner with her in the evening, sitting at her table, and she was a riot. The fact that she's still alive and suffering like she is, is a shame. She really got along good with the troops and made everyone feel relaxed and took your mind off what was going on around you. She was only there the one day. She gave a performance in the evening and that was right after we had chow in the mess hall.

The only thing that I remember about that Dickie Chapelle Memorial hospital was, apparently she was a war correspondent that was either killed or lost on a patrol in and around the Chu Lai area back in 1965.

Bill Turner, GSgt., D Company, May 1966–June 1967, November 1968–June 1969

The press in the states raised around $15,000. They gave it to an officer who was supposed to take care of a monument for Dickie Chapelle. Along with other things, the officer disappeared with the money and the date's rapidly approaching. All they were going to do is build a little thing in-country. Someone got this idea about let's make it a little bigger. So we came up with this seventy bed hospital. My platoon was assigned the job of construction, Delta Company, Third Platoon. There was no material, there was no money, there was nothing. So I went out and started scrounging. In other words, if you're up in 7th Engineers, or 11th Engineers, or the Seabees, or RMK, or wherever we could get materials, we would get it. RMK [Royal Marine Koreans] furnished the commodes, the seabees furnished the cement, and stuff like that. They all knew what it was for. I did some of the asking, the officers, the S3 did most of the arranging for the stuff.

We started this project and the same time we started the project it started raining. We poured the concrete footers in the rain, and you talk about a pretty good size building. I don't remember the dimensions of it. I think it was one-hundred-ten feet one way, and about seventy feet the other way. It was in a "T." So everybody gets a little piece of this. In other words, the whole battalion. If I need some help, I'll get it from whoever. So all the way through this we're starting to work around the clock. We have a deadline. I think it was the date of her death. She went out on a patrol on the date they wanted to dedicate it. We worked around the clock to get the thing done, and we did get it done on time.

But about two weeks before dedication, they came out and introduced me to this young Lieutenant and said, "This is the officer in charge of the project." So I went back to see my skipper and said, "What the hell they trying to pull?" He said, "This is too big a scope for an enlisted man to have anything to do with it. There's got to be an officer in charge." I don't mind if he's in charge. So, what they

Dickie Chapelle Memorial Dispensary. Courtesy of Jim Frank.

did to satisfy me, the battalion PIO (Public Information Officer) came over and took pictures of me and Frank Coward in front of this thing. They ran a story in the Oceanside home town paper about how Bill Turner and Frank Coward did all this stuff and ran the whole story. This beat the national press and everybody coming out.

There was a flag pole right in the front with a plaque. Within two or three days after the dedication the village chief was hung. They hung him right out on the flag pole. We were told it was because all the reading was in English on that plaque. It should have been in Vietnamese.

**Lawrence Stephen Roberge, LCpl.,
Service Company,
June 1966–January 1968**

We had no pets unless you counted the insects, snakes and rats. Damn, I hated those rats. Cats and dogs were very scarce. I always figured they ate them. I remember once while riding the .50 cal. on one of our convoys, I shot a dog running across a rice paddy. Later I thought that I might have destroyed someone's pet or dinner.

I'll always remember the days we convoyed north to do some road and bridge repair. It was during the monsoon season and I was sitting up on the .50 cal. ring mounted atop one of our cargo trucks. I used to love being machine gunner, but never had to use it. John Dedovitch was driver. We made it north all right, but a small bridge south of us was blown out and we couldn't get back. We spent a week or so at some hill base. All that time, same clothes, no showers, C-rats, but a lot of drinking. One morning after having 45 whiskey and beer all night, I was sitting up on the .50 cal. I was wet, cold, hung over, and just hoping someone would shoot me and put me out of my misery. Besides the drinking and the great buddies, there wasn't much of anything.

Jim O'Kelley in front of new 9th Engineer Battalion mess hall. Courtesy of Jim O'Kelley.

Jim O'Kelley, 2 Lt.–1 Lt.–Capt., HQ & D Company, August 1966–May 1968

Late in 1966 I remember constructing a change in the channel of the stream flowing through the airbase. I moved the stream to give us more security and more space. I also remember going down to Binh Son (2d ROKMC Brigade Headquarters) to replace Capt. Jerry Polyasko who had become ill with malaria, I think. I stayed down there for a couple of weeks until Jerry returned from the hospital ship USS *Repose*. During that time, I was the engineer advisor and CO of a small Marine detachment of engineers assigned to support the Korean Marines. We helped them build artillery positions for 155mm towed howitzers, bunkers, fighting trenches, etc. I first learned about Kimchi (fermented cabbage) and 33 beer from these guys. My intestines are still not the same!

Thanksgiving dinner at 9th Engineer Battalion was special in 1966. Up until that time our mess area consisted of wooden picnic tables out in the open. The new Messhall was ready for Thanksgiving, 1966 and that was a big improvement. We got rid of the old metal trays and mess kits and the immersion burners used to clean and sanitize the trays and silverware. The Fall of 1966 was my first experience also with a Monsoon — Southeast Asia style. The rains came sideways and hard. We were drenched for several months — you just learned to live wet! And cold! The only help was a "hot locker" — we built a 4' × 4' × 4' plywood box and installed a single 60 watt bulb in the top of it. We could put wet clothes in there and they would dry in about 24 hours without molding! But we learned to work in the rain and to work with the water — drainage was a big issue — where does all the water go? Usually where you don't want it unless you plan properly (the 7P's again!). So we constructed "beaucoup" culverts, drainage ditches and small bridges. The plywood pallets we had used as walkways to keep us out of the sand even floated away on us, so we had to anchor them down.

1 November 1966 Pay officer, went to ROKMC.

2 November 1966 ROKMC again. Also Quang Ngai bridge site. Turned in pay — the 1st MAR. DIV. disbursing officer refused to accept paperwork because I came up $78 short — (will have to pay out of *my* pay!). Wrote letters home.

3 November 1966 Recon Quang Ngai to ROKMC. Paid disbursing $78 that was missing from payroll.

10 November 1966 Real sick 0100–0300 this morning — maybe food? Gave Col. a utility shirt for Gen. Walt's visit. Sick — nausea, dizziness, diarrhea — Doctor — blood tests, gave me two shots & some pills. USMC birthday.

13 November 1966 Canceled allotment to Mom so could take advantage of 10 percent interest. Good inspection. Still have diarrhea bad.

17 November 1966 Letter from home and scrounge run. Tents burned.

18 November 1966 Malaria pill. No mail. Sent in Lesson 3 — Soils.

22 November 1966 Recon all day. Martha Raye here tonight.

24 November 1966 Thanksgiving, huh?! Slept from 0900 to 1400 — had TB patch checked — got eye ointment. Worked on recon.

25 November 1966 overslept. Very cold & raining in on my rack. Got ponchos & tarp for front of hut. Assigned additional duty as Education OIC for Battalion.

26 November 1966 Lesson 5 — Soils. Very cold & rainy — high winds too. No mail. Very despondent — tired — etc. "I'm sick and tired of being sick and tired."

29 November 1966 Sunshine for first time in daze. 15 pushups.

30 November 1966 Bn OOD. Worked on lesson 6 — Soils. Chow bad. Still raining, windy & cold. 16 pushups.

DECEMBER

Walter Hayes, Platoon Sgt., B Company, 1965–November 1967

We had one of these cranes that move about three miles an hour. We got it out where we were building this road when the monsoon was there. It turned out we didn't get as much done as we thought, so we were going to have to leave the equipment out there. They asked for some volunteers to stay all night with that piece of equipment. Why, I don't know. I don't think it would have been worth one person's life. There were four of us stupid ones that volunteered to stay. As soon as everybody left, it started pouring rain. And I mean pouring. You're sitting there with that poncho over you, and it's pitch black. You can't see anything. You got to check in every twenty minutes, and if you don't, they call you. You're trying to be quiet and listen. You can't hear nothing really.

The radio would go off and my heart would just stop, right there, because I know it's telling everybody where I was. We must have been there until about two o'clock in the morning and we thought we heard something. We're all getting ready to take our safety's off. Here comes some drunk Marine walking down the road. He got lost. He went up in town, went UA (Unauthorized Absence). He was just wandering around out there, in the middle of nowhere, all by himself, trying to get back with the grunt battalion. We didn't know who was more scared, him or us. He sobered up quick when he heard the bolts going. He walked right into us. We kept him there the night. I don't know how a person could get that drunk or that stupid, one of the two.

Ted Zealley, Lt., D Company, 1 November 1965–June 1967

I ended up in the hospital for Christmas 1966. Of course, the Red Cross girls and some movie stars came around to visit the troops in the hospital. Tippi Hedren and Diane McBain came to see us. They chattered with everyone to see what was wrong and how they were doing. Their visit was noticeably short with me when they discovered I was suffering from dysentery.

The mention of hospitals reminds me of Navy Corpsmen. We Marines often reflect on bravery of the members of our Corps. Among the bravest to serve with us were and are Navy Corpsmen. D Company was assigned to clear a "friendly" minefield that had been placed by 1st Engineer Battalion. They had only used metallic mines — no plastic ones. Unfortunately, we found out the hard way that RVN forces that had occupied the position for a short time had indiscriminately laced the minefield with plastic mines. As our clearing teams were working through the minefield, the detector operator on one team stepped on a plastic mine that took off his foot at the ankle. His probing partner was temporarily blinded by the blast. Without regard for his own safety, the Navy Corpsman assigned to that platoon ran through an uncleared portion of the minefield to give life saving aid to those two wounded Marines. It is certain that the one would have bled to death and the other blinded Marine may have wandered about and set off other mines. For this brave act we in D Company were proud to recommend "our Corpsman" for the bronze star which he received shortly thereafter.

At the other end of the Chu Lai strip was the Marine ammo dump. It never appeared to be very well organized. Stuff seemed to be scattered all over the place. There never were any revetments built about the place, but it was a long way from anywhere and I don't recall many hits from the VC, maybe because they got their own resupply from there. When the Army came to Chu Lai, they got organized. They had 9th Engr Bn build a proper ammo dump, complete with revetments, hard stand roads, the works right inside the airfield perimeter across the road from our compound. It was much more convenient to getting ground units in the area resupplied, too. It was also a lot closer to launching sites for VC gunners. I understand there were some real fireworks not long after I left the country.

Fred H. Scheuter, PFC, B Company, May 1966–1967

I remember one time when we were near completion of building a bridge. It was time to eat lunch and everybody except I went back to the 9th Engineer base. I stayed at the bridge site because I had a girlfriend that I liked. I visited her and her brother in her home. We couldn't speak to each other because we didn't know each other's language. We just smiled at each other. After the visit I went outside to wait for the rest of the men to get back. As I was waiting, I bought Coca Cola with ice from the locals. It must have been over one hundred degrees that day. I drank a lot on an empty stomach and I was sick. But the thing that I will never forget is that I was the only American nearby and all of a sudden a couple of Vietnamese men dressed in all black with banana clip type rifles came walking down the road. I only had my M-14 with one magazine. I looked at them and they looked at me. I waved and they waved and walked by. Until this day, I wonder if they were Viet Cong or not. That was the only time I was out by myself.

Lawrence Stephen Roberge, LCpl., Service Company, June 1966–January 1968

I'm not the best judge for food, but I've been told I'm the fussiest guy around. We were very fortunate because we had a mess hall. When we weren't on the road, we could get regular meals. I used to get up and make an effort to get to breakfast because every so often they could have real eggs. Not very often, but I didn't want to take a chance on missing them so I'd always be there.

The food was mostly powdered this or that and very greasy. We could always eat C-rats. They used to have this Kool-aid which was 98 percent of the time lime green. Military, right. Today I wouldn't drink lime Kool-aid for anyone. At Christmas they gave us steak. What a line there was outside that mess hall. Everybody was there, I didn't miss it. I spent two Christmases there. Coffee, well we won't talk about that (but I think it was a secret weapon of the enemy). I used to fill my canteen with coffee. It made a great hot water bottle on guard duty.

**Jim O'Kelley, 2 Lt.–1 Lt.–Capt.,
HQ & D Company,
August 1966–May 1968**

The rest of 1966 was busy — but it seems true that there were "hours of boredom interrupted by moments of stark terror." We were not often as "bored" as the grunts because we had plenty of work to do and I do remember the loneliness and the desire to get back to the "world." And we seldom were in states of "stark terror" as the grunts either because we were often shielded by the grunts or maybe just plain lucky! I think the highlight of 1966 was my trip to Da Nang to hear Dr. Billy Graham preach on Christmas Day. I wrote an article about that. It was published in my local/hometown newspaper, *The Asheville Citizen/Times*. (Appendix A)

1 December 1966 Slept in until 1030 since OD last nite. No mail. Very cold, rainy & very windy. 17 pushups.

2 December 1966 Malaria pill day. Worked on recon all day — went to 1st Engineers for bridge numbers. Assigned Bn Ed Officer. Rainy & very cold (65) & windy. Wearing field jacket. No mail. Finished Lesson 6 — Soils. 18 pushups — 36 sit-ups.

4 December 1966 Sent Christmas cards. Took slide rule exam. Went to communion. Junk on the bunk inspection. Wrote letters and received letters & package.

6 December 1966 Inspecting officer for "D" Company junk on the bunk inspection. Bridge #19 blown — 6 USMC WIA, 7 VC KIA, 4 VCS, 3 Civilian KIA.

8 December 1966 led recon patrol 0400 — 1000. No contact but much water & mud. Showered — first time in ten (?) daze?!

9 December 1966 Malaria pill. Wrote 9 letters.

10 December 1966 Bn OOD. Caught 2 men in Service Co. asleep on post at 0130. Letters and fudge from home.

14 December 1966 Meeting at 0700. 4/11 — 10 KIA — 14 WIA in big fire fight. Went to 3rd Ferry for recon — took 2¾ hrs. up and 2½ hrs. back. Sampan Lt. McCarty & I were using for bridge measurements sank & had to swim out. Appointed defense counsel on Court Martial.

16 December 1966 Talked to Col. about extension of tour in RVN. Invited to Col. Crispen's for steaks. Got brandy from doctor ("Medicinal brandy" — usually given after patrols). 35 pushups. Malaria pill. Got new Calculus book.

20 December 1966 Sent Lesson 4 — Quarrying. Letters from home. Bn OOD. Ted Zealley in hospital. Raining.

24 December 1966 Got call thru to home at 0245. Finished Valley of Wild Horses by Zane Grey. Sent Lesson 2 — Pavements. Up to Tam Ky. Went to Communion. Monopoly.

25 December 1966 Went to Da Nang to hear Billy Graham. Spoke to him — took my address and phone number to call Mother. Talked to Lt. Gen. Walt. Wrote summary for Chaplain. Monopoly.

27 December 1966 An Tan bridge (RR)

Dr. Billy Graham, Christmas, 1966. Courtesy of Jim O'Kelley.

decking. Chewed out SSgt. again. Finished RR bridge report.

28 December 1966 Went to Bob Hope Christmas Show in Da Nang. Left at 0645, returned at 1915.

29 December 1966 Letter home about Bob Hope. Took shower. Monopoly.

Ed Whitaker, PFC, Headquarters Company, December 1966–October 1967

My MOS was to refuel helicopters. When we got there, we weren't assigned in what we were trained for, it was what needed to be done. I worked directly for a Major over there. I worked for him down at the rock quarry. We didn't have gravel so we had to make our own gravel. The United States Government was buying softball size rock from the Vietnamese to put on their road to make Highway One, north of our location. I had to record and keep track of that and then I had to turn in that documentation to this Major everyday. We did that for a long time. If it was raining, we didn't work down there. Then I'd have to work in the office.

I was there from Christmas time until around the 20th of September, then I was transferred to Da Nang because I was working out of my MOS. The funny part was, when I got to Da Nang, I met up with the different people that I had gone to school with back in the States. We all got together there. We were all on a general guard there. The only time I worked on my MOS was the last two months I was in the service which was in the States.

They built the Chu Lai runway while I was there. Did you ever hear of the terminology called beach matting? It is similar to, think of sheets of steel that are eighteen inches wide and twenty feet long. They got round holes in them, but on the side of them, they got like interlocking parts on them so one will latch onto another one. That was the runway when I got there. One night I was on guard duty and one of the planes had gone out on a mission and come back, and he didn't get rid of all his bombs and when he hit the runway, one fell off. When it blew up, it didn't hurt the plane or the pilot, but put a big hole in the runway. Everybody thought we were under attack, so everybody was out on guard duty.

When I was in Vietnam, there was one other thing that happened. Sometimes I believe in this thing called fate, why things happen like they do. After I got to Vietnam I was there for about a week or so and went down to Headquarters Company. If I didn't work down there at the rock quarry, I would be like an extra person and have to run errands or go get people or go give them messages or stuff like this. Well, one time I was in the office and it just happened to be Christmas Day. I was there and we got two planeloads of guys who were going to leave Chu Lai. They were going to fly to Da Nang to see Dr. Billy Graham. Well, when they got ready to go, one guy couldn't go. They had one extra seat and I am standing in the office. "Hey, I can go." So I went in December, 1966.

I couldn't believe it. In the United States I could never see him in person, but I could in Vietnam. I was really pleased. Jim O'Kelley said he went that day, too. And yet, here we are having church services, and you look upon the hill behind us and there's guards. So it is a little different … atmosphere than what I was used to. But I thought it was so unique that it happened like it did. Why did I have to be the last person to fill the roster for the day and how did I happen just to be in the office when someone canceled and couldn't go? It kind of reinforced my faith in God. Here I am, halfway across the world, and could still see Dr. Billy Graham. It was a real highlight of being over there.

**Robert Terry Sperling, LCpl.,
Service Company,
December 1966–December 1967**

On my first patrol, two Sergeants argued for a half an hour as to where we were. They should have asked us peons. We knew where we were, we were lost in Quang Tin Province, I Corps, Vietnam. However, most Sergeants were pretty good on the patrols. On one patrol we apprehended three VC suspects and formed a circle around them. I kept busy looking outward but I could hear the fear of the Vietnamese men's voices and felt good in a way when they were released.

JANUARY–APRIL 1967

North Vietnam Foreign Minister Nguyen Duy Trinh says on January 28 United States must stop bombing North Vietnam before talks can begin. Johnson ends two day meeting on Guam, March 21, with Thieu and Ky. North Vietnamese reveal exchange of letters between Johnson and Ho Chi Minh. Westmoreland confers with Johnson in Washington, April 27; addresses Congress next day.

JANUARY

Walter Hayes, Platoon Sgt., B Company, 1965–November 1967

We went out on a two day operation. Four days later, we were still there and we were begging them to send in water. We didn't have water. A drop tank is an extra tank that looks like a bomb on the bottom of an airplane and it carries extra fuel in it. They were supposed to have washed the fuel out of these tanks before they filled them with water, and then they came in and dropped them. I'd rather drink bomb crater water than what that tasted like. Luckily, they brought in pallets of hot beer and dropped them, too. We were allowed two cans just before darkness. That's why when the kids volunteered to go on these operations, I'd take all the non-drinkers with me so I could get their ration of beer. [laughs] That way the mosquitoes didn't hurt so bad. It was just one of my little schemes.

Ted Zealley, Lt., D Company, 1 November 1965–June 1967

Some of our troops did see action, and regrettably some did not return alive. Each morning D Company had the task to check the road north and drop off personnel who were working on various projects along the way. A truck dropped some folks who were building an access road to the 11th Marines CP (burying burned out amtracks with sand). On the way out to the main road, a controlled mine was detonated and five Marines lost their lives. More than one were thrown far from the vehicle. One landed in the rice paddy and apparently drowned. But even in such a situation, there can be a twinge of humor. When we counted up the casualties (WIA and KIA), we were still missing one Marine. We checked with the hospital to see if anyone else had been medivaced there from a mine incident. No one there. We checked with the 11th Marines aid station. No one had been treated there. Somehow we thought to check back with the hospital. They had no one who had been injured, but they did have someone that the MP's had picked up in the area that they thought was intoxicated or "on something." It turned out that it was our Marine. He had been thrown clear of the truck and had suffered a concussion and temporary loss of memory. The MP's found him staggering around the shops near the scene and just thought he was a Marine who needed to dry out and took him to the hospital.

Wayne McGinnis, L/Cpl., D Company, June 1966–July 1967

This one particular morning they were taking a dump truck and a few men up Highway One. There was a tank battalion up there, but the road hadn't been checked. Gunny told me, load up the dump truck, go down to the main gate and wait on me. He had to stop by the office. Well, they didn't wait. The truck went up the road lickety-split, the driver and a shotgun, three or four guys in the back before the mine sweep teams went out.

They were taking a cook up in there and someone else. Well, when they made the turn there was a little village there. Boom. They think it was electronically detonated. It blew the dump truck. Gunny was maybe only a quarter of a mile down the road, and he saw the explosion and knew what had happened. When he got there, it was all over. It left a big crater and a hole. It turned the dump truck upside down. It took the bed of the dump truck, blew it off and bent it in half. There was a fellow lying over in the rice paddy, face down.

They tell me that one of the guys survived, but to the best of my knowledge, none of them survived. They thought at first that boy was alive, but he wasn't. He was face down in the rice paddy. We got up

Mike Kehoe (center), Don Weinstein (right). ***Courtesy of Jim Frank.***

there much later. Mike Kehoe was on that truck. He was in our squad and that's when they came back and got us.

We were so mad. We went up there to that little village. We said, "If this would have happened to the Koreans or anybody else, they would have burned this damn place down." I remember a Lieutenant saying, "I don't see anything, I'm outta here." We pulled our lighters out and set the place on fire and burned it to the ground. They brought a bulldozer down from up at this outfit where the truck was heading into and buried that village. When they got done, there was nothing left but a sand pile. The people just took off. It was a very emotional time, but to me that wasn't an ordinary circumstance. It didn't happen every day. It was right after that they had Operation Goodwill. You can't do something like that and promote goodwill to the countrymen. Because they're just not gonna buy it. But that was our way of venting our frustration if you will.

We knew Kehoe was from New York. He was the all-American type boy. He was a real genuine, good type guy, where you could get up next to him and have a good time. You felt like, "He's watching my back, I'll watch his back." You always knew where he was coming from. I didn't know anybody that didn't like him. I remember meeting him in California.

**Lawrence Stephen Roberge, LCpl.,
Service Company,
June 1966–January 1968**

We were numbers (2148709), part of the great 9th Engineer Battalion. We carried an M-14 but were not there to seek and destroy. We were there to rebuild roads, bridges, airfields, even schools. It seemed we were there to do some good. We would fix Highway One and the gooks would blow it up. We would build new bridges and again they would destroy them. It seemed to be an endless job. You could almost say it got very boring at times. Then came a little excitement. A few of us were asked to go TAD, Temporary Additional Duty, with the Korean Marine Corps Engineers to help them out south of Chu Lai.

It was great working with the Koreans. We got a chance to meet new people, new foods—"rice and soup," "rice and soup," "rice and soup." I hated that. I lived on C rats and beer. These Koreans were wild. When it came time for discipline, an officer could beat the crap out of an enlisted man and no one cared except the poor bastard being beaten. In our Marine Corps, someone would have been looking for a court martial. They wouldn't take any grief from the small villages either. One day there was some small arms fire coming from a hootch and the Koreans just flattened it with dozers. Nothing bothered them. 'Nam wasn't all work. I spent my fair share of time in the back room of many hootches with some young girl doing boom boom. Boom boom #1 and drinking.

**Jim O'Kelley, 2 Lt.–1 Lt.–Capt.,
HQ & D Company,
August 1966–May 1968**

It's interesting to see what took most of my time—initially a lot of time was spent adapting to the climate, food, and other creature comforts. As things got better in the base camp of the Battalion, the emphasis moved to mission-oriented projects such as bridges, roads, airfields, etc. The combat aspect remained at night, primarily when I took out patrols. Initially we had 3/5 between us and the mountains—but early in 1967 they pulled out and our patrols became more frequent and more important—almost from "internal security" to "external security," although that doesn't fit because it was "360 degrees security" all the time regardless of where we were. As long as the Battalion was in Chu Lai, we found that the camp improved. But when I took Delta Company to the DMZ in Nov. '67, we had to readapt to basic field conditions — primarily what we could carry on our backs.

1 January 67 Had OOD [Battalion Officer of the Day duty] last night. Lt. General Krulak here. Steak. Very hard rain again.

3 January 67 Pistol T. I. (Technical Inspection). Gave Sgt. Fording insect bomb & candles. Corrected bridge report. Went to (site near Chu Lai beach where a Navy) LST beached due to monsoon storm. New plt (platoon) organization given out.

4 January 67 Got paperback books from Special Services to hand out to Headquarters Platoon.

5 January 67 Designed & approved USO stage beam. Designed soils lab for 9th Engr Bn. Got R&R quota for 28 January — 4 Feb. Sent boots for repair. They are literally rotting off my feet due to jungle weather. Got wool shirt.

8 January 67 Generals Greene, Walt, Nickerson, Styles, etc. here at Dickey Chapelle dispensary for dedication. Appointed Co. Training Officer. Went to An Tan (village).

10 January 67 No mail. Major chewed me out for 2 hours.

13 January 67 Malaria pill day. Woke up during night & in AM to heavy gunfire — 2/11 hit badly — had 22 VC KIA on fence & 8 VC captured. 9th Engr dump truck hit mine at Hill 35 — 6 KIA — 1 WIA. Plane crashed on Hill 400 — 6 KIA — we sent demo crew to blow plane & recover bodies — grunts protected us. Recon for patrol. Patrol order issued.

14 January 67 Patrol — 25 rds fired at us — killed bamboo viper (on rice paddy dike we were crossing). Went to memorial services & Col.'s talk. Spot report & patrol report to S-3 & CLDC-COC (Chu Lai Defense Command Combat Operations Center).

20 January 67 Malaria pill. No mail. Ted Rathburn 3/7 back, going to Mo Duc. Checked on pay. ISO sent stories of familygram & patrol. Saw *The Silencers* with Dean Martin. (Appendix B — Familygram)

22 January 67 Raining all day. Went on mine sweep/recon to Tam Ky. Got paratyphoid shot & new shot card.

23 January 67 Got typhus & smallpox shots.

27 January 67 Malaria pill. R & R!!!!! (Bangkok, Thailand) First time out of RVN in 6 months!!!

Ed Whitaker, PFC, Headquarters Company, December 1966–October 1967

One day we were going to go on a patrol up the road and this officer, O'Kelley, he went with us. Any time the Viet Cong had blown up a bridge we had to stop. We had three or four jeeps and two PC's, which are bigger than jeeps. I rode in the back vehicle of the back patrol and we had to stop at every blown bridge. Half of the guys would get out and stand guard. The rest of us would measure the bridge, take a picture of it, tell how it was constructed and what it would take to rebuild it.

Then we went up the road quite a way and we stopped at this army compound. We picked up an army officer and he had gone farther up the road than any of the rest of us ever had. This was in daylight and we stopped at this one bridge. He said, "When we go from this bridge to the next one, there is elephant grass close to the road and there is going to be little towns and hootches out here in the countryside. I have never gone through here and not been shot at. We are going to be zipping right along so don't fall out of the truck because we are not going to stop for you." We went up there and back and never got shot at. Why? Was it because I was there? I don't know. I just have these different feelings sometimes about why things happen like they do.

FEBRUARY

**Ron Rainer, PFC, A Company,
January 1967–October 1967**

After I got there A company moved down to Hill 63 which was between Da Nang and Tam Ky on Route 1. We were in charge of about a twenty mile stretch there between Tam Ky and the main bridge that they were rebuilding. It was really something. It was an infiltration route. There was an awful lot of booby-traps and land mines and something going on all the time in there. We would go down and sweep the roads in the morning. I ran over a land mine about a month before I got hurt. I had some bleeding out of my ear but I refused to apply for a purple heart. The guy that was riding shot gun for me, he got one of his fingers cut or something, and he applied for that. I ran around with a painted purple heart on the side of my vehicle that was issued to me. I drove that and it was the one I hit the mine with. [laughs] In a way you had to laugh those things off. If you didn't, you would go crazy. You were in constant danger, if they missed a mine, then you would get one. Of course, that is what finally happened to me.

We were stationed outside of a little place called Marble Mountain for a while. This was before we moved down to Hill 63. These were grunts. They were way on down the road. We had to sweep to them from the mag area, all the way down. I remember one day they came back in and this guy was missing. I don't know if it was Moore, or who it was, but this guy was missing. They were all going crazy, running around. These were the engineers. They had been out on a sweep, then came back and I can't for the life of me remember if that was him or not.

There was so many that were plugged or just kidnapped right off the road. It was just unreal. If an engineer would wander off somewhere, there was a good chance they would not make it back. I can't say that was all the time, but I do remember that one incident. Then I remember an incident on Marble Mountain where a man was following a mine sweep team and they got ambushed. There was 21 in the vehicle and I think something like 10 or 12 got killed. A lot of these things that I remember were isolated things. I never was involved in any mass attacks or anything like that. Mainly where we were on Hill 63 we were with an artillery unit and then there was grunts on the other side. We would get a lot of sniper fire.

**Jim O'Kelley, 2 Lt.–1 Lt.–Capt.,
HQ & D Company,
August 1966–May 1968**

I made a set of weights and a bench so I could lift. We kept them in the Special Services tent. We could do bench presses and curls and military presses with them. A good diversion and we had a couple of contests to see who was strongest. I even carried them via truck to Ca Lu where we set them up in the Company CP (Command Post) but they didn't get as much use because we were always working all day and guard duty at night. I don't remember taking off Saturdays, Sundays, or holidays at Ca Lu. Just worked dawn to dark and had perimeter guard duty, etc., from dark to dawn for the entire time we were there.

4 February 67 VC blew Binh Son bridge again.

9 February 67 Received heavy AR fire at 1945. 100 percent Alert. Corporal Knowlton back (from emergency leave home).

12 February 67 (Guided) M109's over 2nd Bridge N. Read in afternoon & slept. No mail.

13 February 67 Class on Road recon. W2 form home. Got pay straightened out. PX steward shot in stomach — night med evac.

15 February 67 (Guided) M109 across 2nd Bridge N.

Five Float M4T6 ferry at Binh Son. 6 February 1967. Courtesy of Jim O'Kelley.

17 February 67 Malaria pill. Bridge people brought in 4 Vietnamese children—blown apart by mine. No mail. Disillusioned.

18 February 67 (Checked out) M79 for recon (patrols so I could spot rounds at targets). Rains stopped!

23 February 67 Finished Recon Route 22. Appointed Capt. Blumenkrantz (as Battalion S-2 (intelligence). Turned in utilities to Bn Supply (for new set). ISO for pictures of Colonel. Took beer to 2/5, 3/5. Sick & tired.

24 February 67 Malaria pill. Patrol article in Sea Tiger. Teeth cleaned. Got haircut. Bridge recon #14. Pictures of 175mm guns etc. Wrote up Route 22 recon. Bn Security Officer now—radio setup for Hdqtrs Company. Appointed Bn Security Officer (today—had been "acting" anyway).

28 February 67 Took paint to VMA311—serial # of M79 to recon, III MAF Drum & Bugle Corps here. Worked on Bn Security Order & Task Organization report. Wrote patrol for B Company.

Ed Whitaker, PFC, Headquarters Company, December 1966–October 1967

I'm not pleased to say this, but at one time I got to the frame of mind where I couldn't wait to kill somebody. It was because of the different guys being killed. I thought it was needless, like the time they had six guys in a dump truck and they got blown up. That didn't have to happen.

Where we were at it was so sandy that you could not walk on it barefoot. It would burn your feet. Yet you could dig with your hands and less than a foot down you would find water. That was amazing to me.

It could be so hot and yet you could find water. When we went there they gave us a shot to thin your blood. It wasn't so hard on your heart. On the down side, if you got shot or wounded, you would bleed quicker.

If you shot a cow, it was like ten bucks. If you shot a water buffalo, it was like fifteen. When I was in Chu Lai, they had the bubonic plague. We had to go get a plague shot because of the rats. One night I was on duty right there in the compound. I was walking that night and I heard something and turned around and there was nobody there. I looked again and here is a rat standing on its hind legs like a foot, a foot and a half tall. They were humongus. I think at that particular time there were like seven people that died of the bubonic plague in the village.

John Vasarab, PFC, Service Company, 1967–1968

There was a guy with the Army that had this tank that was broken down. The motor was not running. So they called up and we had to go make a service call. Well, the guy that was driving the tank got impatient. He decided to go across the wooden bridge and it didn't work out. He couldn't wait for us. He went through the damn thing. When the VC found out that the tank was stuck on a bridge, they figured there is only a handful of guys, so we can go blow the damn son of a bitch up. But they didn't make it.

They eventually came down with a big tank retriever and hooked a cable on and jerked them right off the bridge into the water. Then they drug it out of the water. He certainly should have gotten in trouble for that. The worse part was the tank was useless. The barrel was shot out of it. There was nothing good about it. He was taking it back to drop it off and pick up another tank.

MARCH

Lawrence Stephen Roberge, LCpl., Service Company, June 1966–January 1968

I spent 5 days and nights in Japan. I remember those 5 days and fun-filled nights as if they happened yesterday. A friend by the name of Brown, he and I went on R&R together. My hotel and two meals a day were paid for as soon as I got there, and it's good, because three days after I got there I was broke. I spent $650 and had nothing to show for it except great memories. R and R (rest and recuperation) or was it I and I (intercourse and intoxication). What a week I had. Even the last two days when I was broke were great. R and R was one of the greatest gifts we got while being there. I was living like a king for a week.

Jim O'Kelley, 2 Lt.–1 Lt.–Capt., HQ & D Company, August 1966–May 1968

1967 was a strange year — of transitions mostly. We were primarily fighting the Viet Cong (VC) guerrillas throughout 1966 around Chu Lai. But beginning in March 1967 we began facing the North Vietnamese Army (NVA) troops. That affected us in everything we did from minesweeps and road recons to patrols and ambushes. We had to "heavy up" for the NVA as opposed to "lighten up" for the VC. The VC were mostly young men in black pajamas with M-1 carbines and bad aim and homemade mines; the NVA were also young men but in khaki uniforms, Soviet hardware, with good aim (especially their snipers with SKS scopes) and Soviet mines and booby traps. Two different ways to fight within the same war. And the tough part was we never knew in advance, for sure, which group we would be up against.

6 March 67 Turned in other copies Route 22 Recon. Shooting by sniper into berms — caught 1 VCS by L/Cpl. Lochlear — took to ITT. Redid Command Chronology.

Bridge north of Thanh Binh, over Song Ba Ren river. Not repaired—just bring "lowboy" with dozer across—very dangerous job. 3–5 mph. Can't turn wheels or bridge will collapse. Courtesy of Jim O'Kelley.

VC hit airfield at 1240 AM — 57 — 82mm mortar Rds — 7 WIA, 1 plane, 2 generators, several BOQ's, 1 shithouse (destroyed). Got flashlight.

7 March 67 Worked on patrol. Checked on prisoner — ARVN deserter. Went to Kilo Company — saw Bob Tilley about search/sweep ops. Told me Bill Berry KIA yesterday. Patrol tonight.

8 March 67 Patrol action — 2 M-79 at 3–5 VC in paddy. Wrote 3 patrols. Brought in wash.

9 March 67 Another group of VC slipped into An Tan last nite. Wrote 3 patrol orders and patrol report. VC hit 2nd Bridge. Washed clothes. Patrol found tunnel near Tich Tay — went to investigate.

13 March 67 VC blew bridge #16 N of Binh Son. Patrol found 3 tunnels and one large cave — 4 SA incoming — neg results.

14 March 67 Got up early. Breakfast. Chopper recon to Duc Pho. Bn OOD — rough evening with red alert — patrol got 1 VCS.

15 March 67 3/5 for R. P. (Recon patrol checkpoints). Ambush request from Kilo Co. Steve Palmer (TBS roommate) came up. Briefed Col. on Duc Pho Recon. Bridge recon to Bridge #16 and on to ROKMC to check on surveyors. Worked on berm lights & moving berms.

18 March 67 Mailed 10 percent receipt. Checked out caves, tunnels, sleeping areas with Majors & 3/5 XO. Set up 2 patrols and ambush. Patrol & ambush tonight.

20 March 67 Recon bridge #15 &

picked up ROK troops. Wrote 2 patrol orders, went to FAG (1st Field Artillery Group), TKS (1st Tank Bn), 3/5 — Kilo (Kilo Company, 3rd Bn., 5th Marine Regiment) to coordinate patrol routes.

21 March 67 Blew cave — 15' × 25' × 35' with 80 lbs. of C-4. Finished recon #15. Got bed board (for cot). Cleaned up area. Got haircut. Wrote 1 patrol & 1 ambush order. Checked ambush site of last nite — expended 40 SA — 2 grenades w/neg results.

22 March 67 Patrol out. Got Rules of Engagement from 3/5.

24 March 67 No mail. Coordinated fire support procedures with 1st FAG. Worked on Bn Security Order. Birthday — Ugh. Patrol brought in 16 people at 0045H this morning. 8" howitzers firing on hill next to us all night. New CO of Hdqtrs Co.

25 March 67 Wrote 2 patrols. Soil testing. Patrol got 1 VCS. MILK today!

27 March 67 No mail. No work. Wrote patrol order. Had milk & ice cream!

29 March 67 Worked on investigation, abutments for Bridge #19, company meeting. Found out Lt. Glenn McCarty was killed yesterday.

31 March 67 Worked on bridge #19 abutments. Wrote 2 patrol orders. 112 degrees at 1300! Burning up. K Co. got hit, also 4 HE at CLDC. Got 2 new (replacements) 2/Lts today.

**Ed Whitaker, PFC,
Headquarters Company,
December 1966–October 1967**

When I got into boot camp, the letters just came like you wouldn't believe. I was in the service for two years, which is like 730 days. In those two years I got 1,159 letters. When I got transferred to Da Nang, I finally had to throw them away because I couldn't take them with me. There is a picture of me where I'm going to throw them away and I've got all I could handle in my two arms. My mom would write almost every other day and her sister, my aunt, would write the alternate days. Different people in the church would write once a week. One lady, she was almost like a second mother to me, she would write two or three times a week as well.

A few times, mail call was even embarrassing. I think the most I ever got in one day was twenty-one or twenty-three letters. That would be after I would move from one place to another and it would take a while for them all to catch up. It really helped me retain a part of sanity, to keep in touch with the world.

**Robert Terry Sperling, LCpl.,
Service Company,
December 1966–December 1967**

I remember being on a patrol through one of the Tic Tay Hamlets. We were all moving as quietly as we could, looking, listening, moving between the river and the hootches. I could hear people snoring and the water movement in the river. It was very dark. WOWOWOWOWOWO! a small dog barks at me from a distance of only a few feet. Not a single man on the patrol said a word or made a sound.

Ed Whitaker with his mail. Courtesy of Ed Whitaker.

John Vasarab, PFC, Service Company, 1967–1968

I took a motor out of a MRS200 and found out what was wrong with it. They put in an order to Okinawa for parts and it took six months until I got the parts that I needed to rebuild that motor. About the time I got the parts, I forgot what the hell I was doing. Now where are all these pieces that have been laying around for six months?

After a while we got used to the airfield which was like three miles away. It seemed like every minute or so there would be a phantom over there, kicking in the after burners, taking off. Those were just loud. Then, when they come in for a landing, it was just as bad. It would start wheezing and making a real high pitch scream. The planes would either drop the shit on land or out in the ocean, depending on which way they would be coming in. A lot of stuff got wasted because they were afraid the bombs and ordinance would break loose when they landed. They didn't want that to happen.

On Sunday afternoon, if you got a chance, you had like half a day off and we would get into a football game. Some of the guys who had been there a day or two wanted to jump right in because it was the thing to do. It's about 120 degrees, then all of a sudden they would get into a good football game and pass out. The heat takes a little bit of getting used to. By 10:00 in the morning it is already over 100. You get used to that.

We had the opportunity to ride as gunners for the Army on their resupply runs to Da Nang. These were pretty cool because we got to see what new toys the other half

Wrecked MRS 200. Courtesy of Ted Zealley.

had. The Marines are famous for being the last to buy anything new for the boys. I sometimes wondered if they didn't spend their budget money at surplus sales held by the Army.

APRIL

Walter Hayes, Platoon Sgt., B Company, 1965–November 1967

I did see a Staff Sergeant get killed over there when we were on an operation with the grunts. Out in an open field there was an old French building that had one wall standing up. There was an AK-47 sitting out in the middle of the field. We knew it was booby trapped. You could see the fishing line attached to the trigger. This guy wanted it because he was getting short. We looked around and there was some comm wire out in the field, old communication wire for radios. It was long enough to get back behind that wall. Well, I went with the grunts. He tied the wire onto the rifle and got behind that wall and pulled it, and the wall blew up instead of the rifle. They were pretty smart. It was a bad mistake going souvenir hunting.

Jim O'Kelley, 2 Lt.–1 Lt.–Capt., HQ & D Company, August 1966–May 1968

I read a lot of books while in Vietnam — in fact I appealed to everyone at home to send us good reading materials, not "junk" — i.e. novels, etc. versus "shitkickers" and sex books. We were all bored and homesick, etc., normally, so as long as we were "captive," we would read anything, so why not good books. I thought this was a good chance to "force feed" all of us good literature.

3 April 67 Today all we officers began a mustache growing contest. No mail. Col found my M-79 rusty — said never let it happen again!!! Sent bug repellent to Little John.

4 April 67 Wrote patrol orders. Worked on airfield mass diagram. Got new 2/Lt today. 11 VCS — 2 M1 carbines, 2 M2 carbines, 280 rds, 2 grenades, 2 bayonets, etc. from patrol — 2330 took them to ITT.

6 April 67 Slept in until noon. Wrote patrol report. No action last nite. Got in about 0300. Mail. Cleaned M-79.

9 April 67 R & P inspection by Capt. No mail. Early to bed. US Army coming in large groups now.

10 April 67 Promoted to 1st Lt. effective 1 April 1967. Worked on Fuel Tank Tower, Earth Mass/Profile diagrams of ROKMC airfield. Army coming in in force now. 155 guns on FAG hill. No sleep!

11 April 67 Sent out patrol. Found 4 caves and interconnecting tunnels. Got disbursing slip for 1/Lt. No mail. Bad heat rash under arms. Assigned patrol & coordinated Security with K/3/5. Worked on camp layout and new messhall design.

12 April 67 Airfield hit by VC — 6 mortar (82) positions 60+ rds — 2 USAF KIA, 1 USMC, 1 USN and 29 USA — WIA (first report). Went to bed at 1900.

13 April 67 Got survival kit and helmet and two sets of jungle utilities & two sets of boot liners. Got mail. Cut hole in wire for patrols. Started packing gear for move North to DMZ. Sick w/diarrhea, headache.

Helo Ops, in support of 5th Marines, Operation Union II. April 1967. Courtesy Jim O'Kelley.

16 April 67 14 rusty rifles at R & P inspection. Patrol hit by snipers. Mail.

17 April 67 Mine blew up truck near 4/11—4 USMC WIA, 1 Vietnamese critical, 2 Vn KIA. Awful mess!

18 April 67 No mail. Rained almost all day. Worked on patrols and ROKMC airfield. Cleaned gear. 5 New Lts in today.

21 April 67 Malaria pill. Went North 10 miles above Tam Ky with Bridge Platoon & ARVN — FO team in hardened vehicles. 3/5/Kilo moved out on 15 minutes notice to support F Co., 2/1 who was surrounded by NVA. Had to coordinate with new Army Artillery unit (155 Btry) behind us and position reinforced squad on Hill 49.

22 April 67 One WIA from mortars today. Canceled patrols because of US Army convoy. Worked on airfield.

26 April 67 Returned from hospital. Had 97 cases of food poisoning in Bn. No mail. Wrote up meritorious promotion for Cpl. Bailey.

27 April 67 Worked on meritorious promotion. Finished Gant chart of airfield. No appetite. Big fire mission out back. Learned to drive Eimco tractor today. Early in AM — ambush had 1 WIA, 1 MIA. Had 12 VC in "B" Company wire.

28 April 67 Malaria pill. Fixed colonel's map, finished airfield proposal, searched area where VC were last nite — found tracks, shovel marks, etc. Recon of Bridges #19, #18, #15. 155 shells dropped off truck — Vietnamese ran w/them — cordoned off chu Lai ville — search neg. Firefight near "C" Company. Booby trap at "B." No mail again.

Robert Terry Sperling, LCpl., Service Company, December 1966–December 1967

I remember on a patrol where we each had to run across about fifty yards of wide open ground, one at a time. I am no athlete, but there is no question about that being my personal best time for fifty yards under any conditions. I was carrying the additional weight of a flak jacket, M-60 machine gun, 100 rounds, canteen, helmet, boots and running in sand.

One time a patrol leader and a few of us went out during the day to select an ambush site for that night. Someone made the comment that we should be photographing this place for the National Geographic Society instead of choosing an ambush site! It could be a very beautiful country!

Ron Rainer, PFC, A Company, January 1967–October 1967

I think there may have been some marijuana, but as far as heavy drug use with us, we were too busy for any of that. I just don't remember any of that until we got back home and the anti-war movement was going on. That stuff was all over the place then.

John Vasarab, PFC, Service Company, 1967–1968

We were young and impressionable. We never gave much thought to what anybody told us. Just do it, because he said so. Don't think about why he wants it done or why they want it done. We just did our job. They'd tell me we got a dozer or a loader down. There is going to be a convoy coming through, get on it. Get off when they go past the dozer, take the parts with you, take a tool box and you're gone. You'd be on the road for about a hour or two. This is your stop. They stop and let you off and you would go in, take it apart and fix it. They'd say we'll be back around 7:00. Be here. That's it.

Sometimes there would be nobody around, maybe two people. Sometimes there would be maybe ten or twelve. For the most part, you never really thought about it. You just didn't think about it. There was other things on your mind. Unless there was shooting or noise or something, it must be all right. It must be safe here. [laughing] I can't believe we were that dumb.

The most vivid scene in my mind, to this day, is when Sgt. Shickel and I were going to make a service call on a downed bridge boat. We were going north on Highway One when we came to a group of people blocking the highway. We stopped short of them, not knowing the reason for the gathering. It might have been a trap as far as we knew. You only truly trusted your own people. It turned out that an Army convoy had passed through that area shortly before our arrival. One of the trucks hit a little girl of about eight or ten years of age. Please bear with me as this is graphic and very hard for me to tell. The child must have run down the bank on the shoulder of the road and connected with the bumper of one of the convoy trucks.

We found her laying on the roadway with the top portion of her skull taken off. It was as though a surgeon had removed it. I could see her skull because the child's brains were about three feet from the body. We tried to call our people at base, but could not reach them. We were out of range for our radio but another unit was monitoring the nets and sent a helicopter out with some MP's to handle the situation. What is upsetting is that not one per-

Culvert repair north of Chu Lai with MRS 100. Courtesy of Jim O'Kelley.

son stopped to check her out. At least one person had to have seen it happen, or the driver should have had a suspicion about it. The looks on the faces of the locals told me we did not make any friends that day. I can see her body as clear today as when I first saw it twenty-eight years ago. I guess the respect we have for life in this country got lost when we settled in over there. As far as I am concerned, that was a waste of a young life that didn't have a chance to make the choice of what kind of person she was going to be. I will never forget that little girl and if the driver of that truck knows he hit someone, I hope that he lives with it for the rest of his life.

MAY–AUGUST 1967

McNamara, testifying before a Senate subcommittee in August, asserts American bombing of North Vietnam is ineffective.

MAY

**Ted Zealley, Lt., D Company,
1 November 1965–June 1967**

My departure was almost delayed. My career with the 9th Engr Bn started with legal matters, as the first battalion legal officer. It ended as I was appointed as an Article 32 investigating officer for a potential General Court Martial case. There had been a series of thefts throughout the battalion, including the theft of a ring from the hut of Major Fred Paige, the Bn S-3. About a month before I was due to leave, the culprit, a member of the HQ Co., Utilities Platoon, was caught in the act of stealing something in D Company. This person had reason and many opportunities to go throughout the compound to check on utility problems. A check of his belongings in his own hut revealed quite a stash of valuables, including Fred Paige's ring. In any case, I was not to leave the country until the investigation was complete. The accused was entitled to an attorney at all proceedings. The closest Marine attorney was in Da Nang since by late May 1967 there were very few Marines at Chu Lai. I had one heck of a time getting that attorney out of his comfortable palace at Da Nang to get down to tend to business in Chu Lai. I think I had to threaten to come to Da Nang and drag him bodily to Chu Lai. Fortunately he didn't know me well and must have believed the threat. He came. We finished the work, and I left on 1 June 1967.

1 June 1967 was quite memorable. It was probably the best hourly pay I ever received. We flew out of Vietnam about 0330. As a result, I still got my combat pay and the tax exclusion on my pay for the month of June.

**Lawrence Stephen Roberge, LCpl.,
Service Company,
June 1966–January 1968**

The whole country was filled with interesting people. I do remember this one ARVN soldier I met while on convoy south of Chu Lai. The memory always stayed with me because he spoke no English and I spoke no Vietnamese. Interestingly enough, we both spoke French. His was the French language left over when the French were there, mine was a Canadian French from northern New Hampshire. We started talking and I learned that his family was in North Vietnam. He had no way to communicate with them and didn't know if they were okay. I still remember the sorrow on his face as we talked. Here was a young man fighting for his country, his family and home, and not knowing if he would ever see them again. I often thought of the sorrow my family and friends would feel if I didn't come home, but my home was safe and I knew I had a home to go to. This poor individual could have been killed, like any one of us, but also had the possibility of having no one to mourn for him. I still wonder, "Did he ever see his family after the cease fire?" I'll never know, but my thoughts are always with him, and he does have someone to mourn for him if he didn't make it.

Wayne McGinnis, L/Cpl., D Company, June 1966–July 1967

I remember going down an old road one time and there was sugar cane on both sides. We came across an old French fort. It was eerie. It was covered with vines and trees and I remember there was zillions of these little lizards everywhere. It made my skin crawl. They were crawling all around the bricks like the thing was alive.

Jim O'Kelley, 2 Lt.–1 Lt.–Capt., HQ & D Company, August 1966–May 1968

4 May 67 Patrol tonight — Recon. Bad nite. I'm sick and tired of being sick and tired.

6 May 67 Captured VC prisoners on patrol.

7 May 67 Rifle & Pistol inspection. No mail. Played volleyball & ran ½ mile. Signed pay roster.

8 May 67 Finished recons on Bridges #19, #18 & #13.

10 May 67 "B" Company moving to Phu Bai today. Eye still bad. Heard I might go to Charlie company. Got intestinal trouble again!!

11 May 67 Worked on Bridge truss analysis, water tower analysis. Wrote mortar SOP (Standard Operating Procedure) memo. Eye better, now foot swollen.

12 May 67 Malaria pill. Bad day — nothing went right. Got jungle rot on my feet. Airfield mortared.

14 May 67 Patrol 0600–1200 — received 6–8 sniper rounds. No mail. Jack Gracida K-3/5 came by — said Tilley, Earnie Pasquerilla and others hit — GySgt. Armstrong KIA. Very bad report.

15 May 67 Feeling awful — ugh! What a waste! Damn! Saw where D. S. Hackett KIA. Finished An Tan Bridge Truss analysis.

16 May 67 Got val pack for Top Daniels. Got paid. Heard Bob Tilley (Commanding Officer Kilo/3/5) KIA. Big airstrike near 4/11. Yellow alert at 1940.

18 May 67 Not going to a company. Recon S to Mo Duc & S on towards Duc Pho. One man WIA by 82 mortars. Found out from 3/5 rear Tilley not KIA but in

Road to Tich Tay, 9th Engineer patrol with prisoners. 6 May 1967. Courtesy Jim O'Kelley.

good condition (on USS *Repose*—dud mortar shell in his abdomen!!).

21 May 67 Rifle & Pistol inspection. Worked on Court Martial. Worked out drainage on airfield. No mail.

22 May 67 Special court martial, the accused Marine received 3 months confinement at hard labor, 3 mos. forfeiture of pay, and reduced E4 to E1.

23 May 67 104 degrees at 0900. 117 degrees at 1100. 120+ at noon!!! Took reporters to C Company. Sandstorm. Bn OOD. Changed bed & rack.

24 May 67 Slept in from OOD. Sent laundry to An Tan. Got haircut — mustache trimmed.

26 May 67 Malaria pill. No mail. FLSG-B for valpack — no! Sick intestinally again.

27 May 67 No mail. Op Stat orders.

28 May 67 Conducted training inspection of D Co.

29 May 67 No mail. Heavy workout with weights.

30 May 67 Mortar schedule. Job Order Reports. Training schedule.

31 May 67 No mail. Worked on Opstat Rpt., Confidential message about alert status, Task Organization Report and D Co. Inspection Report.

**Robert Terry Sperling, LCpl.,
Service Company,
December 1966–December 1967**

One of my worst patrols was the one where the Army opened up on us with .50 caliber machine guns from their towers on the defensive perimeter of Chu Lai. These towers had been built for the Army's Americal Division by the 9th Engineers U.S.M.C.

**John Vasarab, PFC, Service Company,
1967–1968**

We had weird bugs over there. We never knew what the hell most of them were. We had one of them in the tent and the guys decided to cook it. It was a big white thing and we couldn't recognize it, but it was ugly. It had about four or five legs and each one of them had like little feet. It had about five toes and at the tips of each toe was a little black fingernail. I don't know what the hell it was. After we looked at it for a while, we determined that it didn't belong on the planet anymore, so we decided to get rid of it.

JUNE

**Lawrence Stephen Roberge, LCpl.,
Service Company,
June 1966–January 1968**

The "greatest characters" I recall are the guys I served, lived, worked, played, drank, worried, laughed, chased girls and listened to music with. These are the guys that made 'Nam bearable. Some of the names have since escaped me, but guys like Richard "Dicky-Poo" J. Winn, Billy T. Thigpen, John Dedovitch, Rick "Chief" Ortega, Allen Sizemore, Ray Tingle, Jim Haun, Joe Gilbert, Angelo Santoro, Dale "Rowdy" Garretson, "Hoss" from Mississippi, T.C. Gilmoore, Jim Massey, David Payne, Mawny Perez, Jim Camerow, Torres, Buda, The Brown Boys, and so many more. I could go on forever, but my memory fails me. Those are the characters that were, and even after many years, are still important to me.

**Jim O'Kelley, 2 Lt.–1 Lt.–Capt.,
HQ & D Company,
August 1966–May 1968**

I did a lot of horse trading for gear — we used the word "comshaw" to mean trading for things you could not get through the normal supply system. Interestingly, everything we needed was in country somewhere; the trick was figuring out where and how to get to it. I traded (or comshawed) everything from candles to dump trucks! (other words for this activity: Scrounge — means to beg, borrow, buy, or midnight requisition [aka steal]).

1 June 67 Sold fan, chair for $18.00. Send Op Stat report. Assigned flight dates to platoon. Very heavy rain. Was offered and accepted short R&R to Hong Kong 1–4 June 1967

9 June 67 Returned from R&R Hong Kong at 1500. Got all mail straightened out.

11 June 67 No mail. Played Basketball. Escorted Lana Turner. Read & slept.

12 June 67 Sent Pop Fathers Day note. Planes bombing behind Hill 49. Sent Engineer Ops report. Sent ice cream via UH-34 (helicopter) to 5th Marines at Tam Ky. Bn OOD.

14 June 67 Worked on bridges. No mail. Saw Huey gunships & rocket ships attacking VC who were mortaring end of runway (southside). Artillery going off everywhere — looks like quite a night.

19 June 67 Bad hangover & sick. Got to work 0915! Took Lt. Roberts on recon. No mail except Duke Alum letter for advance tickets for football games!! Right!!

20 June 67 Issued M-16. FAM fire. Wrote Citation for Capt. Lawson for Navy Commendation Medal.

22 June 67 Wrote Navy Commendation Medal proposal on Master Gunnery Sgt. Daniels.

24 June 67 Worked on bridges. Big firefight out back.

26 June 67 Got orders for Camp Pendleton. Ran 5 laps. Went to 3rd Bridge North of An Tan.

27 June 67 Got plague, cholera, GG shots. Worked on bridges again. No mail. Bad day. Got cream for skin diseases from corpsman.

29 June 67 Finished bridge drawings. Calculated abutments. Water tower design at 161st Aviation Company. Bn OOD. Gooks cut wire and ran cattle through the Battalion area this morning.

30 June 67 Slept in AM. Worked out bearing plates & deadmen for bridges. Diarrhea medicine. Got investigation case assigned on 19 missing flak trousers.

Ed Whitaker, PFC,
Headquarters Company,
December 1966–October 1967

This one guy would usually bring me some bananas. When bananas are ripe over there, they are green and they are really short. Like you eat one big banana here, there you would eat three or four for the same amount of food. They are kind of different.

Robert Terry Sperling, LCpl.,
Service Company,
December 1966–December 1967

Most of the time I was a heavy equipment mechanic. I tried my best to repair bulldozers. I also spent four months working for Gunner (CW03) "Seabags" Johnson, keeping records and ordering parts.

John Vasarab, PFC, Service Company,
1967–1968

I went up to Tam Ky one time. They had a dozer that didn't work. They were up there mowing everything down. The Army was up there. I think it was part of the 101st, anyways they had screaming eagle patches on. They were guarding us and the Army was guarding us. There was one mechanic there but he didn't know anything about the dozer and I had gone to school for it. When I got there they had just dug holes in the ground to put the tents up. That was it. There was some barbed wire around it. There was one time when they went out in the morning to check the barbed wire and all the trip flares were tied shut with bamboo. They had a strip of bamboo around them to keep them from going off. Somebody jiggled the hell out of the wire.

When I found that out, I started

wondering, "Who's guarding us? Where the hell are these people when somebody was up there tying this stuff up?" It was just amazing. When I got there, this Army unit had tanks. You know, it made me wonder. Here you go from a place where there are guys with guns, and to a place where there are guys with guns and tanks.

JULY

Jim O'Kelley, 2 Lt.–1 Lt.–Capt., HQ & D Company, August 1966–May 1968

1 July 67 Class on UCMJ (Uniform Code of Military Justice). Worked out bearing plates & piles as deadmen. Got survival knife from MAG 12. Malaria pill late.

3 July 67 Finished Water supply design for 14th Aviation Company, US Army. Went N to 2nd Bridge. Three air strikes out front today.

4 July 67 Went west of Chu Lai — 8 miles to Hill 707 with Recon people. Came back & went north. Scrounged 19 flak trousers (to use on minesweeps).

7 July 67 Malaria pill. No mail. Sent officer data sheet to Camp Pendleton. Worked on Reinforced concrete design for rigid frame box pier all day. Took barbed wire stakes to Recon. Big air strikes near Hill 35. #39 did get hit last nite.

8 July 67 Wrote Bill of Materials for pier. Big air strike out back near Hill 35.

11 July 67 No mail. Went N at 0800. M-54 hit mine — 3 WIA. Took until 1100 to get road swept & truck moved. Then went on N and reconned two bridges. Bridge #2 hit at 1600 on the 10th — 3 USMC KIA — Pete Allen & crew pinned down by 50 cal. fire.

12 July 67 Worked on bridge designs. Bad heat & skin rashes. Rained. Beautiful sunset & double rainbow. D killed VC sniper. Firing MG & SA all around camp about 2030.

Route #1 repairs north of Tam Ky. Courtesy of Jim O'Kelley.

15 July 67 No mail. Da Nang hit hard — 11 planes destroyed, 30 damaged. 8 KIA, 172 WIA — Mail and post office destroyed. No mail in or out for next four days! Went N 32 miles on bridge recon. Saw big airstrike. Heat rash very bad — can't touch shoulders — very painful to wear flak jacket!!

18 July 67 Went N to Thang Binh, found one 45 cal booby trap, two 60 mm booby traps, one homemade mine on road. Got heavy sniper & SA fire up N. Rash very bad & hurts.

19 July 67 Heat rash much worse. Really considering 6 months extension (to get to command a letter company). Bought envelopes & worked on bridges.

25 July 67 Got Basketball net. Worked on grease rack. Bn OOD — received 3 rds SA — report 6 VC to hit us tonight.

26 July 67 No mail. Slept in until noon. No lunch. Eyes swollen almost shut & bad rash. No work at all.

28 July 67 Worked on Trial Counsel for Special Court Martial. Rash very bad. Received another Special Court Martial.

29 July 67 Went N to above 3rd Bridge. Worked on Special Court martials. Rash bad.

31 July 67 4 letters from Mom saying NO to extension ideas. Had one KIA with recon.

D Company building a bridge abutment near Tam Ty. Courtesy of Jim O'Kelley.

**Ed Whitaker, PFC,
Headquarters Company,
December 1966–October 1967**

When you walk around these people, you feel like the jolly green giant. These people are just structured so small. You always felt a little superior to them because you were so much taller. When we worked out of the compound and had the bulldozer, wherever we were at the Vietnamese were all over selling pop or something. But, if you left the bulldozer sitting there, anything that could be carried away would be gone. We had containers on it for oil and for diesel fuel and they would steal it. You would have to take everything that could be carried away with you.

We got c-rations. Well, there are some parts of c-rations you don't want to eat. The one that says Lima Beans on it, you would just throw that up in the air and there would be twenty little hands there after it. They would just scrap for it for survival.

**Robert Terry Sperling, LCpl.,
Service Company,
December 1966–December 1967**

If I only was allowed to tell one story about Vietnam, this is it. Myself and about six other Marines were on a MedCap to a small village. A MedCap is where a Doctor and/or Corpsman will go to a village, announced ahead of time, to help the Vietnamese medically.

We would take turns providing security, searching the Vietnamese before they saw the Corpsman, and playing with the children. I had broken a nail playing catch with the children and sat down with my back to a tree and got out a pair of fingernail clippers. Every one of the two dozen or so children gathered around me and were very interested. They had never seen a pair of fingernail clippers before.

When I was finished, I gave them to one of the boys and he and the others played with it like it was a new computer type game. Just think what other things we Americans have that these Vietnamese or any other 3rd World persons do not have.

Mike Daly, PFC, Hdqtrs. Company, July 1967–April 1969

I spent 2 weeks working in the rock quarry, drilling holes in the rocks all week and blowing them up on Friday. Then cranes would load the blown rock into trucks that took them to the rock crusher. After two weeks of drilling and working with the dynamite, my head felt like it would explode. Leaky nitro will give you a terrible headache.

John Vasarab, PFC, Service Company, 1967–1968

Kool-Aid was the big thing. Everytime you wrote home you asked for Kool-Aid. Families would send it and we would stick it in our canteens. You didn't want to get untreated water. It was like opening a bottle of Clorox and drinking it. It needed Kool-Aid. [laughs] Kool-Aid was a commodity. It could buy anything. [laughs]

On Sunday afternoons they gave us time off to wash our clothes and just unwind a little. On these afternoons you could do your laundry, hang it up and start to remove it almost at the same time. We had some of the local villagers come into our compound to do some cleaning and keep the area as neat as possible. They had one hut that was used to store their lunches and other things. One day I bopped in and took all their chop sticks, just to see what would happen at lunch time. I tell you that it was funny as hell listening to them all trying to figure out what happened to their wooden ware. All that cackling. It only set them back for a few minutes though. They didn't let that stop them from eating.

I guess the biggest thing that pissed a lot of guys off was the mail delivery. The time lag was long and when the main post office in Da Nang got blown up occasionally, it took even longer. This was the hardest thing a man had to face. It made you feel like everyone forgot about you. It's not like you could pick up a phone and call home to find out why they weren't writing you. I think that the depressing feeling from lack of mail messed up some of the troops.

AUGUST

Jim O'Kelley, 2 Lt.–1 Lt.–Capt., HQ & D Company, August 1966–May 1968

3 August 67 Marine in Utilities section killed.

4 August 67 Malaria pill. No mail. Lawyers came down from Da Nang on SCM case. Interrogated witnesses.

5 August 67 Worked on case all day.

6 August 67 Went to beach. Change of command — Maj. Lifset took over from Lt. Col. Babe (as CO, 9th Engineer Battalion).

8 August 67 Trial of Sgt. — found guilty of 2 specs & charge — received reduction to E3.

9 August 67 No mail. Worked on 175 mm platform redecking, 30 x 70 Ammo bunker and 16 x 32 Tropical hut. Sick with diarrhea, cramps, & nausea. Maj. Paige leaving for Okinawa. Bn OOD.

10 August 67 Slept in AM. Went N to Hill 29 in pm. Saw Chuck Tyler — TF (Task Force) X-ray now at Hill 29 for big op that begins tomorrow. Worked with Pete Allen on 3rd Bridge design.

14 August 67 Went S to 3/21 area. W of Nuc Man on road/camp job. No mail.

15 August 67 Capts. list came out — I was on 34th of 53 pages!

16 August 67 Pay day. No mail. Major Paige returned (from Okinawa).

17 August 67 Maj. Bergstrom 3/16 came over about Messhall. Worked out with weights. No mail came. Sgt. Dandar got sniper fire while on recon on Hill 49. Sent special AA form to leave here in August.

19 August 67 VC blew bridge N of Hill 29. No mail again today. Worked on 30 × 70 bunker, laundry & shower buildings.

21 August 67 Went north to new "C" Company campsite near Thang Binh. Went to Mag 13 about USAFI Physics Group Study for troops. Got PPD shot. Raining. Carried dud M-26 from Thang Binh to "B" CP!!

23 August 67 Worked on truss design problem and on problem as to feasibility of using bomb racks as reinforcing for concrete pours.

24 August 67 Orders for home came in. Heading out tomorrow.

25 August 67 Left for home.

Ed Whitaker, PFC, Headquarters Company, December 1966–October 1967

When I went to work in the morning, a lot of times I would have to walk to work. Maybe it was only about half a mile, but you have to understand we could be shot at. It's not likely that close to the compound, but you never know either. You become married to your rifle. You take it everywhere. No matter where you go, it's by your side. You eat with it, you sleep with it. You shower with it. I never had a rifle in my hand until I went into the Marine Corps. I felt comfortable with it after I got used to it.

[laughs] I almost wrecked it one day. In Vietnam you take it with you on your bulldozer. I walked up to the bulldozer and I happened to just lay it up against the side of the blade. I'm checking the oil and stuff before I start it. I jumped on to it and started it up. I raised the blade and when I raised it up, it tipped the rifle away. I remembered and, "Oh, my gosh. Where is it at?" I thought I had ran over it. That would have been embarrassing.

Mike Daly, PFC, Hdqtrs. Company, July 1967–April 1969

I volunteered to go to the field and was sent south somewhere with the Korean Marines. I spent two months with them, a time period that I extremely enjoyed. I remember getting hit one night and my M-14 was gold with rust. I had to kick the charging handle back to break the rust. It worked the rest of the night with no problems. The next night I decided to clean it good and when it was all apart, we got hit again. With the lights completely out, I had to put the gun together again. Thank God for ruthless D.I.'s. Their training paid off.

SEPTEMBER–DECEMBER 1967

Communists begin major actions in September. Westmoreland starts to fortify Khe Sanh. Johnson, in San Antonio on September 29, says United States will stop bombing in exchange for "productive discussions." Foreign Minister Trinh says on December 29 that North Vietnam "will" talk once the United States halts its bombing.

American troop strength in Vietnam approaches 500,000 by year-end. Domestic protests against the war rise.

SEPTEMBER

**Lawrence Stephen Roberge, LCpl.,
Service Company,
June 1966–January 1968**

Every damn Marine was heroic to me. Every day giving his best to try to build so much out of so little. I still remember the time that we were working nights to help build a new school in Chu Lai after working all day. We in Service Company were hauling gravel. All of a sudden one of our trucks blew up. Someone had thrown a grenade in the battery box of Rick "Chief" Ortega's truck. He was all right, just minor shrapnel. Maybe it's not worthy of the silver star, but getting hurt while helping others must mean something. Chief is a great guy and I was glad that he was okay.

OCTOBER

**Jim O'Kelley, 2 Lt.–1 Lt.–Capt.,
HQ & D Company,
August 1966–May 1968**

2 October 67 Returned to Chu Lai. Assigned to "D" Company.

**Edward L. Casper, Cpl.,
Headquarters Company,
August 1967–August 1968**

Most of the time was boring. Sandbags were filled until it was too hot to work. Guard duty filled up a month by standing bunker watch on the perimeter. There are always little details that had to be done. We had a outdoor movie, NCO club and a basketball court to entertain yourself when off duty. The songs I remember well are "Give Me a Ticket on an Airplane," "Detroit City," "Can't Get No Satisfaction," and "Paint It Black," as well as others.

If it was not for good friends like then Corporal Freddy Wood, PFC Hard, Heavy Savare, Lance Corporal Bill Wallick, Lance Corporal Steven Sprague and Lance Corporal Jim Hitsmen, the time would have drug by. Freddy was a jokester and prankster and kept things lively.

One huge thing happened to Freddy and Jim up the trail one night. It could have turned out bad, but it all worked out well. Freddy and Jim were on a squad size patrol. Their fire team comprised of them and one other guy were set up in an ambush and the rest of the patrol went off and

Ed Casper. Courtesy of Ed Casper.

left them in the woods alone and lost. You could hear them on the radio, but they all got back safely.

Ron Rainer, PFC, A Company, January 1967–October 1967

We spent a week on a bridge and this typhoon came through. The water rose and rose and it got to about a foot below the bridge and then stopped. This was the river and the banks would flood through the rice paddies. We were anchored up on this bridge and they would drop c-rations to us from a helicopter. We were sitting ducks up there. They would shoot at us all the time. At night, it was scary because you could see the tracer rounds coming in towards you. You could see them coming. They would just fire at that bridge all the time. We were laying the ground work for that longest bridge.

Rick McCan, a good friend of mine, was hurt and I was following him when he ran across the mine. There was a Staff Sergeant that was riding on the running board which they always told us never to do. But he was riding on the running board of this vehicle and he hit the land mine on that side, the front wheel, and we got down and pulled him out of that rice paddy. Both of his arms and both of his legs were gone. We put him on the chopper and got him out of there. Before the chopper came I went down and McCan was spurting blood out of one of his arms, so I wrapped it up.

Two days later I was following a sweep team when I pulled into an area to backup and hit a mine. They pulled a big chain out of the ground and thought that was what was causing the reading. They told me that there was com wire that was run underneath that chain, about four foot down. It was run out to the tree line from the rice paddies, and they just touch those wires together. They were really trying to block construction of the road. I was thrown out and can't remember too much there. I remember waking up a couple times in Da Nang. A Gunny Sergeant was standing over me asking me why I didn't sandbag my truck properly. [laughs] He wasn't even in the field or anything. Maybe he was doing that to just get me riled up. I was injured two days before my birthday. It was October 20, 1967. They reported me as a 20 year old at that time.

I never did take an R&R. What I wanted to do was extend for six months and get an early out of the Marine Corps. I had an option to go spend seven days in Australia, go home for thirty days, come back to Vietnam for six months and then after that I'd get the early out. That was the process they had if you were willing to spend an additional six months in Vietnam. When I got hurt, I was waiting for the R&R to Australia to be approved. I had everything in the works, paperwork and everything. But then I got hurt.

John Vasarab, PFC, Service Company, 1967–1968

I was sitting in one of the outhouses we had and Terry Little was playing games. I never saw him. He snuck up behind me and opened the door on the back and he's got a God damn fire extinguisher and set the son of a bitch off. It scared the hell out of me. Froze my marbles.

I went down to see the Korean Marines once. I watched them have an inspection. They were a sick bunch. I was down there for a couple of days and they were going out in the field. This officer was checking out their equipment. He went behind this one guy and he was checking the entrenching tools. I don't know if it was loose but something didn't suit him. He took the son of a bitch out and he clubbed the soldier with it. He dropped him right there and nobody moved. The guy laid there, he's got a little bit of blood coming out the side of his head from getting hit with this tool and nobody moved until the formation was over. Then a couple of his buddies came over and picked his ass up and hauled him to the doctor. I thought we had it bad.

One of the Korean Marines was a pretty good artist. I had a little picture of The Last Supper in my wallet and I showed it to him. He made a big copy of it on some kind of a fuzzy canvas. I sent it home to my mother. It was hanging there for a long time. He did a beautiful job on it. He won't take anything for it, other than I paid for the paint and whatever it cost him to get the paint sent to him. It took about six months until he got it finished. He mailed it up to where we were. I put it into a cylinder canister and mailed it home.

NOVEMBER

Jim O'Kelley, 2 Lt.–1 Lt.–Capt., HQ & D Company, August 1966–May 1968

Every Friday we had to take the big orange Malaria pill. The Corpsman normally brought them around. They were about twice the size of a vitamin pill. Most of us usually were sick for the next couple of days with intestinal cramps, diarrhea, etc. When we got up North on the DMZ, we also took the small white pills the Army used (of course the Army and the Navy couldn't even agree on Malaria pills). Unfortunately, neither pill worked very well—I had one young Marine die from Malaria at Ca Lu and I got Malaria myself.

Robert Terry Sperling, LCpl., Service Company, December 1966–December 1967

One night the firing was getting pretty

Driving pilings for bridge. Lt. Pete Allen on right. Courtesy of Jim O'Kelley.

bad and a tank rolled in from Chu Lai Defense which guards the airbase at Chu Lai. The tank stopped and slowly turned its turret gun and search light back and forth searching the village like this for over ten minutes. At first we were very grateful for that tank. However, after awhile we imagined ourselves as a Vietnamese in one of the huts in the village. We definitely had it better in our bunker!

Mike Daly, PFC, Hdqtrs. Company, July 1967–April 1969

I begged to be sent on Operation Pineapple Jungle. This was quite an experience. It was an Army and ARVN operation. My job was to clear jungle so ground traffic could be spotted from helicopters. Jungle was cleared approximately one mile wide and ten miles long. During this time period we got hit almost every night. We lost five bulldozers and one operator. The operator was Oliee, from Sweden, who served with us to gain his citizenship. At one point, while clearing the jungle, I fell completely into a tunnel complex. The dozer slid into the cavern with me on board. This place was later to be named Hog Back Ridge because we found a small barnyard under ground there. My dozer had shrapnel holes in the torque converter, therefore had no high range. I had been sent to clear the mine field below the ARVN hill. Oliee came in early and began to help me. He hit a grenade on a trip wire and it blew right next to him, peppering him with shrapnel. Lucky Oliee for taking my grenade, he was able to get front row seats when Bob Hope came to town and the rest of us were still in the jungle. This operation ended just before Christmas.

Paul Kozak, PFC, D Company, September 1967–September 1968

(November '67 while Delta Company, 9th Engr. Battalion was TAD to 11th Eng. Bn. 3rd Mar. Div.—bivouacked with 3/9 at Ca Lu in Northern I Corps. Ca Lu was approx. 8 mi. north east of Khe Shan along Highway 9.)

My first glimpse of combat, and introduction to fear came shortly after we turned in. While laying in the fetal position, I clung tightly to the inside of my sleeping bag. I never thought I would be cold in Vietnam.

Suddenly, the damp night air erupted with the sound of machine-gun fire. My desire for warmth was no longer a concern. Tracer rounds glowed as they ripped through the tent. I made my exit and joined the platoon in the fighting positions. Everyone chambered a round at the same time. The magnified sound of rifle bolts slamming home was intense. My baptism of fire was upon me; I married the sandbags and aimed my rifle.

As my knees bore into the earth, a strange feeling came over me. The aroma of rifle-cleaning fluid, lubriplate, and canvas stimulated my senses. In addition, I became aware of my air passages and equilibrium. These sensations were unfamiliar and frightening; I was totally absorbed by the intensity.

A red flare popped, then descended in front of us. Behind me and up the hill the company commander shouted, "They're coming up the ravine; fix bayonets!" Someone whispered what I was thinking, "Bayonets?" I snapped mine into place and prepared for the worst.

There was a commotion over in Second Platoon's position. A new guy from that platoon charged up the hill in retreat. At that moment an illumination mortar ignited overhead. The guy who had turned coward rolled back down the hill. He was then dragged to the line and thrown into a connecting trench. My squad leader, who was directly in front of me, buried his head in prayer; this was not a good sign.

Miraculously, silence fell upon us. A cautious relief flowed through me. Another

Rockpile in foreground and road to Ca Lu. Courtesy of Jim O'Kelley.

"Rough Rider" resupply convoy between Rockpile and Ca Lu, near 13 January 1968 ambush site. Courtesy of Jim O'Kelley.

illumination round lit the area. The elephant grass was still. I could not hear any movement. A short time later, the company gunny broke the silence; "Scabbard those bayonets Marines. Platoon sergeants, secure your men."

Later we would learn that North Vietnamese sappers had probed and penetrated Lima Company's positions. There was no major attack.

I didn't shoot a round that night, nor did I see the enemy. However, I was a different man. I had had my first glimpse of what was to come.

John Vasarab, PFC, Service Company, 1967–1968

There was one period that the post office up at Da Nang got hammered and we didn't get mail for two or three weeks. There is nothing worse than not getting mail. You didn't have much to start with, but when you don't get your mail, that's really a bummer. So, this one guy takes it upon himself to write my mother a letter. He tells her that every time I hear a MRS200 start up I just kind of slink off into a corner somewhere, and I sit there, curl up and a little tear comes out of my eye. Well, my mom did not understand and she gets hold of the Red Cross, who gets a hold of some psychiatrist unit over there and they sick a shrink on me. Well, a friend tells me he heard through a company clerk that this doctor is coming to check my head. He tells me to stop crying so for two weeks I didn't go near anybody. For two weeks they hounded me to get my head shrunk. That was all because of him.

In the meantime, the same guy got a hernia. He was in the hospital and got operated on. When he came back I was across the compound. It was a big open area and there was like a broom stick. I started yelling at him because of this shrink chasing me down. I told him I was going to kick his ass. I picked this broom stick up and I hurled it

9th Engineer Battalion at Chu Lai during monsoon, December, 1967. Courtesy of Jim O'Kelley.

like a spear. I mean there was no way I knew I could hit him. Not even remotely possible. So, I threw this stick and there was a hood from a tractor laying in the sand and the stick hit the hood and ricocheted up. He was about five feet from it when it was on its way up and it hit him in the nuts. This is like his first day out of the hospital. I figure we are even now. I spent two weeks trying to keep from getting my head shrunk and he got rapped in the nuts. It was even.

DECEMBER

Paul E. Virtue, LCpl., D Company, March 1967–March 1968

31 December 1967 Cloudy

Peterman medivaced. Stepped on M-14 blast type mine when re-entering live mine field to finish camouflage of other mines. Firebase Ca Lu (DMZ)

Charles King, Sgt., B Company, September 1967–September 1968

The best day in-country for me personally was Christmas Eve night.

It was just guys away from home and kids never out grow their toys. For some reason or another somebody put up a little old palm tree. They put cotton balls on it and they put an M-60 machine gun underneath this tree. Then they put an M-16 and a couple grenades and kind of decorated it. Little boys with their toys was my interpretation, only we were grown men. Then somebody started singing, [pause] and we all started singing Christmas carols. It was lights out in the tents. Once somebody started singing it wasn't long before four or five guys got there. Then here comes ten or twelve more and before it was over the whole company was outside singing. And to this day, it's something that's really stuck in my memory. The good things and the same song, "Silent Night, Holy Night." We all broke up and to this day it tears me up. When I hear "Silent Night, Holy Night," if it wasn't for my wife, I don't know what I'd do sometimes.

**Robert Terry Sperling, LCpl.,
Service Company,
December 1966–December 1967**

My last week in Vietnam, while Corporal of the Guard, a Staff Sergeant kept telling me to be extra careful because of unusual enemy movement in the area. I thought him to be overly concerned and I was upset with him for making me so nervous my last few days in Vietnam. I forgave him when I heard about Tet in late January 1968.

John Vasarab, PFC, Service Company, 1967–1968

They have the spring and the winter monsoons. The winter ones are the longest. The spring one wasn't too bad. That was just maybe a month. During the winter one, you may get an hour or two of no rain during the day, and the rest of the time, it rained almost constantly. You couldn't ever get anything dried out. There would be stuff hanging all over the tent. It was like walking into an old gym locker. Everyday it just stinks.

JANUARY–APRIL 1968

In January Sihanouk tells Johnson's emissary, Chester Bowles, that he will not stop American forces from pursuing the Vietcong over the Cambodian border. Tet offensive begins January 31 as North Vietnamese and Vietcong attack South Vietnamese cities and towns.

American and South Vietnamese troops recapture Hue on February 25 after twenty-six days of fighting. General Earle Wheeler, chairman of the joint chiefs of staff, brings request from Westmoreland in Saigon for 206,000 additional American troops. Clark Clifford, succeeding McNamara as secretary of defense, begins study of troop request; soon favors rejection of buildup.

Westmoreland appointed army chief of staff, replaced in Vietnam by General Creighton Abrams. On March 25 "wise men" meet in Washington; advise Johnson against further escalation. On March 31 Johnson announces partial bombing halt, offers talks, and says he will not run for re-election.

Martin Luther King, Jr. assassinated in Memphis April 4.

JANUARY

Paul E. Virtue, LCpl., D Company, March 1967–March 1968

Monday, 1 January 1968 at Ca Lu

Opened 80 cases of M-16's and 11 M-14 mines for stock piling of mine field #6. Made dump run and picked up 1,000 drift pins from CB's. Minefield detail replaced mine Peterman detonated and 2 M-16's the enemy set off with mortar two mornings ago. Found wire cut in three places yesterday and tunnels. 48 sniper rounds last night, first of any real sign of enemy aggressiveness. A booby trap near cut fence. It was most likely one of our M-16's with trip wire that they got from ambush on the 19th of December on our mine convoy.

Tuesday, January 2, 1968 Clear/Cloudy

It was one of those days that things just didn't go as planned. Taking mines out of my staging trailer messing up my count. Transportation seems to mess us up the most. There is always something happening to delay or switch around vehicles.

Thursday, January 4, 1968 Clear/Cloudy

Helicopter shot down about four hundred meters to our west. Ran out of gas with tractor just after getting started. Told Gunny at NCO meeting that mines wouldn't be ready to go at 6:30 in the morning. I had been telling him for the last three days that we needed more help. This really shut him down. Twenty days before my 21st birthday. It seems hard to accept, but that's life.

Friday, January 5, 1968 Clear/Cloudy

Tractor wouldn't start. Got another tractor but had no pin for towbar. Finally got the first tractor started. On the way back from dropping the mines off at mine field, tractor stalled out. It was too late to make to the mess hall for chow so we ate C-rats. Started working out of dumps on

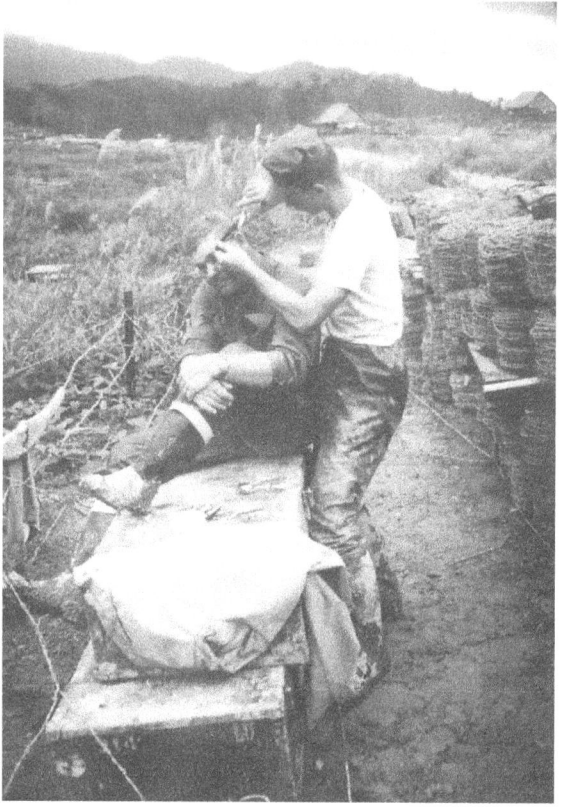

L/Cpl. Molossi cutting M. St. E.V. LeDuc's hair at Ca Lu, January 1968. Courtesy of Jim O'Kelley.

the hill. Finished three of the mine dumps on the road this morning.

Sunday, January 7, 1968 Rain

Blew 225 M2A4 (Bouncing Bettys) mines which were destroyed because they are now obsolete. Used 120 lbs. of C4.

Wednesday, January 10, 1968 Rain

We had plenty of mines ready but they didn't plant too many mines because of the rain we got last night making the hillsides very slippery. The mine trailer returned without being cleared of trash. I had brought this problem up before the NCO meeting last night but what good did it do? I let the Lt. know about this and he said that it would be taken care of by a work party after dinner. Two of my own men ended up doing it. I told the Lt. of this because it wasn't up to the mine dump crew to do this in the first place. We went to the Right Guide and gave him a chewing out.

Thursday, January 11, 1968 Clear

Completed perimeter mine field about two miles in circumference. It was a busy morning for the reason that we had to have 2,016 mines out by 10:00. I was given four extra men for the morning to help. But one was a Corporal which didn't like to do or follow the plans of a Lance Corporal, myself. He took another man with him without my consult, and messed out my man power.

Saturday, January 13, 1968 Cloudy/Rain

Blew 191 M-16's. Convoy was hit hard. About 25 or more Marines died. About 45 wounded. Most of our platoon and the rest of the Company had to stand the grunts' guard. So 3rd Plt. didn't move out like it was planned. NVA (North Vietnamese Army) used our mines against us which we lost on a convoy they last hit the 17th of Dec. "Send the corn on the next convoy, we are ready to plant."

Sunday, January 14, 1968 Clear/Cloudy/Rain

A day of rest. We don't know what date we will be leaving now. We may all have to become grunts. We had gotten word about Bob Molossi's rifle being among many others after the convoy had been hit. Later it was confirmed that he was a KIA. It was so hard to accept, but it was one of those things you have to face up to about war. He was the best man that had ever worked for me in the mine dump. He acted like a carefree happy-go-lucky Californian that actually down deep cared!

Monday, January 15, 1968 Cloudy/Rain

All three squads were assigned details. 2nd Squad was to crate up mines on helinets and pallets. We had just finished half of the detail when our Captain O'Kelley gave us the word that we were being helo-lifted out as soon as we finished. It was confirmed that there was 20 KIA's and about 80 medevacs from January 13 ambush.

Thursday, January 18, 1968 Cloudy

Had a rifle inspection this morning. Nobody passed it. The Lt. was keyed off because they weren't Garrison clean like they have to be when we get back to Chu Lai.

Wednesday, January 24, 1968 Clear

A plane finally came in at 10:00. It was a good feeling to touch down at Chu Lai. We are now told that the Company is moving to Hill #63 Sunday.

Thursday, January 25, 1968 Clear

This morning we went over to sick bay for shots. After lunch the Captain told us (2nd Plt) that we are moving out tomorrow morning as the advance party. Also that we wouldn't be moving back to this area ever again. It looks like they are going to move the Battalion north in the near future. I think that all Marines are going north. The Lt. told me that I had gotten R&R to Hawaii, but I didn't want Hawaii mainly because it is expensive. So he came back later and asked if I wanted Tai Pai. I heard that it was really good so I took it.

Saturday, January 27, 1968 Clear

Today I took a package to the post office, but it was too heavy. It was disappointing, but I had more gear to send so I just let it go until Sunday when my spirits would be on the better side.

Sunday, January 28, 1968 Clear

Went to church this morning, but now the Doggies have even taken over that too. There is an Army engineer Bn. just forming up here. The 26th Engr's. I haven't felt too much like eating lately, but I went to lunch anyway today. After lunch I started tearing down the package which was too heavy to send. I had to make another box from a luggage container. I have finally gotten all of my junk packaged and ready to try again.

Wednesday, January 31, 1968 Clear

The convoy with the rest of our company was supposed to leave this afternoon, but didn't because of trouble on Route 1 north from Chu Lai to Da Nang. Mag 12 Air Support was hit hard with rockets and mortars tonight. Two secondary explosions occurred. The second one lit the dark sky like daylight for about 5 seconds. It really packed a shock wave.

Mike Daly, PFC, Hdqtrs. Company, July 1967–April 1969

Upon returning to Chu Lai, we were given five days of no duty. We used this time to go to supply for new clothes, visit sick bay, write letters and go to the Korean Club on the beach. I never received my five days. SSgt. Blackshire came to get me to go back to work. I explained my situation to him in an undiplomatic manner and was immediately given thirty days mess duty. To say the least, I was upset, but after doing the time I volunteered for another thirty days, and missed most of the monsoon season that year.

Peter Allon, PFC, Service Company, November 1967–December 1968

I went over in September of '67. I was there for Tet of '68 with Service Company. First Sergeant Marshall and Gunny Calhoun would come in the bunker every

Scene of 13 January 1968 ambush. Courtesy of Jim O'Kelley.

9th Engineers building helcopter pads at Chu Lai. Courtesy of Reno Rizzo.

time we were hit by mortars. They'd dig under the sand. We just about got fragged a couple of times. That used to be our escape hole at night. If nothing was happening, we'd go through the wire into An Tan.

Dan Diridoni, LCpl., Service Company, December 1967–December 1968

They just picked me out and said you're going with B Company. You are going north to build roads up near Hue City. Of course, I had never heard of Hue City. I didn't know where it was or where anything was there. I met up with B Company in Tam Ky, which is halfway between Da Nang and Chu Lai. That's where they had been for a while.

Robert Handley, LCpl., D Company, January 1968–February 1969

When I got there, I was assigned to the motor pool right away. I remember there was a Sergeant Dura in charge of the motor pool at that time. Our assignments were to go out with the mine sweep teams every morning. Then, depending on how the sweep went, we'd pull other duties. Sometimes it was a convoy to Da Nang or Chu Lai for resupply or ammo or something. There was some training over there also.

Dave Nichols, LCpl., B Company, January 1968–February 1969

We spent many months in the area of Hue, Phu Bai and the A-Shau Valley. Much of that time was spent working with the Army's 101st Airborne Division. We constructed much of Camp Eagle and cleared most of the land for Fire Base Bastogne near the border of Laos. Late in my tour we were assigned the job of paving Highway 1 from Chu Lai to Da Nang, approx. 50 miles.

When we arrived in the Phu Bai area, we set up a small compound to the west of Phu Bai and Hue. We shared this compound with a 105 artillery battery and a group of Seabees. The Tet Offensive of 1968 started shortly after we set up in the area. We were in a strange situation during Tet. We were never really attacked by VC or NVA while in our compound except when a helicopter tried to re-supply us. Every time a helicopter tried to land, the LZ was heavily mortared. This caused us to go for a very long time without getting supplies. There were some times that the helicopters would drop artillery and small arms ammunition from the air, but we were very low on food.

FEBRUARY

Paul E. Virtue, LCpl., D Company, March 1967–March 1968

Thursday, 1 February 1968 Clear

The convoy got on its way this afternoon. We had a full scale firefight at the rear of Delta Co. The "Doggies" made it that way anyhow. I was the only one left behind except for Gunny Buck. So I got stuck with cleaning out four of the huts which were lastly used by the men leaving on the convoy. It didn't take too long but it was just the idea of it. The Top said I could move to the Staff Hut tomorrow morning. The "Doggies" start moving in in full force tomorrow. Went to hospital today, but they were too busy to take care of my follow-up. Have to return tomorrow.

Friday, 2 February 1968 Clear

Went to hospital first thing this morning. They had quite a few patients. I went into Patient Affairs, but they didn't have any transportation available. So I walked down to the USO after briefly looking through the new PX at Div. They had built a new USO which is something else. They now have free cold milk and juice and free hot dogs. When I returned, shortly after the Top got back on the convoy, so he had me run some of his petty ass errands. It must be an awful strain on him to have to walk 100 yds. to mail a letter.

Saturday, 3 February 1968 Clear

Arrived at Da Nang at noon. First thing this morning I turned in my rifle. Then we went to disbursing to draw money for R&R. What I didn't realize was that I could only draw half a months' pay. So this really left me short. Then I mailed the second package which cost me $10.60. Top Culp lent me the money until next pay day.

Sunday, 4 February 1968 Rain

It was raining when we arrived at Tai Pei. I guess that it is the rainy season here now. I just got a haircut and manicure. Of course I have my hotel room. The first thing I knew was that someone was trying to sell me clothes. Boy, have these people got a line. I have always heard that they have been very successful businessmen and now I can see why.

Sunday, 11 February 1968 Cloudy

We were supposed to leave for Hill #63 at no later than 08:30, but because of the usual delays we got underway at about 11:30. We arrived there around 15:00. It is a lot bigger build-up here than I ever expected. The tents have plywood decking on the ground. This is the best we have ever lived in tents. Also we have electricity 24 hours except when taps go at 22:00.

Living conditions at Ca Lu. Courtesy of Jim O'Kelley.

The fall-out bunkers are very well constructed of sandbags. The best thing about it all is that we didn't have to build it like everyplace else we have been. I thought that I had packed up all of my gear and sent it home. Somehow I seem to have gotten more.

Monday, 12 February 1968 Clear

Well, the Gunny was up to his sly games again. He tried to make me the toolman. I just had to flatly refuse him. I don't think it is right for someone not having the proper rank to tell others that outrank him what to do. I just want to be out on the job with the rest of the guys!

Thursday, 15 February 1968 Clear

Made up floor sections and cut flooring.

Friday, 16 February 1968 Clear

Completed ordnance bunker with sandbags. Then helped with the club flooring.

Saturday, 17 February 1968 Clear

This morning I was sent out to the rock crusher to work. But seeing as how they wanted me to bend and lift heavy rocks with my bad knee, I went back and helped put up the rafters.

Monday, 19 February 1968 Clear

My squad had the mine-sweep south this morning. We didn't find any mines. After the sweep, we went on work parties.

After lunch, we all went to the rock quarry and loaded six dump trucks with rock by hand. After this, we had a fan-fire consisting of: M-16's, M-60, M-72 (log), M-79 grenade-launcher, smoke, WP, and frag grenades.

Wednesday, 21 February 1968 Clear
Put on the sides of dump trucks. This is so they may carry more each load.

Thursday, 22 February 1968 Clear
Took mine-sweep to rock quarry first thing in the morning, and then assisted in finished sweep on Route 1 South. After lunch, three of us put in a training-aid minefield. This included a culvert to practice checking for mines and booby-traps.

Friday, 23 February 1968 Clear/Cloudy
Went on south mine-sweep this morning. Finished at 10:30 and had until lunch off. After lunch, two of us had to stand guard on a dozer. This was where we fire our rifles, so I let rip about 300 rounds. So, of course, I gave my rifle a good cleaning in diesel, tearing it down to the last part. After standing guard on a tractor for about 45 minutes, we came back and cleaned up the outer side of the berm-line. After this, I reloaded my magazines and wiped off my rifle.

Saturday, 24 February 1968 Rain
There was a misty rain most of the day, while the sun was divided by the heavy overcast all day. Four of us used cratering, shaped and regular demo charges for blasting rock at the quarry this morning. After lunch we did some more of the same. I fan-fired 180 more rounds with my rifle. I had just about completed cleaning my rifle when I got the cleaning rod hung up in the barrel. I guess I'll have to go the armor tomorrow and possibly get a new rifle or barrel. I had this one so nicely broken in. Tomorrow I will be carrying the M-60 machine gun on the north sweep which we will have for a week. The other platoons have been running into a lot of mines and contact on this 13 mile sweep!

Sunday, 25 February 1968 Clear
About half way on the northern sweep this morning we got pinned down by sniper fire. They like to shoot at the mine detectors. No one got hurt, but our cargo truck got two flats. One round hit two feet to the left of my shoulder while I was prone on the road. We continued on through once nice towns. War torn and burned out, it is almost lifeless now except for Koreans keeping out VC looking for concealment. During the sniper fire I re-injured my knee which has never gotten completely better.

Monday, 26 February 1968 Cloudy
This morning after formation I went over to the camp hospital to have my knee looked at. They in turn sent me to Chu Lai 2nd Surgical Hospital. Myself and other patients waited all morning for a helicopter. We got one about 12:30. The view on our way was really something. Too bad I didn't have a camera with me at the time. They didn't have time to look at my knee today and so I get an appointment for Wednesday.

Wednesday, 28 February 1968 Clear
Had splint applied to right leg. About three hours later I had unbearable pain in leg and knee.

Thursday, 29 February 1968 Clear
Took it easy.

Charles King, Sgt., B Company, September 1967–September 1968

It wasn't long after we went up to where the rock crusher was outside of Phu Bai that we lost three guys up there. They were ambushed on a truck convoy. I always have memories of that.

Dan Diridoni, LCpl., Service Company, December 1967–December 1968

We took off, went to Da Nang and stayed there. We stayed with the Seventh Engineers there for a night. The next morning we took off and went up over the

"An RPG (rocket) round went through the door Swede was sitting next to. Doc Collier was not killed in this truck as he was shot in the back of the head attending a wounded Marine nearby." Courtesy of Dan Diridoni.

Hai Van Pass and down on the other side of it, and that's where I had my first experience with war. I think you might have read a little bit about what happened with the truck that hit the mine. That was a kind of bizarre turn of events.

We were on a convoy heading north and were probably about twenty-five miles north of Da Nang when we hit a command detonated mine. They caught the guy that ignited the detonator and we were halfway back in the convoy when this happened. The only person that got hurt there was the guy that was sitting in the shot gun seat. Myself and another guy were sitting up on top of this dump truck. It knocked it damn near on its side. It was an antitank mine and the guy that was riding shot gun broke his arm. We stayed there for a short time, pondered the situation and then took off. There was about 50 trucks in this convoy and when we got to Phu Bai, we stayed there for about two days. Then we headed into Hue City.

I didn't know "Doc" Collier and Swede Hedlund very well as I was new with B Company. I was physically detached from them, but they were real nice people. I remember myself and Alan McNeese waving good-bye to them on the ill fated convoy that crossed in front of us and crossed the pontoon bridge to try and get back to Phu Bai. We heard the ambush unfold very shortly after they left. I was only one-quarter of a mile from our spot around a bend in the road. What a helpless feeling this was. We all knew what was happening. Very shortly after this, what was left of the convoy came streaming back across the bridge and most were completely frantic and scared to death.

At this point the war became reality to me. They stopped and had me hose out all the blood in the bed of a dump truck where the bodies of Corpsman Collier and Swede were. Swede was not dead yet, but he should have been, the poor guy had so many holes in him. I remember Doc Collier's eyes, as they were wide open and I remember the look of astonishment in them. He was shot in the back of the head and some say it was an executional type of wound. I do know that he was found slumped over Swede's body in an attempt to assist him. This is factual, as Elroy Schultz who was on that convoy witnessed this. Why this dedicated man was never put up for a medal is beyond me. But, in remembering Doc Collier's dedication to "his Marines," as he would call us, if he had to die in that place, this was the only acceptable way.

When we headed through the city of Hue, we went directly through and across this big bridge that goes across the Perfume into the city itself. The Citadel is just on the other side of the main city. Then we took a direct left and went west about half a mile and that's where we stayed. When we went through the city, we didn't realize it but that was on the 31st of January, or the 1st of February. There were two regiments of NVA that had infiltrated the city already. They were in there on February the second when Tet broke.

There was myself and one other fellow and we were running this water purification equipment. They stuck us on a floating pontoon bridge on the Perfume River about a half mile outside of the city. There was a ridge line between where the river went through a pass in this ridge. Just on the other side of the ridge was where the city was. We used to go up to this ridge with a platoon of grunts that were with us. They were 1st Marines, 1/1, Charlie Company and they used to go up on the ridge and look for people that were trying to infiltrate. Obviously, communications were letting them know to watch their backside and watch everywhere around you because they were still infiltrating. We used to go up there almost every day, and watch what was going on. It was like a low seat in a theater. I know I had no business being up there, but I was young and stupid and I'm glad I did as I got to witness history.

We did go on patrols while we were on that pontoon bridge. We went with our security force (Charlie Company, 1st Marine Reg., 1st Battalion). The reason we did was because they were understaffed and weren't expecting Tet to break out in Hue in '68. They took any able-bodied men. The patrols were mainly to spot NVA coming and going into the city and calling in artillery and air strikes on them.

We saw a lot of explosions. It was always during the day time when we went up on the ridge. It was funny, the Americans were not allowed to use any air power there because the city was considered a sacred city. All the structures were ancient. The Vietnamese people had their own little air force, but they didn't have jets. They had the old Korean war and some second world war prop planes. They would be buzzing around there with their little prop planes and would be strafing it. They would drop a few bombs here and there. But what was interesting, when the battle ships opened up on it from off the coast, they were lobbing thousand pound bombs into the city. You could actually see the projectiles coming in. It was incredible. Absolutely incredible. That was when they had the NVA all pretty well cornered and encircled. When it first started out, you could see from one part of the city to the other.

Much later in the process of trying to take the city back and after there was so much destruction already, the Vietnamese government said to just go ahead and do whatever it takes because this is dragging on too long. It was a disaster. For the NVA to go into the city and to take control of it like they did, and for the American forces to try to root them out, it was a terrible thing. Losses were no where near as bad for us as they were for the North Vietnamese. Coming back out through the city we saw the amount of bodies that were North Vietnamese. Bodies were piled everywhere.

Probably one of the saddest things that I remember seeing was a cathedral there. The North Vietnamese had gathered up all the people they had on their list and assassinated them. There was 100–150 people that just were slaughtered in this church. So they are pretty ruthless in the way that they went about doing things. What they said was the NVA were cleansing the city. Anybody that provided support for the Americans was on their list. That's how they went about making villages tremble when they came through. That's one thing that really kind of pisses me off. I don't think any atrocity is a very good mark for any civilization.

Dave Nichols, LCpl., B Company, January 1968–February 1969

We tried to get a convoy of trucks to Phu Bai for supplies. The convoy had to go through Hue and met with disaster. It was attacked by a large force of NVA. A reactionary group was sent to rescue them. Fortunately this group had an Ontos (tracked vehicle that fired six 106mm recoilless rifles) and the Army provided a quad fifty truck (6 by 6 truck with four 50 caliber machine guns mounted on a turntable, like an antiaircraft set up). They were able to drive the NVA off, but we had several men killed, including our Corpsman. These were the only men killed in our company the entire time I was there.

MARCH

Mike Daly, PFC, Hdqtrs. Company, July 1967–April 1969

Upon returning to the platoon, I had my fill of bulldozers and tried my hand at crane operation. I constantly broke the cables and had to find another piece of equipment or return to the dozer. I became the tar truck operator which took me all over Southern I Corp. We would shoot diesel on the roads to keep dust down, tar to keep the VC from digging up the road for mines and tar on LZ's to keep down everything. I spent the rest of my tour on the tar truck. Its operation was so important and the undercarriage so low, they would carry the truck on the back of a lowboy to our destination.

Edward L. Casper, Cpl., Headquarters Company, August 1967–August 1968

The time I always will remember was

25 minutes after midnight on March 25, 1968. The Viet Cong launched a coordinated mortar attack on our battalion and rocket attack on the Marine airwing on the main base. I was on duty at the Com Center when the officer of the day ran in, his eyes wide open and said that they were walking mortar rounds toward our perimeter. I had heard muffled explosions, but I figured they were at a distance. Explosions were commonplace in Vietnam. I grabbed my rifle and pistol belt and ran across the ground to a billeting area to ensure our commo men were up and safe. They were to come to defend the commo bunker should we be threatened to be overrun. I heard what I thought was raindrops hitting the roof and later found out it was shrapnel falling. As I entered the door of the first hut, a mortar round hit the tin roof at the back of the hut. I guess it knocked me unconscious and later I heard moaning, came to and searched for the men.

It was dark. Following the moaning, I located a wounded Marine and was aiding him out of the hootch by carrying him on my shoulder just in case the mortaring began again. As I got outside I yelled at the medics to go inside and see if there were any more wounded. I took the one wounded Marine up to the medics aid station and turned him over to them. I told them that they may need to go down to the hootch area because they may be of more assistance down there. I then went over to the commo bunker to report to the communications CO and the battalion CO the extent of the damage and casualties as I knew it. The colonel told me to get treated, as I had blood all over my T-shirt. I said I was okay and was going back to duty. He ordered me to get treated and had two other Marines escort me to the aid station for treatment. It was then that I learned that the body covered up was that of Heavy Savare, a good friend. It was a sad time after that and I do not feel that I ever recovered. It just seemed that all the wind went out of your sails. All I wanted to do was get out of Vietnam alive in one piece.

Dan Diridoni, LCpl., Service Company, December 1967–December 1968

In early March McNeese and I were sent to LZ Sally which was just below Camp Carroll. It was a staging area for the 101st Airborne. Every day we would leave our base camp and drive ourselves and our equipment down by some river and make water all day. They gave us a semi to haul our equipment as nobody wanted to drive us to this area. Very shortly we found out why.

A group of inept ARVN's were our security, if you want to call it that. We would receive sniper fire and the ARVN's would scatter and we would hide underneath of our erdalator. Eventually, in about an hour or so, they would come back and we would start working. This was almost a daily occurrence and was quite comical thinking back on it now.

You know they made an example out of one thing that happened there, and as a result the American people stereotyped the veterans. I'm talking about the Calley incident obviously. There was a man who was probably half psycho before he went in the service, who knows, and that probably pushed him over the edge. That was one thing that I always found interesting. Your reaction to this sort of thing and what you would think when you see things like that. They would be so horrible, so bone chilling that you would just crawl up inside of yourself and just feel terrible about what you saw. But it does just the opposite. I spoke to a lot of people that said the same thing. It doesn't make you crawl up inside or anything like that. It makes you very angry. It makes you very, very angry. It's an anger like you never felt before, that you never thought you were even capable of feeling.

I think that is why things like that happened. You just lose it. You quit becoming a human being at that point. I think that probably happens in every hostile situation. It has probably happened throughout history. You take kids eighteen or nineteen years old, what do you think they are going to do? I look at some of these kids today. My daughter's boyfriend is in the Marine Corps. He just went through boot camp. I love this kid. He is just great, but I look at this kid and there is no way we were that young.

Robert Handley, LCpl., D Company, January 1968–February 1969

I remember the country was very beautiful. The people were standoffish and distrustful. I didn't make any friends over there. Usually if you got friendly with them, they wanted something. Ungracious.

Brian Althouse, PFC, A Company, March 1968–October 1969

I reported to Alpha Company and I was still scared and shook up from the flight. It was a hootch and it was all full of holes. They had boardwalks, not boardwalks like Atlantic City, but walkways made out of wood. You walk on them over the sand and that was all blown apart in front of the hootch. They had a big coffee urn in the window and that was all full of holes. And it was like "WOW." This guy nicknamed Short Round, was the first guy I came in contact with. Everybody was out to chow so he told me what happened. They had a mortar attack the night before. There were 3 KIA's and 11 WIA's and one of the rounds hit right in front of the hootch. That's what the holes were from. I thought, "I'm going to die."

APRIL

Dan Diridoni, LCpl., Service Company, December 1967–December 1968

Then the powers that be decided that we were to go out into the A Shau Valley to a firebase called Bastogne. This was due west of firebase Birmingham and about a mile or two from Laos. A Staff Sergeant by the name of Moore and our old friend Elroy Schultz picked us up from LZ Sally and drove us to Birmingham on the road that B Company had cleared. From there we and our equipment were helilifted into the thickest jungle I have ever seen. They had 175mm and 155mm guns there in support of the 101st troops who were running an operation called Carentan II.

At that point we were attached to the 101st Airborne. It was very interesting how we got attached to them. They didn't have any mobile equipment. They had to helo lift our stuff in there and there was some streams around there. They set us up down by these streams and basically set up a fire base around it. There was a battalion of 101st Airborne, the 3/27. If you are interested in any of that stuff out there, I got copies of the operations that they performed. B Company is the one that cleared the road from Hue City west on Route 547. There was a ancient road there that had been there for a long time, that the French had maintained while they were there. After fifteen years in that thick jungle it grows over, and it was B Company's responsibility under task force X-ray to clear that road. There was a haven out there for the North Vietnamese soldiers. That's where they had their hospitals, their recreation and their staging area. That's how they ended up hitting Hue and from there they hit Khe Sanh. It was central and it was very remote. This was the start of clearing it out.

Once I got out to the A Shau valley I saw how bad the situation was for water. The North Vietnamese had anti-aircraft weaponry all around and every time they would fly helicopters out there they got shot down. The chances of them flying water in there were not good. They figured that they were going to be losing helicopters bringing in supplies. What they did is just drop us in there because we had that mobile equipment. Most of the equipment that the 101st had was still down at the central highlands at Pleiku. They didn't come up north until around the end of the summer. They were engineers so they used whatever was at their means. We were all task force X-ray.

You heard the term triple canopy? That's exactly what it was or else it was clear. We had to clear a knob away on a hill so that we would be able to defend it. But, if you would walk out anywhere where it was not cleared, you couldn't see the sun. It was that thick. It was very thick. The battalion was running continual operations around the fire base to keep it cleared. We were about two or three miles from the Laosian border. It was funny because on a daily basis we would receive anywhere between twenty to thirty rockets a day. It was always around the same time. They were very predictable. I don't know why it was that way, but it was. They all came from that direction because they were firing from across the border.

We had to stand guard duty and stuff out there. There was no barb wire at all around the thing. I don't think I should tell you this story. Are you very sensitive?

We were novelty out there. We were in the Marines and these guys were in the Army, but they treated us well. There was no problem. Anyway, they always stick new guys on the perimeter the first night for guard duty. They put me and McNeese in this one bunker and told us to maintain our fire because there is no barb wire. If you start shooting before flares are put up or something, they would obviously pinpoint your bunker and start firing on you. So we got out there and I will have to tell you, I was scared to death. It was two hours on, two hours off and one guy would sleep. I was sound asleep and the next thing I know Mac's waking me up. "Wake up, wake up." I said, "What's the matter?" He said, "There's somebody out there and they're talking to us." I said, "What are you talking about?" He said, "Listen." I didn't hear nothing. I didn't hear nothing. All of a sudden I hear what sounded like, "fuck you, fuck you." Like I said, I hope you are not sensitive.

Holy shit. They're harassing us. He said, "We're not supposed to fire." This went on, back and forth, back and forth and we kept hearing this. Before long he started firing. We had an M60 in there and he started firing at the sound. The officer of the day came storming down there, "Who the hell is firing down here?" "We were, sir. They're out there, swearing and cussing at us." "Damn, stupid, sons of bitches, those are lizards." They got these lizards out there that have this big pouch and when they blow their pouch up and let it out, that's what it sounds like. It's a big joke. It breaks the monotony with everybody laughing their asses off. Needless to say, we had to spend a week out there. They did that to all the new guys. Of course, they wouldn't tell you. [laughs] After a while we got to sit back and watch the next guys do it. You get a little trigger happy out there. That's why I had to check with you first, so you wouldn't be offended.

A lot of strange things happened like that. There is a lot of things you can laugh about now. Some things you couldn't. They were constantly, constantly bringing in their dead and wounded from the surrounding area where they were fighting every day. The means that they brought some of these guys in haunts me to this day. Where they would have a hard time extracting some of the guys, they would just drop a line down through the jungle. They could get it down through there with a heavy weight and they would just tie the body by their feet, pull it up out of there and haul it back to the base. You would see them coming back in with this thing swinging off this big long rope upside down and you knew what it was. It was the only way to get them out of there. I saw a lot of things over there. That was one of the things that bothered the hell out of me. They didn't want to leave anybody behind.

We had what was called an erdalator. It's a Coleman tent trailer and it had a couple of vats in it. There was a system to it. You had these great big rubber tanks that would hold 3,000 gallons of water. We were capable of purifying up to 3,000 gallons a day if we were able to incorporate our 3,000 gallon rubber flocking tank. If not, we could only produce about 1,000 gallons a day. The flocking tank was used to dump the raw water into. We had a water buffalo that would go suck up water from wherever the murky stuff could be found. We would pump it from there into this rubber tank and we would try to fill it as much as we could.

Then we would do what was called flocking. We would add the chemicals alum, soda ash and Hth (chlorine) to coagulate the dirt, mud, etc., etc. into large clumps that would sink to the bottom of the tank. We would then suck from the surface of the tank, which was fairly clear water, into the erdalator unit tanks and further agitate it and coagulate it to remove any remaining impurities. Then we would run it through these sophisticated filters that we would coat with diatomaceous earth. These would remove any organisms that remained in the water such as schistosomes, which would cause diarrhea, malaria, etc., etc. All kinds of nasty illnesses for the troops.

We would then pump this clean chlorinated water into another 3,000 gallon tank or a water buffalo which is a 500 gallon tank on a trailer. The water would then be dispersed to the men. My friend, Alan, and I worked twenty-four hours a day, eight hour shifts. It was kind of a slow

A Shau Valley. Erdalator in process of being bunkered because of rocket attacks. Courtesy of Dan Diridoni.

process actually. Flocking the water and getting all that stuff clear was not that big of a deal. But the equipment was so small it would take a long time. But we could keep a battalion in water for an indefinite period of time as long as they kept people off our back and kept our equipment from getting blown up, which they did. It was very important to them. You get out there in a remote area like that and you can take all those holizone tablets you want but you're still going to get sick. You start getting men coming down with the trots and you are in trouble.

At the time we were out there it was anywhere between 100–115 degrees. The guys needed a lot of water. They were sweating bullets. They would fly the chemicals and stuff in. After three months they unceremoniously pulled us out of there. By that time the balance of B Company, 9th Engr. Bn., had the road pretty well completed out to the base. In other words, they started having some convoys come out.

The bunker where the erdalator was located was deep because of the rockets that were coming in daily. They were the big ones. They were the 122 millimeter rockets and you could hear them coming for miles. They could shoot them from 10–15 miles away. You heard the whistling coming and you knew it was time. They dig the bunkers deep. They would put I don't know how many layers and layers of bags on top of their command post and all that. We were ten feet underground with huge beams over the top and metal and sand bags. We got a steady diet of 122mm rockets and artillery from Laos daily depending on the NVA's supply situation. There wasn't anything that would stop those rockets. Nothing. Maybe it was something that helped you psychologically get through it. Obviously, you didn't want to get caught out in the open when those rockets started coming in because they would walk them around.

By that time they had the base pinpointed. They knew exactly where everything was at because of the area being so thick around it, they had people spotting it all the time. That's why those guys were out there trying to clear around it all the time. This was their country and they were masters at hiding in it. You would hear that whistling coming in, you're a long ways away from wherever your bunker was, and it's not like we wanted to stay inside the water point bunker. It was so big, you would look for a smaller bunker. We had a couple of them we dug ourselves. We would jump out of the bunker with the water point in it, and to hell with that we would just go get in a smaller hole. I don't know how many times I went to go jump into a bunker that was closest to me and ended up having my nose up some guy's butt. [laughs] Get in there man. [laughs] I'm not kidding you. Push, push, I didn't care either. [laughs] That's a terrible thing to say, but it's the truth.

Those rockets would throw off some humongous pieces of shrapnel. They were just gigantic. Those things would be whistling around there and would chop you right in half without a doubt. The thing that was really frustrating and really made you mad about this was the fact that you just didn't know where to fire back. They had some big guns in there. They obviously had artillery in there. They had 155 and 175 millimeter guns but they couldn't reach it. They couldn't reach where those guys were. The range of those guns was not anywhere near what the rockets were. First of all, we weren't supposed to be firing into Laos. Second of all, we couldn't even reach them. Very rarely did they fire any of their artillery rounds in because those could be spotted. Our guys would then start firing our guns at them. The guns that were there, that's why they called it a fire base, they were in support of the troops that were working the area. If they called in artillery because they got hit by a company of NVA, they would call it in from that fire base. Eventually, they leap frogged it into another area in the A Shau from Bastogne.

Dan Diridoni and Erdalator below ground. Courtesy of Dan Diridoni.

One thing that I thought would explode when I was there was when Martin Luther King was assassinated. It was very, very strange. All the blacks and whites got along. Period. No question about it. But it was funny after that, nothing hostile happened, but the attitudes kind of changed. It was like the blacks started hanging out more with blacks. It was really weird because up to that time everybody was equally tight. You wouldn't think twice about spending time in a bunker or on guard duty or having someone watch your back. I think that changed things quite a bit. It was too much to handle. First, Bobby Kennedy, then Martin Luther King, I mean, what's going on back there.

We heard the news from *Stars and Stripes*, the armed forces newspaper. I don't believe I ever recall listening to a radio out in the A Shau. We did get the *Stars and Stripes* occasionally. We'd get mail occasionally. We would keep informed. My parents even had my local newspaper sent to me. I would get ten or fifteen of them at a time, because we wouldn't get mail for awhile. It was kind of interesting reading some of the stuff that was going on and I hardly ever read what was going on in the world. I wanted to find out what was going on in sports. Who was winning the pennant, and football and all that stuff. I missed the sports. To this day I still don't read the front page. My wife gets so damn mad at me. "Why don't you read what is going on in the world?" Because I don't really care. Now I'm not happy with the sports world. Baseball guys are on strike.

Robert Handley, LCpl., D Company, January 1968–February 1969

I'd have either security in the back on mine sweeps or I'd have engineer supplies. It would either be a five-ton cargo truck or it would be a dump truck. It was just transportation. They wanted a truck there. They didn't put me in front. [laughs]

Brian Althouse and a buddy on a minesweep south of Hill 10. Courtesy of Brian Althouse.

There were usually two or three guys up in front with metal detectors and I recall two or three times that I was actually there when they'd find a mine.

Dave Nichols, LCpl., B Company, January 1968–February 1969

After Tet of '68, we moved into the large base of Phu Bai. We were on the west side of the area and sort of joined up with the Army's 101st Airborne Division. We helped them construct Camp Eagle when they moved in. We did a daily mine sweep for the 101st each morning. This was on a road that ran west from Phu Bai to the river. I drove a 6 by 6, five-ton dump truck. Three or four guys walked ahead of the truck with the mine sweeping equipment. The Army provided security. This usually meant they sent one jeep with two people with an M-60 machine gun mounted on a tall tripod in the back. This jeep was usually about ¼ mile behind us because they were afraid that someone might step on a mine. They didn't want to be caught in the blast. I tried to explain to them that if the guys didn't detect a mine, which was unlikely, and they didn't step on it, the jeep might run over it. They were no safer being farther back. I also explained that the reason I stayed so close was so the men would have some cover if we were attacked. They could get under or behind the truck.

Brian Althouse, PFC, A Company, March 1968–October 1969

J.R. was a buddy of mine from Georgia. He was definitely a rebel and being Marines together we used to pick on each other. We became pretty good buddies. He was on patrol one night and was getting ready. I walked out of the hootch to go to the club and about a eight round spurt blew off out of an M-60 machine gun. I kissed a lot of sand. Then it stopped. I got up, brushed myself off, and went back in the hootch and it was all smoky. I said, "What are you doing?" J.R. was standing there with his mouth open, like "God, I don't know." He was just loading it, checking it out and he chambered it, and he must have had his finger on the trigger or something. There was MP's there real quick. Nobody was hurt. He thought he was going to get in trouble, which realistically he should have, but it was cool. He was all right, just shook up. At least he was smart enough to have the weapon pointed down. He shouldn't have been loading it in the hootch anyway. I guess he was checking the chamber because he was carrying an M-60.

MAY–AUGUST 1968

North Vietnamese diplomats arrive in Paris in mid–May for talks with American delegation headed by Averell Harriman.

Senator Robert F. Kennedy assassinated in Los Angeles, June 5, after winning the California primary.

Richard Nixon wins Republican nomination for president in Miami, August 8.

Vice-President Hubert Humphrey wins Democratic nomination for president in Chicago amid riots outside the convention hall.

Johnson stops all bombing of North Vietnam.

MAY

Charles King, Sgt., B Company, September 1967–September 1968

We had our beer and our bourbon, but I don't recall any guys that messed with the dope. I think some of them did. I'm almost positive some of them did.

Dan Diridoni, LCpl., Service Company, December 1967–December 1968

I had my hair stand up about three years ago. My neighbor had one of his friends over one night and we got to talking about the service. We were in the service about the same time and in Vietnam about the same time. He was interested in seeing my photo album, so I started showing it to him. He started looking at the pictures of Bastogne. He said, "That's fire base Bastogne in the A Shau, isn't it?" He said, "I was there." I said, "When were you there?" He was on that hill when I was there. Honest to God's truth. He was involved in Operation Carentan I, Carentan II, Delaware, all of those. In a battalion there are a lot of guys and I didn't know him. He does remember me because we were the only two Marines there. He does remember that aspect of it. He remembers this water point that we had. You talk about a small world. We are rather tight now. It was pretty neat.

Robert Handley, LCpl., D Company, January 1968–February 1969

One time we took a convoy into Hoi An, that's an old French city, and we got stuck in there. The streets are so narrow we couldn't turn the vehicles. [laughs] I don't think we were supposed to be in there though. Somebody took a wrong turn or something and we eventually got out of there with no harm done. It was like a rose in the middle of a weed patch. It was just a beautiful little city. It was all French architecture with very little damage.

Dave Nichols, LCpl., B Company, January 1968 — February 1969

During the spring of '68, some of us were moved to the A Shau Valley about seven miles from Laos. The Army wanted to build an artillery base named Bastogne. I was told that this base was used to shell an airstrip in Laos. It was partially completed when I got there because a group from our company had gone in earlier. They flew us in on a Chinook (large dual rotor helicopter) because the road was "impassable." The earlier group had been hit pretty hard going into the jungle to build the base. Because of this, they were moving everyone by helicopter. Three days after I got to Bastogne I was informed that we would be taking a convoy back to Phu Bai. I mentioned that we had just flown in because the road was impassable and wondered what had happened to all the NVA that were supposed to be along the road. I was told we would have plenty of security. This was true. In order to move three trucks to Phu Bai the Army provided two tanks and three armored personnel carriers. After this, we used bulldozers with large "rome plows" and cages over the top to clear the jungle back from both sides of the road which significantly reduced the ambushes to convoys.

Brian Althouse, PFC, A Company, March 1968–October 1969

The first four months I was there, we were in Chu Lai. We ran north sweeps and patrols outside the perimeter. But we were right there next to the air field so it was kind of heavy duty. We got incoming sometimes, but most of the time it was to the air field. We'd sit in the hole during the alert and we'd watch the 122 mike-mikes (millimeter) go overhead. You could hear them coming and could look up and see them. Then you'd hear them hit. The only thing we really had to worry about was one falling short.

There was a lot of nights when there was mortars coming in. They would hit us from the hill. We had a gunner on every corner post with a .50 caliber machine gun. One night Charlie was walking mortars in and he saw the tube. He could see the flashes of the tube and he opened up on it. They were walking them right down the berm. We are in holes on the berm, so if one hits next to you and you're in a hole, you're cool. But if one falls in the hole, you're history. And this guy opened up from the north bunker with that .50 cal. He knocked that mortar tube out. I don't know if he killed them, or if he just hit around the area enough to move them, but he stopped it. Then he got in trouble for that because he didn't have permission to open fire. That's the honest to God truth. I don't think he got busted, but I know he got in trouble. He got office hours for it.

JUNE

Dan Diridoni, LCpl., Service Company, December 1967–December 1968

When we left the A Shau valley, we took all the equipment with us. We left Bastogne and went back to Phu Bai where B Company was now working with the 101st. They were doing some work around Camp Eagle which they had built in the meantime. It was just west of Hue. That's where they based most of the division, so

Installing culverts. Left to right: *O'Casio, "Dog," "Indian," J.R. Clure. Courtesy of Brian Althouse.*

it was a huge base. They were putting in runways all around there and keeping the roads clear from Phu Bai down to Phu Loc. It was real pretty country down near Phu Loc. McNeese and I stayed at Phu Bai until October, then we went back down to Chu Lai.

Dave Nichols, LCpl., B Company, January 1968–February 1969

One of the most important things we received over there was mail and "care packages" from home. In most cases the delivery of mail was pretty good, but there were exceptions. My best friend from back home was killed by a land mine in April of 1968. He went into the Marines a couple of months before me. The last time I saw him was when I was in Boot Camp. We only had a few seconds to ask each other how it was going and then went our separate ways. The mail at the time was screwed up, so I hadn't heard from home about his death. I first read about it in *Stars and Stripes* newspaper. He was listed under the KIA column. The first mail I received about it was actually the second letter written about it. My dad wrote that "we are still waiting for Bob Peckham's body to be flown home for the funeral." This is a terrible way to find out that your best buddy was killed. Several days later I received the letter that was mailed first that told of Bob's death and how he was killed. The news would have been easier if I had gotten this letter before the other letter or the newspaper article.

Mail from home was extremely important. It was our only contact with our friends and loved ones. It really didn't matter who it was from. It was just great to hear from the "world." Of course, some letters were more important than others. Letters from a special girlfriend would be read over and over.

I must admit that I never cared for the civilians. I didn't trust them. I still believe that many of them were Viet Cong or at least sympathizers. I hated getting a haircut and having the guy shave my neck with a straight razor. I was always nervous that he might slit my throat. One time we had stopped in a village and were talking to some kids. We left and just down the road there was an explosion behind another guy's truck. Someone had tied a hand grenade to his rear axle. The string was attached to the grenade pin. I guess they expected the pin to pull out and blow the truck up. Fortunately, he had built enough speed that the grenade was far behind him when it exploded. The string and pin were still attached to the axle.

Wayne Hansen, PFC, A Company, May 1968–February 1969

The combat engineers were the ones that did most of the work there. On Hill 63 we lived in tents, but on Hill 10 we had to sleep in bunkers because they would drop mortars on us at night. When we got there the bunkers were all beat up. We built these big rocket proof bunkers out of bridge timbers. That's where we stayed. It was [pause] quite an experience.

Bill Spadafora, Cpl., C Company, A Company, June 1968–July 1969

I was the Adman Chief from Headquarters Company in charge of all administration for the C.O. and First Sergeant of A Company. Alpha company had about 15–20 miles of road to mine sweep every day. Our company was broken up into three different locations. The 1st platoon was at Hill 10, 2nd platoon was at Hill 29 and 3rd platoon was on Hill 59. A company would hook up with two other companies, Delta Company to the north of us, and either Bravo Company or Charlie company to the south of us. Our responsibility was to keep Highway One open between Chu Lai and Da Nang so that the

Bunker (home) on Hill 10. Courtesy of Bill Spadafora.

"Cannonball Express," a big Army convoy, could get through. They would come down from Da Nang and bring the supplies to Chu Lai. Then in the afternoon, they would take the empty trucks back or take some supplies from Chu Lai up to Da Nang.

When I first got there, we had between 175 and 185 men in the Company. When I left, we were down to about 125–135 men in Alpha Company.

I really had no fear of being shot and killed, but it was on my mind a few times [laugh] that I would be maimed, lose an arm, lose a leg or something like that. One of the biggest fears that I had was the darkness of the night. I can remember the very first patrol I was ever on. We were out walking single file across the rice paddies. There was no moon out. It was pitch dark. I guess the best way I could describe the feeling is when you stick yourself in a closet and close the door. It was so dark that you couldn't even see your hand, let alone see the Marine that was in front of you or behind you. I can't remember how many times I would fall off a rice paddy dike wall into the rice paddy or just trip over something and not be able to see. Even today, whenever it gets dark, [pause] that feeling comes over me because I remember that first patrol that I was on.

I'm an avid outdoorsman. I enjoy hunting, fishing and the outdoors, but even when I go hunting I try to avoid being in the woods after dark. When I'm carrying my gun, I get that feeling that I'm back in the jungle. It's kind of hard to explain. I know where I am. I know I'm back in the States. I know I'm in a controlled environment. I know I'm not in enemy territory. But at certain times it just comes over me. It starts to get still, starts to get dark, and I have this rifle in my hand. I'm walking through the woods in heavy brush and I get a flashback of my first patrol. I guess sometimes when we do things for the first time it leaves a deep impression. Sort of like having a boyfriend or a girlfriend for the first time, or riding a bicycle for the first time, or driving a car for the first time. Those things you don't remember. Well, I can't forget my first patrol.

I can remember sitting in a rice paddy [pause] waiting for the ambush to take place. We were just waiting and waiting and waiting and waiting and nothing happened. There was tension and the anticipation of something happening, and whether I would be able to do what I was trained to do on my first contact with the enemy. Whether or not I would just turn tail and run, or whether I would die, or whether I would get blown up. All those things go through your mind. Every time you go out on a patrol, or every time you go out on a mine sweep, or every time you hear about something stupid where someone gets killed because their rifle falls down, or someone gets hurt or injured because they ran over a mine with a jeep or a truck, there was always that tension, always that apprehension or anticipation of something could happen. That was a lot of pressure on a lot of fellows. I know I used to feel a lot of it myself.

I believe my experience in Vietnam has carried me through some of my more difficult times as a civilian. When I hear people complain about how hard things are, I have to reflect back to the things that I saw and the things that happened to me while I was in Vietnam. I can honestly say that one of the biggest injuries I received was the fact that I have this phobia for the dark. When I'm driving sometimes in the dark, with my lights on, with my family, even then I can't help but reflect back to that first patrol when it was so dark and so mysterious. It really had a lasting impression on me.

It's very interesting to me that every time I stop the tape and I reflect back on some of the things that I've spoken to you about, I think about things that I never thought I'd remember. Just recently we celebrated the Fourth of July. Everybody had firecrackers, and sparklers and that type of thing. You wouldn't think in the environment of Vietnam, where rockets and bombs and machine guns and M-16 and hand grenades are being thrown and all kinds of flashes are going off, that we'd want to celebrate the Fourth of July.

On the contrary, some of the fellows had taken the tracer rounds from their guns and put them into magazines so all they had was just straight tracers. Then they would fire their guns on automatic, so there would be like an orange stream going up into the air. Someone else would be throwing off illumination grenades. Some of the increments from 81 mortars would be taking like a nitrate packet, that propelled the mortars, and stick them in the tube, light them and they'd be like sparklers. It's funny to think about that. It's not a funny incident, but something that you think would never occur in Vietnam where guys would actually think about celebrating when they're getting shot at and killed.

JULY

Dave Nichols, LCpl., B Company, January 1968–February 1969

In the summer our company moved to the south end of Phu Bai. We were located next to the south gate where Highway One passed through the base. We were responsible for manning one guard bunker each night. We also provided "listening posts" each evening. This involved four men going outside the perimeter about three hundred yards to observe. Basically you just sat very still and watched to see what was going on. If you saw enemy movement, you radioed this information back to the command post. Artillery would fire on the movement. I volunteered for listening post quite often. If you were up on the listening post, you got the next day off. This was probably a warped thought process on my part, but I did it so I could get the next day off. Otherwise you pretty much worked seven days a week, sometimes getting Sunday off. The most regular problem with going out on a listening post was trying to come back into the compound. The Army manned one of the guard bunkers on the perimeter and it seemed like they would shoot at anything. We always radioed to the command post that we were coming in and then we fired a "five star cluster" of the appropriate color before approaching the wire. This is like a hand-held fireworks that shot five stars of either red, green or white into the air. In spite of this the Army would open fire on us as soon as they saw or heard us. It got to the point that we aimed the cluster at their bunker. While they were scrambling out of the path of these hot "stars," we would come in.

One other time someone fired mortar or artillery illumination over us. It lit us up like it was daytime. We had very little cover and were sitting ducks. A couple of huts in the village near us opened fire on us and kept us pinned down behind a rice paddy dike for awhile. Artillery took care of that problem.

Brian Althouse, PFC, A Company, March 1968–October 1969

On mine sweeps, we'd have three guys running detectors and three probers. You'd have seven or eight guys because we were always short-handed. A full squad is supposed to be thirteen people. We never had a full thirteen. If somebody got killed or got wounded, they'd get replacements in for them but it never went up to full squad. There was just not enough people. You never had enough people to do what you were supposed to do, but you did what you had to do.

You'd have two guys out in the field dragging for electrical wires. They'd go along with the sweep. Everyday you would take turns doing different things. One day I could be dragging, another day I could be running a mine detector. If you're running a mine detector, usually you got two guys who used to team up. One would run the detector for awhile and the other one would probe. Then we would switch. That's how it worked. But the two draggers would be out there for that morning unless something happened.

Building sick bay bunker at Hill 10. Pictured left to right: Brian Althouse, "Peabody," J.R. Clure. Courtesy of Brian Althouse.

Wayne Hansen, PFC, A Company, May 1968–February 1969

The MOS number was 1371 and that was a combat engineer. Basically you were trained for carpentry, bridge building, mines, booby traps and heavy explosives. We built these big bridges, too, but it was a big waste of time as far as I was concerned. Once the bridges were done, Charlie blew 'em up. They were all wood. I'm looking at it from a PFC's perspective. I wasn't a Captain or a Major. I thought it would have been easier putting up a pontoon bridge or something like that, rather than waste a lot of time and energy and have the wooden bridge blown up.

Bill Spadafora, Cpl., C Company, A Company, June 1968–July 1969

About two weeks after I was assigned to A Company was my first contact with death over there. There was a mine sweep that was out and the word came back to the Compound that one of our men had stepped on a land mine. This particular Marine was a Lance Corporal or Corporal. I don't recall which, and for the life of me I can't remember his name. I didn't really know too many people because I just got over there. The VC or the NVA had a nice little trick. They used to bury their mines right where the end of the bridge would meet the road. They would dig it down pretty deep, but not too far, and then they would loosely pack the sand on top of the mine and the detonator. Once the traffic started to flow over and come off the bridge, it would slowly pound the dirt down and compact it.

The first Vietnamese bus came across the bridge. The front two wheels came down off the bridge, ignited the mine and blew the little Vietnamese bus to Kingdom come. We had civilian casualties all over the place. Naturally, the Marines went into a reactionary defense. At that time I think they had two APC's with them and a tank. This particular Corporal and a couple of other Marines ran back to see if they could assist these civilians that had been wounded. One Marine stepped off on the other side of the bridge and ignited the other mine. He lost both his legs, but he died en route to the hospital. I can't for the life of me remember that man's name, but he'll be remembered in my brain for the rest of my life.

At the end of the day I recall the company CO telling us exactly what had happened and we had a little service for the Marine. I remember him ordering a couple of the men from his squad to get whatever belongings he had and put them together so we could ship them down to Battalion. I remember going out with the CO and a couple of others and reconnoitering the area, seeing exactly what happened and documenting everything. The CO wrote a letter. But I can't remember what the guy's name was.

AUGUST

Robert Handley, LCpl., D Company, January 1968–February 1969

I met my wife in Hawaii for R&R. It was in August of '68 and went too fast.

Dave Nichols, LCpl., B Company, January 1968–February 1969

The weather was "bad" most of the time. It was always too hot, too cold, or raining too hard. I don't want to sound like I'm whining, but the weather was pretty extreme. In the summer the temperatures would go over 100 [degrees] F. with very high humidity. It was oppressive. You just could not find any place to cool off. Sweat constantly poured off your body. In the winter, it seemed very cold. It was also damp which made it feel even colder. The monsoon season was miserable. You were

Building new five-strand bridge. Left to right: Blackford, Reilly, "Peter Pan," Smith. Courtesy of Brian Althouse.

always wet. It also made an engineer's job even harder. Everything turned to mud because we had scraped the cover off the ground.

Brian Althouse, PFC, A Company, March 1968–October 1969

We built a five-span bridge and Charlie blew half of it. He blew two spans out and then burned the rest of it. We were out there for security that night. Then they called up another unit, a bridge platoon from Chu Lai, to put in a pontoon bridge and we were security for them. We were out at the perimeter along with the Army.

Bill Spadafora, Cpl., C Company, A Company, June 1968–July 1969

When we used to go out on patrol, we used to run a lot of combined action patrols with the Popular Forces and the South Vietnamese Army. Guys would kid around. They would say, "Listen, Bill, if you don't come back, could I have your watch? If you don't come back, could I date your girl? Or, could I marry your wife?" If someone said that to you on the street today, you'd probably want to pop him in the face. But you live with these guys, you eat with them, you sweat with

Same five-strand bridge after enemy blew two strands and burned three strands. Courtesy of Brian Althouse.

them, you suffered with them. They were your brothers and it didn't matter whether they were white, green, yellow, purple, you took it as a joke. Guys were really serious when they went out of the wire on a patrol. The sentry would say, "Good luck, we'll see you when you come back" type of thing. It was just one of those things. It's kind of hard to explain the camaraderie to someone that's never been there, especially when you're in a dangerous situation. Men rely on each other and they'll watch out for each others' back. You become very close. It's nothing for guys to come back off patrol or to be in some kind of combat or firefight and they'll hug each other and just look at each other and check each other over to make sure everything's there.

I was twenty years old. I was probably one of the oldest men in the platoon at the time. We had a lot of eighteen and nineteen year olds. When we went out on a mine sweep, sometimes it became routine. We let our guards down sometimes. Maybe that was wrong, and maybe that was right, but it became a way of life. There were a lot of incidents where Marines would be grading a road and they'd run over a mine. The shrapnel would come through the land grader or the bulldozer that they were working on and they would be medevaced out. We'd be on a mine sweep and be taking enemy sniper fire for a few minutes and all of a sudden it would stop.

Sometimes it was very hard to believe that there really was a war going on in certain portions of Vietnam. Occasionally we'd get the opportunity to go up to Da

Nang. On one occasion, the Company Commander, myself, a Navy Corpsman and another Marine had the opportunity to go. He brought us along so that we'd have an opportunity to go over to Freedom Hill and get a hamburger and a hot dog or a malted or something like this.

Even though Hill 10 was an Army water purification center also, the showers were only turned on at certain times of the day and that was in the evening. It wasn't too often that you had the opportunity to take a shower in the middle of the daytime. This particular time was during the monsoon season. We would get pretty muddy and wet and we were kind of grungy looking. I remember having mud and grime and stuff up to my waist and crust on my boots. My utilities looked like I had been in them for a hundred years. I might add that in our particular outfit, especially on Hill 10, the officers never wore their officer bars. The reason being is that the VC or the NVA would put bounties on the officers' heads. If they shot an officer they would get a reward from their commanding officer.

The C.O. dropped us off at Freedom Hill and they wouldn't allow us to come into the PX. First of all we had our weapons with us, and second of all we looked like we had just gone through hell. We had to sit outside for about two hours until the C.O. came. When the Captain came, he said, "Hey guys! Have you all had your fill of hamburgers and hot dogs?" We told him what had happened and he became very furious. In Freedom Hill they had M.P.s at the door of the PX and you had to check your weapons and do certain things. You had to meet certain criteria. I remember him going up to the MP and telling him that he wanted us to go in there to get something to eat because we were going back out in the field. The MP had these nice, clean starched utilities on. He was clean shaven with a clean hair cut.

The MP looked at us like, "Where the heck have you guys been? Is there really a war going on outside the city limits of Da Nang?" The Captain said that he wanted us to go in there. The MP wouldn't let him go in. I remember the Captain pulling out his .45 and cocking it and pointing it at the MP and saying, "Listen, if you don't let my men get in there to have something to eat, I'm going to shoot you right here and now." Before anything else happened the MP realized that he'd better let us in there. The Captain and ourselves went into the PX and as we walked in the whole place stopped. Everyone stopped dead in their tracks. First of all because we had our weapons with us. We were supposed to check them in and we were under strict orders never to go anywhere without our weapons. It just had a lasting effect on me. It seemed like there was two different wars going on. A support war and a combat war, I guess you would say.

Robert Handley, LCpl., D Company, January 1968–February 1969

I remember the ambush that Rizzo was in. An acquaintance I went to motor transport school with was driving the jeep. It was kind of a surprise to see Rizzo at the reunion because we all thought he was dead. We left late and were coming south out of Da Nang. We were with a convoy. There were supposedly a large number of VC or North Vietnamese army regulars in the area that we were going through between Da Nang and Baldy. We were going down the road and we started taking fire. The convoy stopped and one half went somewhere and the other half went back to Da Nang. Three of our guys got wounded and we lost the lead jeep, but all the supplies made it back.

Jim Tagye, PFC, D Company, August 1968–February 1969

When I first got there some of the guys

were taking mines out because the captain we had over there at the time wanted some souvenirs. Now I was only there a short time when we were in an ambush and he got hit in the stomach. I thought he was killed, but he was not. If it wasn't for the Huey's coming in, spraying the area with machine gun fire, we never would have made it out. They started walking mortars in on us, and I thought, "I'm a dead man." Then all of a sudden these Huey's, or Puff, came and they shot the hell out of that village. That's how it all stopped and we got out. It was getting real late that night. That's the reason why the captain wanted to get through that village, to get back to the compound before dark. He wanted to go through there even though he was warned by this Recon not to go through there. It was heavily fortified by VC. He said "Hell, we're going to go through." He took a round in the stomach. One of our guys got a bronze star out of it, the guy running the .50 caliber.

We were riding security for the truck drivers. Convoy security. We were grunts at that point. But we did catch hell. It was very scary. I was only there seven days, and what is this? I see guys getting shot, guys getting killed, and I'm saying, "Oh No!" I had to go up in front of the line for this recon team because I had the M-79. He said, "Okay, we're going to bloop some shells into the little hootches that they have." Then the rounds were hitting the well. I was saying, "Are they bullets?," being real naive, new in-country and he said, "Yes, they are." But he didn't say it like that. [laughs] I said, "Good-bye." My sergeant took my M-16 from me because I had the M-79. His ran out of ammunition, or maybe his jammed on him. He said, "If anyone comes close, just use the M-79 on them." Well the M-79 only went off after it made three revolutions. That's when it would go off. So if someone was standing in front of me it wouldn't go off. It wouldn't activate. But I'm new.

We used to provide security for truck drivers a lot of times, too. One time we did get hit and my rifle jammed on me. That was a scary feeling. I thought, what am I going to do now? You go through all this training and it scared the hell out of me. After I got out of that truck, the truck driver came around and said to me, "Man, you're lucky, because there's a round right behind where you were sitting." I can still remember seeing that hole. A lot of the times you're there, you don't really realize that you are frightened or scared. You're just doing your job. I don't remember being scared except that first time I was in an ambush. Then I was very scared.

Martin L. Brown, PFC, D Company, August 1968–August 1969

I did get in one good firefight. It was in the morning out of the Korean compound. I was driving and they took a .50 caliber and sandbagged it in the back end of the truck. The VC set up an ambush where we stopped to grab sodas and stuff. The ARVN's ran into this thing just before we got there and they chased them out. They did start quite a firefight. I turned the truck around right on the edge of the vil and backed it out. They opened up with that .50 caliber. Looking at the treeline, I could see the sun shining off some the VC equipment, so I started shooting at them. When they opened up with that 50 in the back of the truck, they all started shooting at the truck. I just laid down on the floor. [laughs] I'd stick a rifle up over the door once in awhile and shoot off a few. Then they sent in some aircraft. They found thirty-four bodies out there and they gave the ARVN's seventeen and gave us seventeen.

We built this humongous bridge over there. It's actually the biggest bridge the Marine Corps ever built. Once we finished it they changed our platoon to 1st Platoon from 3rd Platoon. It was kind of a morale booster.

It started out as a 120-ton class bridge and we cut it down to 60-ton. There were nineteen spans in that thing, five of them are close together on the south end, then it like doubles. That's one of the reasons we finished it so fast. We got rid of half the spans. (Appendix C)

They sent a crane over on the north bank and drove the pylons in for the north abutment. There was a black guy from New Haven, Connecticut named Earl Haynes. He and I went over there by ourselves, and in a day and a half we built the entire north end abutment. We put all the dead men in, all the timbers, everything, and then they back filled it before they got the bridge to it. Both he and I got a Meritorious mast for doing that. I used to be a logger up north before I went in. I used to climb up those pylons and saw them off with the chain saw. That saw dust used to cover me and it was all full of creosote. I used to burn. My skin used to peel off from creosote.

We used to go up on convoys up to Da Nang and pick supplies up. I drove a security truck and had a 2nd Lt. with me. We had him to sign a piece of paper so we could buy an eighty case pallet of beer, and stick it on the back of the truck for the return trip. We hid that stuff all over the place. You could buy it in clubs for ten cents. We charged twenty cents so we'd have enough to go get another pallet. After you guys all left, there was $450 in the safe, in our little kitty fund. I think five of us split it. [laughs]

SEPTEMBER–DECEMBER 1968

Nixon elected president of the United States, November 5, with Spiro Agnew as vice-president. Henry Kissinger chosen by Nixon as national security adviser, December 2.

American troop strength in Vietnam at year-end is 540,000.

SEPTEMBER

Paul Kozak, PFC, D Company, September 1967–September 1968

Vietnam, September 19, 1968. I eased the truck forward and nudged through a group of hot and tired Marines. We had just completed a mine sweep and I was to drive ahead, turn around and pick the Marines up. The truck accompanied the platoon during the mine sweeps and today it was my job to drive. The truck carried with it a .50 cal. machine gun which gave extra cover to the flanks should we get hit. It was not a good practice, but today, like other days, some would climb on early. "Doc," our Navy Corpsman, would be no exception. He climbed in the cab and sat along side of me. Also, this was a special day. It was my three hundred and sixty-fifth day in Vietnam; however, I did not expect it to be such a chilling, painful and deadly experience.

Whom! Without warning the Southeast Asian air erupted in a furious cloud of red earth. I had hit a land mine, and so powerful was the blast that I was knocked unconscious and literally taken back to my childhood... "Draw!" I shouted to my mother as she entered my bedroom. Excited with laughter I drew my six guns and while running backwards hit the back of my head on the bureau. Tears ran down my face and my voice stammered as I cried out, "Mommie I hit my head." Rushing to my aid she lifted the red cowboy hat, which now covered my face, and hugged me ever so tightly ... reality returned. Stunned and semi-conscious I began to hear sporadic rifle fire—soft sounds at first then becoming louder. Suddenly, and with my hearing now restored, the rifle fire intensified and was now joined by the sounds of rapid machine gun fire. Simultaneously, my sight returned; however, all I could see was a light brown mist. Then, with the force of a left hook to the jaw, it hit me what had happened. "Oh my God! I've got to get out of here!" I shouted. I believe I then stood straight up since the truck was now on its side. The door was now overhead and I climbed out.

Although I had survived the main blast, I was still to meet agony at its worst. An explosion occurred when one of the fuel tanks ignited capturing my entire body in a vicious breath of flames. I stood motionless, frozen for the moment while observing a fellow Marine, named Yearwood, taking cover behind a pillar. He turned his nervous and trembling face towards me then shouted, "Koz! You're on fire!" With that he ran towards me and in an attempt to pull me to safety, instead pulled the skin off my arm. Together, Yearwood and I ran toward a rice paddy as the sounds of rifle fire and explosions continued. When we reached the paddy we found it was dry. I rolled feverishly absorbing what moisture was left in the mud. After I extinguished the flames I stood to my feet stunned and in a semi-shock. With seventy percent of my body burned and a severe wound to my left leg, I stood in want of a sniper round. The shock value which helped suppress the pain was now wearing thin. An anger grew in me. I think it was my body's attempt to counter the torment. I turned toward the tree line and screamed. Enemy rounds cracked as they passed close to my ear. "Get down, get down" someone shouted. I next heard my platoon leader's voice, "Kozak, we called you in as KIA (Killed in action)." I could see the look of surprise on his face. I then saw my pain in his face. "Kozak, you're going home" he exclaimed.

Death greeted me as I made my way to the waiting chopper; it was my final review. Boom! Boom! Boom! Grenades, trapped in the fire, exploded as me and some others passed the burning truck. Just beyond lie two fallen Marines. One, a machine gunner, would die a week later. It was sad that I could not remember his name. Platoon members to my right returned my glance with quiet stares. Their stunned expressions seemed to bid me farewell. Farther along and to my left two Marines stood over a lifeless figure. It was the body of "Doc" [Corpsman Kurt Duncan]. Minutes earlier he and I had been only inches apart. Now he was far away; never would I see him again. I reached the chopper and joined the wounded. My raw skin stuck to the diamond plate deck as the aircraft ascended. Looking down I viewed the fatal scene for the last time.

So close were the tree tops, I thought to myself, as the helicopter made its way to the rear base camp. The trauma had been so overwhelming, the pain so intense and the result so final, that I thought it so absurd that I would notice the tree tops. I was leaving Vietnam, but the struggle had only begun. The journey would be very far; I would often think of how much easier it might have been had my life ended that September day.

Today, I can honestly say I'm grateful to be alive.

Dave Nichols, LCpl., B Company, January 1968–February 1969

I think one of the stupidest things I saw over there were "radar traps." Late summer of 1968 my company was given the job of paving Highway One from Chu Lai to Da Nang, about fifty miles. We hauled the gravel then graded and rolled it on the roadbed. Then we hauled the hot asphalt from the asphalt plant to where it was spread and rolled. The Seabees provided the asphalt spreader. It was just like what you see today when you see a road being resurfaced. At one point we were spreading the asphalt twenty-five miles away from the asphalt plant. We hauled the asphalt in dump trucks. If it is kept hot, it dumps out like gravel. If we didn't hurry, the asphalt cooled too much and it wouldn't dump properly. It came out in a big lump and was useless. The military established a speed limit of fifteen miles per hour in villages and sixty miles per hour everywhere else. We had just been given new diesel powered five ton dump trucks and these trucks would run seventy mph if you had room to get your speed built up. If we would have driven the exact speed limit, all the asphalt would have been useless, so most of the time we ran as fast as the trucks would go.

The 82nd Airborne Division (Army) Military Police invented a system that used two mirrors and a stop watch to establish your speed. When they saw you in the first mirror, they started the watch and when you appeared in the second mirror, they stopped the watch. This enabled them to calculate your speed. The next thing you knew there was this stupid little jeep with red lights flashing trying to pull you over. They wrote you a ticket and a copy went to your commanding officer, so he could punish you. Our CO threw them away because we had to speed or we couldn't complete our mission. Most of the time we just kept the pedal down until we got to the site of the spreader. The MPs would then stand on our running board writing a ticket while the spreader was pushing us along. We refused to pull over for them, and we were much bigger than they were, and in some cases we would use a different truck to block the jeep while the other truck got away. What a waste of manpower. We were in the middle of a war and they were writing speeding tickets.

Brian Althouse, PFC, A Company, March 1968–October 1969

In July, we had word come down that we were going to go out on Hill 29, or Hotel 29er. We knew we were going out in the bush. That's where it got heavy. On Hotel 29er they had an artillery battery which was part of Americal Division. There you slept in bunkers, and you had bunkers you could fall out in. We reached there and disembarked, and the other platoon that was there stayed that first night. The other platoon was going back to Chu Lai. The first night we got incoming and it looked like the Fourth of July. It was heavy duty.

We did mine sweeps every day and the south sweep went to Bridge 35. That was the bad one. That's where we lost Jaybird. He was blown up. They blew the bridge and he was standing on it when it blew. We lost an Army 6-by that had fourteen guys on it. They were pretty well damaged. There were a couple of KIA's on that. But this was an everyday thing. This was the bad part because we knew we weren't playing. There was so many rounds fired that day I can't even tell you what we were shooting at. Rounds were just going everywhere.

At the end of the day we discovered one water buffalo, a little girl and a mama-san and Yarborough. But there was nothing left of him. Every day after that on the south sweep you never knew. We'd clear the road, we'd get back on the tanks and start pulling away, BOOM, we missed one. Then you got to go back and where there was one, there was always three.

The day that Yarborough was killed they swore that was electronically blown. But if it was, then why didn't they blow it earlier because we were all on that bridge. We had the whole squad on that bridge. Plus, the north sweep coming up from Tam Ky was there. Then we cleared the road and everything was fine. We all got back on the tanks and were going to head back to the CP and then, BOOM. Yarborough was the only one there. That's when all hell broke loose.

Wayne Hansen, PFC, A Company, May 1968–February 1969

From what I've heard, mine sweeping was like one of the worst jobs there was. When we ran a mine detector you have these earphones you wear. We used to have to wear a flak jacket. We couldn't wear the helmet because of the earphones. We couldn't carry a pistol because we weren't authorized. Marines are funny that way. I'm very proud that I was a Marine, but they have some stupid rules. You couldn't carry a rifle because it would get in the way. So if you got ambushed or got pinned down by ground fire, all you got is a mine detector. Sometimes they'd only fire one clip of ammo, but you don't know. You hit the deck, you're spread out with no weapon, no hand grenade, not even a helmet.

I really didn't think I was that afraid until one time when I found a mine. I looked on the ground and I said, I bet you there's a mine here. I told the probe man to be real careful and he clipped the mine. I saw the fear in his eyes and I thought I was going to die. That's how it would work on you. I've got like major high blood pressure.

Bill Spadafora, Cpl.,
C Company, A Company,
June 1968–July 1969

Word came back one evening that one of the fellows was killed setting out the trip flares. We found out he was just seriously burned. The trip flares were sort of like a roman candle, and it had a little string or a cord that you could pull or hook up to an area. If the enemy came through they would kick it or trip it off, and it would send up something similar to a roman candle and light to illuminate the area. Well, he was out in the wire setting these trip flares out and one of the trip flares got caught on the barbed wire. As he stepped away, the trip wire caught on the barbed wire and the trip flare went off. The flare was like white phosphorus and it went right up his back and burned him pretty bad. He was medevaced out. So a simple thing of just going out there and setting something up was dangerous over there.

On that same location, on Hill 29, we had a Marine that was killed by a kind of self-inflicted wound. He didn't commit suicide, don't get me wrong. I never met a Marine over there that was a coward. I never met a Marine over there that didn't do his job. What had happened was, he was standing watch in one of the bunkers on Hill 29, and his M-16 was loaded. He had it leaned up against the bunker wall and was sitting next to it. The rifle fell over or was knocked over and it fell into his body and went off. He was killed. I don't remember if he was killed instantly, but I remember the fact that he was killed by his own weapon. That was really tragic. It made a lot of fellows really sad.

It was bad enough that we had to be over there. It was bad enough that the enemy was shooting at us. But to be killed by your own weapon because it fell down and bumped into you or something was a rotten way to go.

Martin L. Brown, PFC, D Company,
August 1968–August 1969

When we were on that bridge, we used to get sniped at all the time. We were like twenty feet over the water, hanging out there like ducks in a shooting gallery. They used to snipe us every day out there.

Jim Tagye, PFC, D Company,
August 1968–February 1969

One day we did get hit.

PFC Martin L. Brown We used to set up machine guns on the bridge. The ARVN's from the compound went out and they were all sleeping out in the weeds. The VC were on the back side of them and shot over their heads at us. We just opened up and shot up a bunch of ARVN's. The VC wanted us to do that. They were always thinking like that. We wounded two ARVN's and the rest of them got the hell out of there.

PFC Jim Tagye I was carrying that M-16 and M-79. I remember blooping them and shooting my M-16.

Sometimes we would get stuck doing guard duty at nighttime. So you're up all night, then go out the next morning and do your mine sweep and then go build the bridge. So I don't think we got any sleep for twenty-four hours. That was when we were on Baldy.

PFC Martin L. Brown We started out behind schedule and ended up ahead of schedule. We were devoted I guess. [laughs] We used to go crazy on that thing. I used to get so thirsty, my mouth would taste bitter. I would just keep going. We used to sweat so much it was like a white crust all over us from salt.

PFC Jim Tagye We used to use a lot of Kool-aid, too, to sweeten the water. The water was bad. I thought it tasted bad.

PFC Martin L. Brown We drank a lot of beer and a lot of soda.

PFC Jim Tagye I drank a lot of soda, because the beer was warm. I didn't like warm beer. We drove trucks and did mine sweeps. He drove a truck longer than I did. I drove it the last month I was there.

PFC Martin L. Brown I took Kozak's place driving the truck. I had to go down and get the last gasoline truck the battalion had. Kozak had the next to last one. About two weeks after Kozak hit that mine, we were doing a south sweep out of the Korean compound, the triple culvert section, and they blew a hole in the road. It left just enough space to drive through. I knew there was a mine in there. I made these guys probe it three times.

PFC Jim Tagye I was on the headset that day.

PFC Martin L. Brown They couldn't find it but I knew it was in there. I started to hench through there. I slammed in the clutch, then I started to push it in a second time and I felt like I took off in a fast elevator. I didn't hear anything. Next thing I know I'm about a hundred yards off the road, standing on a rice paddy dike, shakin' so hard because I had so much adrenaline in me. I remember thinking Geez! I must have ran across the top of that water. [laughs]

PFC Jim Tagye I remember that day because I was the guy with the headset on, and I really felt bad when Marty hit that mine. We swept it, and we kept on sweeping it. Guys kept on probing it, sweeping, probing it … three times. Then we said, "Come on Marty, get in the damn truck and go." There's nothing there. When he hit it, I really felt bad. I felt very guilty about the whole thing. Thank God he wasn't hurt.

PFC Martin L. Brown Half of it didn't go off. If the other half had gone off, it probably would have blown the gas tank and I probably would have been cooked.

PFC Jim Tagye After he drove the truck, I took over for him. I guess that was the very last month I was there. I thought it was more stressful driving a truck than doing the mine sweep.

PFC Martin L. Brown It was. The next day after I hit that mine was the day I started drinking in the morning. You used to be able to lift the seat up where the driver sat and there was a hollow space under it. I used to sneak out at night and put about ten beers in there.

PFC Jim Tagye I never knew that. [both laugh] The day I was wounded though, someone else wanted to drive the truck. I was walking point that day. I don't know who took over the truck driving duties after I left.

The day that Kozak got it we were working the drag teams. Marty was walking on the right side and I was walking the left side. The drag teams got there so far in advance of the rest of the sweep team.

PFC Martin L. Brown We were actually

slow because that VC guy was looking and watching us. I checked his ID. On the right drag team we used to have to walk through bushes. It was one of the rare areas where we lost contact with the sweep team. In fact I don't understand why none of us got shot over there.

PFC Jim Tagye I think we got there before you did.

PFC Martin L. Brown You did. We stopped and checked a guy. I told them he was a VC, but I didn't know. I didn't know anything. I was still kind of new. He was leaning over watching the sweep team. So I checked his ID. I made him wait. I didn't know how to read them, but I did it just to screw with his head, to make him think I knew something. That was that morning and he was watching to see if the truck was going to blow. I was too naive. I should have brought him with us and had him interrogated. I was too stupid back then, so we got there a little late.

PFC Jim Tagye I remember getting there early and waiting and waiting, just me and this guy Schaeffer. He went and jumped on the truck. He got hurt pretty bad. I thought he was killed, but according to the records, it does not indicate that.

PFC Martin L. Brown He was sick. That's why he got on the truck. He was tired. He had pneumonia.

PFC Jim Tagye He told me to get on it and I said no. We weren't allowed to do that. I know the "Doc" got in the cab with Kozak. Then they went into the school yard there, the little driveway, and that's when they hit the mine.

PFC Martin L. Brown We'd stop and the truck would pull in about a hundred feet and turn around in the school yard. They watched us every morning and they figured out we didn't sweep that, so they laid a mine in there. It was right next to a Buddhist Temple. There were a lot of monks in there and they'd ring these gongs all the time and burn incense. We thought it was a secure area. The VC were pretty smart.

We all stopped right there at the pillars. The soda boys came up and I remember I bought a can of Sprite. Usually I got on the truck so I'd get a good seat, right there, but it was so hot that morning and miserable, that I bought a can of Sprite. I remember tipping the can back and that's when he hit it. The concussion almost knocked me on my ass. After that I went over by the wall around the school as close as I could get to the truck. I didn't know if they were going to ambush us. About that time the rounds started cooking off. Jim started shooting the roof off the school house and yelling obscenities.

PFC Jim Tagye That's the day I played "John Wayne." I ran into the school yard, jumped through the window, rolled over and nobody was there.

PFC Martin L. Brown Then we kind of sat there. An ARVN captain came over, grabbed my arm and pulled me over. About a hundred feet in front of the school there's a stairs going up, and the corpsman was laying there on his back. I thought he was a black guy because the explosion frizzed his hair and...

PFC Jim Tagye Deformed his face. I checked him first, before I went into the school house. When I was running towards the school I saw him and stopped. I thought it was Schaeffer and not "Doc," and here it wasn't. Later on I found out. After it was all over, we had to set up a perimeter out back and all over the place because we had to get the helicopter in. We didn't know if there were VC in the area or not. There was a lot of firing going on. As it turned out, it was mostly the ammo going off. But we had to set up a perimeter to get the guys medevaced out. Kozak, "Doc" and Schaeffer.

OCTOBER

Mike Daly, PFC, Hdqtrs. Company, July 1967–April 1969

I extended my tour in August but caught malaria and could not go home until September. Upon returning, I was sent up to the Hill north of 29 with C Company. Someone did not close the valve on the diesel and gas blivets. They became mixed together and I was to shoot them on the road to get rid of it. I began shooting right outside of the compound, past a village where my spray bars struck the porch of a hootch built right next to the road. Thinking nothing of it, we stopped the truck and I straightened the bar. Since I did not turn off the spray bars, we left a puddle. We continued on over three bridges. My driver began going faster and faster. I tried to signal him that at the speed he was traveling we could not do a good job. He screamed to look behind me as he continued to pick up speed. When I looked, there was a wall of flame twelve feet high following us at thirty miles per hour. I shut down the spray bars. Evidently, someone in the village put a match to the puddle we left and we just burned three miles of road, three bridges and a village. The site commander sent us back to Chu Lai immediately before the villagers formed a lynch party. That truck was never a very popular sight to the Vietnamese after that. Upon arriving back at the base they decided to get me out of the area for awhile, and I was given a dozer and sent to the 7th Engineers in Da Nang to work on Operation Da Nang Barrier.

Dan Diridoni, LCpl., Service Company, December 1967–December 1968

Some of the tractors and stuff they had were pretty old. They were Korean War vintage stuff and fortunately they had some guys that were really good at fabricating things, welders and stuff. Our unit later received an Army unit commendation for our effort.

They were having a real problem getting parts. As a matter of fact, when we went back down to Chu Lai in October, most of the equipment was shot. They had to get refitted completely with new stuff when they went back down there. It was pretty ancient stuff, but the old erdalator made it. We figured out how to use it because it had never been used before. It was brand new. It had cosmoline and everything on it. We took that from Chu Lai when we left and fortunately it had a manual in it. Neither one of us remembered how to use it. We did not know how to use the damn thing. We learned just by trial and error. Thank God nobody got sick on us.

In the school they kind of skirted around this erdalator thing, which was a mobile source of purification. It was so new and it was very portable. I did not know that they didn't know how to use it themselves. They just went through it very briefly. You'll never need to use this. If you're on a water point somewhere, you will have stationary permanent equipment with big towers and huge equipment. That's not the way it turned out. You get into remote areas where you have to bring in portable stuff and that was ideal. From what I understand later on, the Army Engineers brought in something that was similar to what we had except twice as big. It was a very, very modern water purification system.

It was weird. It certainly wasn't like you were in a war zone. I don't know if you ever saw pictures of the country, but it was the most beautiful greens and blues and colors that I've ever seen. It was just gorgeous country.

Robert Handley, LCpl., D Company, January 1968–February 1969

My wife was pretty good about sending mail, but I wasn't too good with her. I know she called the Red Cross on me. It gets to a point where you just don't want to write. You don't want to do anything. The days just keep dragging and dragging before we were considered even getting short. A lot of guys got called into the CO because they weren't writing home, usually because they got a call from the Red Cross saying a family member was wondering what the hell was going on. After that I wrote home pretty regularly again.

Dave Nichols, LCpl., B Company, January 1968–February 1969

The food was okay to me, but I was one of the few people who liked C-rations. We had a problem with supplies during Tet. The one thing they had success getting to us was C-rations. Being with an engineer company we usually had a supply of C-4 plastic explosive. This could be used to heat the C-rations. As long as it had ventilation, it only burned and didn't explode when lit with a match. It burned very hot and fast, so you had to stir your food or it would burn in the bottom of the can. I wouldn't have been as fond of C-rations if we hadn't been able to heat them. The one exception was when somebody must have gotten a good price on "Spam." For a while we had Spam and powdered eggs for breakfast, Spam sandwiches for lunch, and Spam and potatoes for supper. I had so much of it that I still cannot eat Spam.

Bill Spadafora, Cpl., C Company, A Company, June 1968–July 1969

I remember the very first time that I actually saw a civilian casualty from the war. It happened to be a young child [pause] and to me that was really a rude awakening to the war. I never really gave it a thought that the civilians really were affected by it. Where we were on Hill 10, aside from the little village of To An, there really weren't too many civilians. However, I remember seeing this Vietnamese father carrying this young child into the compound one day. The Corpsman was rushing with them and going into the sick bay which was a bunker almost beneath the ground. The child had been out in the rice paddy and apparently there was an M-79 grenade launcher round that had not exploded. He had the misfortune of picking it up, and it went off in his face. It … took part of his face away and part of his shoulder and part of his arm. I remember them calling in a medevac and taking the child out to Da Nang or Chu Lai.

But we used to get quite a few civilians into the compound. Once in awhile the Popular Forces would come into the compound that had some casualties from the patrol the night before. Or just the civilians would come in if a child had hurt themselves in some way. Some of it was just everyday scratches and bruises and others were caused by the armaments of war. The Navy Corpsmen that we had were great. They were the best. I don't think I ever met a Navy FMF Corpsman that I didn't like. These guys really stuck their neck out and really did a great job. They were always the first ones there.

Martin L. Brown, PFC, D Company, August 1968–August 1969

We had those five gallon igloo water cans. We'd put ice in there and throw the beer in and all the officers would come up and get water. We'd pull the top off and get beer. They didn't know it was in there. [laughs] It was a lot of hard labor, but our morale was pretty good then. There wasn't any racism, hardly at all. It was just before the '68 draft boys got over there and the racism started. It started getting bad just four months before I left.

**Jim Tagye, PFC, D Company,
August 1968–February 1969**

I only remember one guy smoking a joint the whole time I was in Vietnam. Afterwards they started sending in different guys and I guess those guys were smoking pot and stuff. The Army did it. We were with the Americal Division, 196th Light Infantry and they were shitbirds. They weren't very good troops at all. They had very low morale. They were draftees. I think that made a big difference.

PFC Martin L. Brown There were one hundred thousand black and Hispanic illiterates that they were supposed to put on Okinawa and Guam and train them in vocational skills. They sent them over there to Vietnam and gave them white NCO's. That was Lt. Calley's people. We used them for mine sweep security.

PFC Jim Tagye They weren't worth...

PFC Martin L. Brown The Sergeant used to tell them to get out and walk flank with the drag teams and they'd say, "Fuck you" and light up a joint. They didn't care.

PFC Jim Tagye The only personal experience I had with them was one day I was on drag. We took some incoming and these guys dropped their rifles and actually ran. They left me there, standing there. A couple of guys dropped their rifles and ran and we had those guys with us for security. I picked their rifles up and I threatened to shoot everyone of them. They apologized to me. I said, "Well it's a little late to apologize to me now." Nobody got hit, thank God, but there was a lot of sniper fire coming in on me and these guys just hightailed it. I never felt safe, ever again, with those guys.

NOVEMBER

**Dave Nichols, LCpl., B Company,
January 1968–February 1969**

I remember one time when it had been raining for quite a while and I tried to take a truck load of mortar ammunition to the top of a very high hill. This was west of Phu Bai and the "road" up the side of the hill made several switch-backs as it wound up the hill. It was very muddy and slippery. At one particularly steep portion all of my tires began to spin, including the front ones. Once they started spinning the truck actually began to slide back down the hill. The problem was that about fifty feet behind me the road made a hard 90 turn. If I didn't make the turn, the truck would go over the edge and drop about two hundred feet straight down. I tried several times, but I always slid backwards. I finally told the Sergeant from Mortars that he was going to have to have his people come down and carry the ammunition to the top. This led to quite an argument that finally ended when I told him his people could unload my truck or I would dump it right there on the road. He finally saw things my way. There was no way to get the truck up the hill and I wasn't about to go over the edge of that cliff.

**Brian Althouse, PFC, A Company,
March 1968–October 1969**

One day on the north sweep we found an eight-inch round. It came from a ship and it didn't detonate. So Sarge, me and this other guy, named Reds, were together. Sarge says, "You guys pick that up and put it on my shoulder." I said, "Sarge, what if we drop it?" He chewed my ass out. He told me, "When you think about things like that, that's when they happen. Now pick the *!?&#@ and put it on my shoulder." Reds and I picked it up and put it on the Staff Sergeant's shoulder. He carried it up to the road and he got a couple of other guys up there help him lay it down on the road. It was on a slope and it went down into a deep pond like a bowl of water. He put a piece of flex-x on it, a time fuse, lit it and rolled it down the hill. It was raining that day and we were standing back behind a tank. It blew the water sixty feet high, if not higher. Honest to God. That thing went BA-WOOM. And I picked that thing up? But I'll tell you one thing, I did learn something from Sarge. I never argued with him again. He knew I was scared. You get so scared, you can't help it. You do what you gotta do, but you're scared, because you don't want to die. You don't want to get hurt. He was really cool. I wish I remembered his name, but I can't. He got promoted to Warrant Officer.

Wayne Hansen, PFC, A Company, May 1968–February 1969

We used to do some stupid pranks. On Thanksgiving they sent us a big container of eggnog. It was supposed to be for Thanksgiving Day when the colonel was going to fly in and have Thanksgiving dinner with the troops in the field. They sent turkeys in these big thermal containers so we'd have regular turkey. The Army guys camped out on our hill. They drove up in these tanks and one of them had a bottle of rum. And they said, "Hey, look what we got." So, somebody says, "Too bad we couldn't have some eggnog and we could have a real Thanksgiving feast." So me and one or two other guys say, "We got eggnog," and they say, "Yeah, right." So we snuck up to the top of the hill, we broke the lock and took the eggnog back. All the guys got a cup of eggnog with rum in it and we put the empty container back in the cooler. The next day when the colonel came, we were all standing out there trying not to laugh at the captain trying to get the stupid eggnog to come out. There was nothing in there, just an empty container. That was like one of the fun things. It was little things like that that you had to do to keep your sanity.

Jim Tagye, PFC, D Company, August 1968–February 1969

On the Marine Corps birthday we all got drunk in the Korean compound. I was drinking Vietnamese rum and we all got smashed.

Martin L. Brown, PFC, D Company, August 1968–August 1969

The Lieutenant gave me a whole quart of Old Crow.

PFC Jim Tagye We all were smashed and got hit that night by the VC. Thank God that the Koreans were there. We had a good time before we got hit. There were some good times. There was a lot of laughter. It wasn't all bad. I grew up in a fairly nice catholic neighborhood. The conditions over there with the flies during the day and mosquitoes at nighttime was not what I was used to. I never even shot a rifle in my life. You go over there and you're put in this situation and you don't even have bathrooms. You don't have a proper place to eat or drink water and it's just totally different. It was so foreign.

PFC Martin L. Brown We'd come out the main gate on Baldy, go to the right and there was a sand pit. We'd all gather up at the gate and go out on the sweep. We started going down in the pit because we figured they'd start laying mines in there because we had started using it. These guys, Larry and this other guy, went down there by themselves with the detector. They did it about three mornings in a row and the VC were watching them. They set up an ambush for our guys. They got down there and shot them up. I saw the VC take off running.

PFC Jim Tagye We took off running after them. We got one. We didn't find a rifle on them, naturally. You're not going to find that. He just tried to blend in. So we picked him up.

PFC Martin L. Brown That's how they got us, though. They used to watch us continuously. They would just watch us until we made a mistake. If we'd do it more than once, they'd get us. We never knew when it was going to happen.

PFC Jim Tagye That's why it was a three-hundred-and-sixty degree war. You never knew.

PFC Martin L. Brown It wasn't like they were coming to get us big time. They just picked at us. We used to find things like C-4 with a blasting cap stuck between the leaf springs on my truck all the time. They'd just stick it in there, so when the truck came down on it, it'd blow the spring out. I found one of those in there one time because I was up-chucking between the tires. I was drunk from the night before. [laughs]

PFC Jim Tagye That wasn't the VC that did that. That was us. [both laugh]

I remember those kids were always over by those dumps picking out food, the mamasans were picking out food and flies were all over the place. Unbelievable.

PFC Martin L. Brown The VC used to set speakers up out in the woods for propaganda. They would tell us to surrender. They'd do it in three languages, Korean, English and Vietnamese. Koreans used to try to feel them out with mortars to see if they could get the guy. One night they got real close because they shot some out and

Christmas Day, 1968. From left: *Joe Harran, Marty Brown and Thomas Costello. Courtesy of Marty Brown.*

it landed, and the guy's voice stopped for a couple seconds. That was pretty interesting. I was surprised they used to do that.

That area had a lot of VC and a lot of VC sympathizers. A little bit north of there was all VC sympathizers. Hanoi Island was out in the river there. We were up there when they B-52'd that. That was Pipe Stone Canyon. That was an operation we went on. There were five thousand VC taking R&R on that island. They started sending in B-52's to bomb it. Of course, when they do that, the VC know they're coming, so they all leave. We went out on an Op. We did mine sweeps right next to the Op for about four days. They just worked their way in. It was pretty interesting to see them going in. They used APC's and infantry and had a lot stuff going in. They didn't find much out there when they got there. I guess the VC knew they were there.

DECEMBER

Peter Allon, PFC, Service Company, November 1967–December 1968

I did my time with the 9th, then I

volunteered to stay over, so I went to Okinawa. I was Third FSR and I requested mast after about three months to get back to 'Nam because it was mickey mouse. An officer has you scrubbing the deck in the barracks at four in the morning. I think there was about four or five of us returnees from 'Nam. We were all from different outfits, but all assigned to FSR. It was just too much mickey mouse bullshit after 'Nam. Most of the Marines were too young to go to 'Nam so they left them in Okinawa. I got my ass back into 'Nam and I went to 7th motors. I did seven months with them and then I woke up in Guam. From there I went to Bremerton.

Dan Diridoni, LCpl., Service Company, December 1967–December 1968

I was Service company, but I was TAD and spent basically almost my whole tour with B Company, and in my heart I've always considered myself B company. What a great group of men, ones who I will never forget. My MOS was 1121, water purification.

They call it TAD, Tour of Additional Duty. They had communications people and radio men that were Headquarters Company people but were attached to B Company. We had electricians that were out of Service Company and were attached to B Company. There was a lot of different things that went into making up a letter company. It wasn't just truck drivers or heavy equipment guys, it was a multitude of these support people. Service company people or Headquarters people, depending on what their job description was, were all over the place.

Dave Nichols, LCpl., B Company, January 1968–February 1969

I think my best day, other than the day I left, was at Christmas of 1968. I went to see the Bob Hope Show. I was so far back that I had to use binoculars, but I didn't care. We had many USO shows, but most of them were oriental bands trying to sing American songs. Their accent made it impossible to understand the words, but most of us recognized the music and knew what the words were supposed to be. With the Bob Hope show it was all "round eyed" girls and English without the Oriental accent. The girls were beautiful and Bob was funny. Bob Hope is a true American hero. When I think of all the Christmases he gave up to bring some cheer to thousands of service people each year, it gives him a special place in my heart. It saddens me to see how old and frail he has become. It will be an especially sad day for me and thousands of former military personnel when he passes away.

I listened to music over there whenever I could. My favorite group was the Everly brothers. Their music was so smooth and calm. It always reminded me of home. I also liked the Beach Boys, Four Seasons and Jan & Dean. We listened to Armed Forces Vietnam Radio. There was a blond female disk jockey that played the music every night. I can't remember her name (maybe Chris something), but we all had pictures of her. She was really good looking and she had a way of talking that drove us all nuts. It was like she was talking directly to just you.

Brian Althouse, PFC, A Company, March 1968–October 1969

During the monsoons it would drop down to 70-some degrees and it was really cold. You'd freeze. You could go outside your bunker and take a shower. You go outside with your bar of soap and take a shower because it would be downpouring. It just rained every day and every night continuously. All the fields you used to drag in, filled up with water like a lake. Then if you were a dragger, you were in water up above your butt, dragging.

I remember this one time I was dragging. This was not during the monsoons, this was dry. I was walking along a dike, and the rice is still pretty high. It's almost up to your knees. This critter flew in. I swear it had a wing span of fifteen feet, but that's exaggerating. I have never seen a bug that big in my life. Well, I pulled the gun down off my shoulder and I'm ready. I sight right on it and threw it on fully-automatic. I didn't fire a round though. I had the M-16 in my right hand, drag pole in my left hand, and I started to walk around and I look up on the road. And I thought, if I shoot at this bug, these guys up on the road are liable to open up, too. So I did a 180 around him. But I've never seen a bug that big. I don't know to this day what kind of bug it was. He just landed on one of the rice paddy stalks. There was some times that there was humor. I told the boys about that when the sweep was over and we had secured the road and everything was cool, and they howled at me. They said, "Oh, yeah." I told them that I was going to shoot but I looked up at you guys and thought I better not. "That's right, we would have shot you." That was one of the fun stories.

Wayne Hansen, PFC, A Company, May 1968–February 1969

A lot of times, some of the things they did by the book were like gray areas. One time we got a new Colonel. That was the day I found that mine in Tam Ky. They gave us all new camouflage fatigues. He was gonna fly in his helicopter to Hill 10. It was about 20 miles, maybe 15 miles away. The day before we found a cluster of mines. That morning I found at least that one mine. So the road was mined. All week long we had to work on getting our brand new fatigues all cleaned and spiffed up. That afternoon we cleaned up our M-16s and had to wrap them in towels, [pause] okay...

We got on the truck with all our gear, all the way it was supposed to be and we all looked like we're going for a parade. But our [speaking slowly] our weapons were wrapped in towels so we wouldn't get dust on them. If you want to talk about being angry! I didn't have any animosity towards the officers, but it was like the rationale was so stupid. We're going up a road that we know is mined ... and you've got to cover up your weapons. What happens if we get fired upon? But that was one of the stupid things that was done, and I guess maybe they didn't think it was that stupid. But those little things sometimes make you wonder. Why?

But you're 20 years old and you don't have the rank, so you can't say nothing. You just go along with the program. But after awhile you start learning. You start seeing those things and that's how it was. Those were the things that would get on your nerves and yet we had a lot of good times.

Bill Spadafora, Cpl., C Company, A Company, June 1968–July 1969

The Battalion had allotted so many men from each one of the companies to go see Bob Hope. I wasn't one of the fortunate ones to go, however there was some fellows from Hill 10 and Hill 29 and LZ Baldy, 59, that had the opportunity to go see Bob Hope. This was one of the things that occurred that was kind of funny, maybe ironic or maybe daring or stupid. I remember the fellows taking a 6-by from Hill 10 down to Chu Lai to see the Bob Hope show. They were under orders to make sure they returned to the compound before it got dark. The CO didn't want anyone driving on the road when it was dark. Naturally, for reasons we all know, was that the enemy places bombs and mines on the road then. The roads that we normally mine sweep in the morning would be unguarded and unprotected. The CO wanted the fellows back from the show before dark. I guess it was around Christmas time and it was not getting dark very late.

They went off to the show, they saw Bob Hope, they had a great time, and they were having such a good time they went over to the club that was in Chu Lai and had a couple of brewskies. Meanwhile the truck did not get back to the compound until about 10:00 or 10:30 that night. Apparently most of them were so tanked up that they were singing and yelling, having a good time and carousing from the time they left Chu Lai until the time they got to Hill 10. If there was any enemy or VC on the road, it must have scared the hell out of them to think these crazy Marines were driving on this road in the dark. As they pulled up into the compound, they were just having a good time for themselves, and singing and laughing and just forgetting about exactly where they were. Whether or not that was such a good idea, I don't think the CO liked it. Immediately after that he had the NCO's and the Lieutenant that was with them standing tall in front of him and he was reaming them up and down. He was telling them why and giving them a riot act about not being back when they were supposed to be back. Other than that [laughs] they did have a good time for themselves.

Jim Tagye, PFC, D Company, August 1968–February 1969

I know once we built the bridge, they didn't blow it at all during the time I was there. We finished the bridge in December and I was hit the first of February.

JANUARY–JUNE 1969

In January Paris talks expanded to include Saigon government and Vietcong representatives. Nixon begins secret bombing of Cambodia, March 18. Secretary of Defense Melvin Laird invents term "Vietnamization" in March to cover American troop withdrawals.

Nixon proposes simultaneous withdrawal from South Vietnam of American and North Vietnamese forces, May 14. Nixon, with Thieu on Midway, June 8, announces withdrawal of 25,000 American troops from Vietnam.

JANUARY

**Bill Spadafora, Cpl.,
C Company, A Company,
June 1968–July 1969**

I have a letter from Nixon. My parents were involved in politics at the time I was over there. Nixon was running for President at the time and I had a sticker up on my bunker. My dad had sent a picture to him, and he had sent a letter back, to me, in care of my father. He said after he got elected he would try to bring everybody home. My mother was the other gentleman's campaign manager at the time. Farrell and Nixon were running at the same time. I didn't know too much about Nixon then. I knew he had been vice-president under Eisenhower and had been in public office for most of his life.

My dad had sent me a letter telling me that he had received something from Nixon after the election was over but I didn't see it until I got home. I just thought it was nice that he responded. I really didn't have any kind of political convictions in those days. When you're nineteen years old, [laughs] I wasn't even old enough to vote. [laughs] That's before they changed

Bill Spadafora during 1968 Presidential Campaign. Courtesy of Bill Spadafora.

the voting age. When I was stationed in California, I wasn't even old enough to drink, unless you were on the base. You couldn't drink in California unless you were twenty-one. So it made it a little difficult. So whether I liked the man or not, I don't think it made a difference. I guess Nixon did like seeing the picture.

Martin L. Brown, PFC, D Company, August 1968–August 1969

We had young guys there who were pissed off they were there, so they used to take it out on the people. You used to see that a lot.

Jim Tagye, PFC, D Company, August 1968–February 1969

We had such a cross section of people. The first time you see one of your friends get killed, you really start turning against people. You don't know if they're friendlies or the enemy. I think you become angry and we did take it out on the people. We always used the word "gook" for everybody, the enemy and the friendlies.

PFC Martin L. Brown I was pulling the drag hook one time and this guy came out with this green uniform on. It was a dark green uniform like Dickies you work in. He was walking along the dikes as I was pulling the hook. He asked me for a cigarette. I used to carry about five packs on me so I just gave him the whole pack and lit it for him. We walked up and got to check point one and he reaches in his pocket and handed me a surrender pass. He was NVA. I didn't know it. I had only been there a couple weeks. I didn't even know what they looked like. Everybody else saw him and they didn't know it either. His uniform looked like it had just come out of the package. Most NVA uniforms that I ever saw were bleached out until they were almost light green. He was an older guy, too. He had graduated from Berkley in California. He was an NVA Staff Sergeant. He was pretty amazing.

PFC Jim Tagye We interviewed him. I asked him why he surrendered, and he just showed me his money and said he wanted to spend some money. He showed me a picture of his kids and wanted to go back to his family.

PFC Martin L. Brown He said they started out and got blown up by bombs and were sick and miserable. There were thirty-five guys out there that wanted to come in. They just wanted to surrender because they were so miserable. I guess they went out and got them.

The ARVN's used to have a pit that was probably three feet deep. When they captured somebody, they'd stick them in the bottom of the pit. They'd have an armed guard there. We used to all hang around there sometimes. I used to jump in, see who they were and see if they could speak English. I used to feel sorry for them. I used to put a cigarette in their mouth and light it. Some of them didn't like that. Then I realized they always had those cone hats on and all the smoke would get up there [laughs] in their eyes. I stopped doing it.

People were superstitious if a bus hit a mine or something. When they bury somebody, they have to have their whole body there, or I guess they don't go to heaven. So they'd spend days just combing through the rice paddies finding pieces, etc. One time, I guess it was a VC that got his head blown off by a little ARVN compound. They wouldn't move him because he didn't have a head. So we'd walk by in the morning and the first morning it wasn't too bad. The second morning he was black with flies. The third morning he was shriveling up. It was probably the fifth morning before he was gone. Somebody just couldn't stand it anymore, so they got him out of there. The Vietnamese weren't going to touch him because he didn't have a head.

We used to see all kinds of stuff. Mongooses running around and we would always see two, mates. They were hard to see, but when you saw them, there was always two. It was nice.

I got everything confiscated, pictures, etc. through customs when I got back.

PFC Jim Tagye All of my pictures were

lost when I got wounded. I got maybe ten pictures. I was wounded February 1st. I read the Command Chronology and I believe it said there were seven Marines and one Army person wounded that day.

FEBRUARY

**Wayne Hansen, PFC, A Company,
May 1968–February 1969**

I had a rough time. I lost a real close friend. We were together in Alpha Company and I had a knee injury. [pause] I had gone down like three times during incoming and I chipped some bones in my knee. I didn't really think anything of it. Sometimes it would hurt real bad and other times it wouldn't. There was times when I was limping around and they wouldn't let me go on a mine sweep. It was towards the end. The company up on Hill 63 was Delta Company. They were nicknamed Dyin' Delta because every day they went on a mine sweep they'd get ambushed and four or five guys would get it. So all the new guys would go to Delta Company. Then they sent me and this guy named Frenchie. We were in Tam Ky at that time. We thought what did we do wrong to be sent to Delta Company. The lieutenant says, "They need you guys because you've got experience and they're all new guys." They knew I had a bum leg when I got there and I told them to just give me a couple of days. Well, I went on one mine sweep. We got a little bit of ground fire and I was running, but it was obvious that I couldn't keep up too much. The next day they flew me to Da Nang and I was on my way to Guam for surgery.

My buddy stayed, and a couple months later he got killed.

I'm still dealing with his getting killed. I haven't really dealt with this. I've tried and it's such tremendous feelings. I felt when I got medevaced [pause] that I shouldn't have gone. Even though it wasn't my decision. You can go through all that rationale, but those feelings are still strong. [pause] He used to put on a show for us. We made him a costume and they'd play a record and he'd make like he was singing. We made strobe lights and stuff and called it the "Frenchie Show." Everybody would come, even the Army guys on the hill. It was a good time.

His name was Norman Chavarie. He was from Massachusetts. He was there for 18 months. He just came back from leave. He had extended, gone home to the states and come back. He was only there one or two days. The VC threw a hand grenade and he got hit with the blast.

When I was in California and heard about it, that set me off. God, I gotta go back, and I tried to go back to Vietnam. They gave me an early out so then I tried to go into the Army and they rejected me. That's when I did the suicide thing. But the irony was, I would've already been home a whole month ... before that would've happened.

**Bill Spadafora, Cpl.,
C Company, A Company,
June 1968–July 1969**

On Sunday afternoons, usually myself

Bridge #29 built by A Company. Courtesy of Bill Spadafora.

and several men from the platoon and two of the Navy Corpsmen would don some of our equipment and go down the road to a French Orphanage that was not too far from Hill 10. This was called a Med-Cap. A Medical Combined Action Patrol was usually done with the Popular Forces of South Vietnam. The reason for this was goodwill, naturally, but also we would go there and repair the orphanage for the nuns. The Navy Corpsmen would go and try to patch up the kids. Some of the kids would have open wounds and sores that never seemed to heal because of the fact that they lacked the nutrients and vitamins in their body to combat any type of bacteria. The Corpsmen would go and change bandages or put Band-Aids on or give shots to kids that may need some kind of shot and drop off some medicine to the nuns. There were French and South Vietnamese nuns. Very little English was spoken. I think the Mother Superior knew how to speak English and French and South Vietnamese. But one of the nice things about that was how much we looked forward to that.

One of the nice things about going on the Med-Cap on Sunday afternoons was it gave you an opportunity to get out of the compound. We never walked on the road because of the fact that the VC or NVA might mine the road, so we used to walk through the rice paddies. We would visit the orphanage, see the kids, speak to the Vietnamese nuns and sometimes we would get lunch or dinner. I recall one incident when we were all sitting around this table and the nuns had served some food. I think it was potatoes and cabbage, a couple of other things and meat. The meat was pretty good. I remember one of the Marines saying, "Sister, what kind of meat was this?" We ended up eating monkey. Some of the fellows immediately excused themselves from the table and proceeded to throw up outside the building. [laughs] But other than that, it was a pretty good occurrence. We enjoyed going there.

After leaving the orphanage, we never walked back on the road. We used to walk through the rice paddies or in-between the villages. There was a village by the name of To An, which was between Hill 10 and the orphanage. We'd take a short cut through this village. Well, one afternoon, in full combat gear, with our rifles and our packs and full medical gear and everything else that we were carrying, we were going through a rice paddy. It was a dry time of year, sometime in February or March of '69. As we were coming around one of these hootches (a house in Vietnamese) this gigantic water buffalo decided that he was going to start charging this Marine squad. There was about seven or eight Marines, two or three Corpsmen and maybe four or five Popular Forces, or South Vietnamese troops. Now with all that firepower we could definitely have annihilated this water buffalo. But just previously, down in Battalion area, they had shot some livestock of the South Vietnamese and the word was out that no Marines would shoot at livestock.

So here we have several Marines in full combat gear, able to take down anything, immediately do a turn around and start

Remains of Bridge #29 after VC/NVA blew it. Courtesy of Bill Spadafora.

running across this rice paddy. I guess the temperature was about 130 degrees or so with this water buffalo in full stride chasing after us. I wish I had one of those home videos at the time, we probably could have won a lot of money. In the mean time this water buffalo is catching up to us, getting closer and closer, and everybody is yelling and screaming and cursing and saying things like, "If this goddamned buffalo gets any closer, we're going to blow him to kingdom come," maybe not in those exact words, but you get the idea. Meanwhile, as we round another hootch, this little Vietnamese kid comes out and says something in Vietnamese, and this water buffalo stops dead in his tracks. The rest of us are laying out, spread out across the rice paddy, panting and trying to catch our breath and sweating to death. We're laughing our heads off because we have this gigantic water buffalo chasing after us and we could have annihilated the thing. It wasn't funny at the time, but it's a funny situation now when you look back at it. It's the kind of story I always tell. The word got out that some of the Marines from the 9th Engineer Battalion got chased by water buffaloes. It took us a little while to live that down. But, all in all, we had a good laugh about it.

The best time of the day for me was probably mail call. Everybody was happy to get mail from home and see what was going on. I didn't have a girlfriend, so I really wasn't expecting mail from any particular woman. My mother used to send me "care" packages. Everybody had a "care" package sent to them. My mother used to send me chocolate-chip cookies in a canister. Everytime I used to get them, they would all be broken up into crumbs. It used to be a joke. I used to send her letters back and tell her that instead of sending me the whole cookies, she should just send them in crumbs, maybe then they'll come whole.

I think one of the nicest things was my brother. I'm ten years older than my brother. At the time I was nineteen, twenty years old, and my brother was only nine and ten years old. He used to write me letters once or twice a week. He'd write me a letter and never put a stamp on it. I thought that was very nice because in the corner where you would put the stamp on the envelope he would just put "Free to my brother in Vietnam." That letter always got to me. I saved a couple of those. I thought it was pretty neat that the Post Office would allow that to go through. I always enjoyed getting letters from my brother. He kind of looked up to me and I appreciated that so much.

My mom used to send me liquor sometimes. We used to get Jack Daniels, and she used to send it to me in Aunt Jemima plastic containers that the syrup came in. That way the bottles wouldn't be broken through all the freight and mail and handling. Sometimes I got them, sometimes I didn't. I guess somebody in the mail room knew exactly what it was and helped themselves to it once in awhile.

Aeiral view of Hill 10 from 80-foot tower. Courtesy of Bill Spadafora.

During the holidays, like at Christmas time, once in awhile you'd get a letter from a group of kids or a Christmas card from a group of kids. Sometimes it was from some kind of a civic organization saying, "We support you. We hope you are well during the Holidays." That was pretty nice to get something like that. We'd get something like a little "care" package from somebody, once in awhile, who you didn't even know, from someplace in the United States somewhere. It was writing paper or [pause] just little stuff. It was nice.

MARCH

Robert Handley, LCpl., D Company, January 1968–February 1969

I lost a good friend over there named Randy Molkentine. He died of malaria. That sticks in my mind. He died after I left. I lost some money in a card game shortly before I went back to the states. I asked him if I could borrow some money because I wouldn't have any to get from L.A. home. He lent me one hundred bucks. He was fine. He wasn't sick then. He was a weight lifter and a short guy, but real stocky build. He was real healthy. I got home a week, ten days later, and stopped at his parents home. They lived in a suburb of Milwaukee. They told me then and I was shocked. Literally shocked. You wouldn't figure it for Randy. He was just real healthy. But I guess malaria, some strains of it, your temperature just goes up and that's it. As far as I know, he's the only one that I knew of that actually died over there.

**Bill Spadafora, Cpl.,
C Company, A Company,
June 1968–July 1969**

When I was over there about nine months, I had an opportunity to go on R&R. I was glad that I waited about nine months before I went, because a lot of fellows had difficulty coming back from R&R. Some guys went on R&R when they had three or four months in-country and after going on R&R and having a good time, didn't want to come back to an environment that wasn't too healthy. Sometimes some of the fellows didn't come back. They went AWOL. There weren't too many places you could go to that were seven days long. You could go to Bangkok or you could go to Australia and Hawaii. Our CO wouldn't allow single guys to go whenever an allotment came in for an R&R to Hawaii. It would be only married guys who could go to Hawaii. He felt that this way the married guys would have an opportunity to meet their wives there in Hawaii and see them for a short period of time. Hawaii was a seven day R&R.

I had the opportunity to go to Australia. I thought that was very interesting and a lot of fun. Australia is a beautiful country. They welcomed the Americans there with open arms. We had a great time. I was there for seven days. I spent some time in Sydney and in Bondii Beach, which is like a resort area outside of Sydney. Like all servicemen, a lot of fellows went to Australia and I met up with two other Marines from different parts of Vietnam and we kind of hung out together. This particular incident happened one day as we were crossing one of the main streets in Sydney. We were all walking abreast of each other and a truck or car backfired. All of a sudden you found the three of us laying flat out on the main thoroughfare of a street in Sydney. All the traffic stopped. Everybody was looking at us as if what had happened to these three people who were laying flat out on the road? It's kind of funny to think about it now, but at that point it wasn't. For us being so trained and so tuned to reacting to artillery fire or mortar fire or incoming rounds, that the sound of this backfire from this vehicle, and the three of us would automatically react to the same thing by diving on the ground. I guess we were so conditioned to combat that we weren't even relaxed while we were there. It's an interesting theory, an interesting thing. I never really gave it too much thought, but it's funny that sometimes that happens. Even now, today, when you hear a loud noise, or a plane or a helicopter flying overhead, or something that's out of the ordinary, that's loud and boisterous, it reflects back to some of your training. I thought maybe I would just mention that.

APRIL

**Bill Spadafora, Cpl.,
C Company, A Company,
June 1968–July 1969**

Many times after we were done with the mine sweep and traffic would be flowing on Highway One, we would head back to the compound. We'd come across a bridge once in awhile and the little Vietnamese kids would be swimming in the rivers. The main diet for the South Vietnamese is mostly rice. I didn't see too many chickens over there. I saw a lot of ducks. They had duck eggs and ducks and sometimes they ate cat and dogs and monkey. But a lot of times they liked to have fish. We'd come across one of these bridges and the kids would want us to throw hand grenades into the river. So we would get the kids out of the water and throw hand grenades into the river. The hand grenades would go off underneath the water and the concussion would knock the fish out and they would float to the surface of the water. Then these Vietnamese kids would jump in the river and go after the fish that were floating on the surface. After awhile it became a normal routine for the sweep teams to come to a particular bridge, the kids would be waiting there for them, and they'd throw a couple of grenades in the river. Several fish would float to the surface and these kids would just jump in and pull the fish out. We called that fishing Vietnamese-style, or Marine-style, and that was just an incident that I thought I'd tell you about. I recall throwing a grenade once or twice over the bridge myself and popping up a couple of fish. Vietnamese kids appreciated it, and we had an opportunity to throw a grenade in the water, so … [laughs] it worked out both ways.

You know when I tell these stories, especially the ones about the water buffalo and the hand grenades in the river, most people think that being over there wasn't so bad. But aside from the heat, and aside from the dysentery, and aside from the mosquitoes, and aside from the malaria, and the leeches when you walk through the streams, I guess it wasn't a very bad place to be. Unfortunately, the enemy was shooting at you. There were occurrences where we had Marines in the 9th Engineer Battalion get killed by Vietnamese, North Vietnamese, NVA, VC, whatever you want to call them. We just called them "gooks" or VC.

MAY

**Brian Althouse, PFC, A Company,
March 1968–October 1969**

When I was up on Hotel 10, we always had Americal Division with the tanks and APC's. I knew a guy named Randy Candle. He was from Reading, Pennsylvania. That is just twenty minutes from where I live right now. He and I became good friends. We used to drink beer together and stuff like that. He was on a tank. But you had different people every day. You might have one tank crew one day and then have another crew the next day. But whenever he would be up there, we'd get together and became good friends. We were from the same state and lived close because I was from West Chester and he was from Reading.

When we were up on Hotel 10, we were on the east sweep. That was run towards China Beach, towards the ocean. The Americal held an area out there. Well, they had a problem one night. The east sweep was a sandy road, an easy place to put mines. They ran into difficulty one night. There was a whole lot of crap going on and they were our security every night. They'd come up and we'd have them around our perimeter along with our guard duties. Randy wasn't with his tank. So I went and asked, "Where's Randy?" One guy told me what happened. And I was like, "Wow, man." And I'm going to tell you this.

He went out and they were doing an operation. They were pulling an op and they came under heavy fire. He was on an APC. It hit a mine. It blew the APC and he was wounded. Guy picked him up and put him on another APC. That APC hit a mine. Those guys ran. They pulled back, everybody was pulled back. But they left him. They left him. That guy told me you could hear Randy keying the mike ... Randy ... Randy was a good guy. He was a normal, average dude. He just wanted to be like the rest of us and they left him out there. They could hear him keying the mike so they knew he was still alive. They told me that the commanders wouldn't let them go out and get him. They wouldn't let them go. I don't know. That might be true. I don't know. But he died.

When I was home before that on special leave, I called his parents because I had his phone number. This was when I lived in West Chester. I called his parents and talked to his dad. I told him I knew Randy but I was going back to Vietnam. I was only home for thirty days and I was going back. He said, "Well, stop by." I told him, "When I come home, I'll stop." But now I lost his address. I tried through the VFW and I can't find him. I couldn't even locate him at the Wall. I can't find him to this day. [Brian has since located and been in touch with the family of Randy Truman Kendle.]

He was a good guy but the way he died, the way those guys told me, it was insane. Insane. I just can't believe they couldn't get him. In the Marines, if you have a fallen comrade, you pick him up. You don't leave a comrade down because if you get hit, you don't want to be left there. I always had a hard time understanding that. I still do. But like I said, I wasn't there. I just can't comprehend. I always had a downfall about the Army for that. In the Marine Corps they train that you don't leave a guy dying there. You just don't do it.

**Bill Spadafora, Cpl.,
C Company, A Company,
June 1968–July 1969**

[speaking slowly] One experience that I'll never forget was one of the most fierce firefights that I've ever been in and it lasted a good twenty-five, thirty, maybe even forty-five minutes. We had set in on a bridge and it was suspected that the enemy was either going to blow it up or pass through, but it was our responsibility to intercept them. The Commanding Officer, a couple of South Vietnamese soldiers and an Officer, myself and several other Marines were spread out across a rice paddy. All of a sudden all hell broke loose. We ambushed them. While the firefights pursued, the enemy started to throw hand grenades and one hand grenade exploded pretty close, if not almost on top of my CO. Fortunately, he was in a crater already, so he wasn't hurt, but there were three Vietnamese soldiers that were killed instantly. With that the remaining Vietnamese soldiers just got up and left. The South Vietnamese soldiers got up and left us.

We had nine Marines spread out across the rice paddy with a limited amount of ammunition. I was operating an M-60 machine gun at the time. I think if the NVA or the VC would have known there was only nine Marines, they would have took off and charged us. We were surrounded. We pulled back to a tree line and were taking small arms fire for a period of time and were surrounded. You could actually see them through the silhouettes off the light from the flares and the illuminations that were going off because we called in support from Hill 10. We had a mortar there that they sent up for illumination and you could see the VC or the NVA jumping the rice paddy walls, getting closer and closer to us. Needless to say, we were surrounded for a couple hours and [pause] it was quite a harrowing experience. There was a Navy Corpsman with us who carried two wounded South Vietnamese troops across a rice paddy during this whole incident. I know he was put up for a medal, I don't know whether he received it or not. I don't know if it was a Navy Cross or the Silver Star, but that was quite a sight to see.

It's kind of hard to explain what goes on in your mind when you're experiencing something as horrifying as that. All I know is that the Army came out with a tank and a couple of APC's came out onto the rice paddy. The tanks used to have a big light on the top of the tank. They lit up the rice paddy and it was like a John Wayne movie. The enemy was spread out across the rice paddy and it was like a free-for-all there for a little while. It's funny that sometimes I remember that a lot. We were ... pulled back to a tree line, and a lot of things go through your mind. Whether you're going to make it through or you're not going to make it through. [pause] I think that's an experience that I'll never forget and it's probably carried me through a lot of hard times after I got out of the service.

I sent you a little clipping about that patrol and how I won my Bronze star, but [pause] I think someone becomes a hero because of the situation that they're in. We were in a situation that if we didn't fight we would have died. We had no choice but to fight. I just happened to be there and happened to have the M-60 machine gun and held off the enemy while the rest of the patrol moved back. It's quite an experience to hear bullets hitting all around you and hitting the trees and hitting the dirt and flying by you so close that you can hear them whizzing. I don't think anybody can really understand that. It's not something that I've ever talked to too many people about because they don't really know what it really means.

JULY–DECEMBER 1969

Nixon unveils "Nixon Doctrine" in Guam on July 25. In August Kissinger meets covertly in Paris with North Vietnamese negotiator Xuan Thuy.

Ho Chi Minh dies in Hanoi at age of seventy-nine, September 3. Massive antiwar demonstrations in Washington, October 15. Nixon delivers "silent majority" speech on November 3.

Another big antiwar demonstration in Washington, November 15. On November 16, revelation of the My Lai massacre which took place the year before.

American troop strength in Vietnam reduced by 60,000 by December.

AUGUST

Brian Althouse, PFC, A Company, March 1968–October 1969

The best opportunities were Sunday afternoon if nothing happened. Once you cleared the road, and there was no problem, when you got back to the CP they gave you Sunday afternoon off. Then you play and act like a bunch of teenagers because that's what we were. We would do stupid things, a bunch of kids until the sun started going down, then you had to start getting ready again.

Edwin J. Raley, PFC, D Company, 1969–1970

D Company was located on LZ Baldy about half way between Da Nang and Chu Lai at the intersection of Highway One and Route 535. When I arrived in-country, the 196th Light Infantry Brigade had Baldy and D Company was a tenant USMC unit whose mission it was to keep open about 10 miles of Highway One and about 10-15 miles of Route 535 west to LZ Ross doing mine sweeps and bridge construction and repair.

William C. Jung, Sgt., August 1969–July 1970

(letter home at start of second tour — 13 August 1969)

"Dear folks,

"I've finally found time to drop a line from my new outfit, the 9th Engineer Battalion in Chu Lai, South Vietnam. Before telling you about this place, I'll tell about the trip over.

"We left Pendleton on the 7th and went by bus to Norton Air Force Base near San Bernadino. Bill Meekma (sister-in-law's brother, also a Marine) drove over and paid me a visit before I departed Staging Battalion. From Norton we flew to Anchorage, Alaska. We were able to disembark for a few minutes, and believe me, that cool fresh Alaskan air felt good. Then we flew to Tokyo, Japan. Here we developed engine trouble, so they let our plane load (nearly 200 men, mostly Marines) loose in the terminal bar for awhile. We drank the bar dry. After half an hour they were out of cold beer. Finally our group "stumbled" back on to the jet and flew to Okinawa. Here we remained for two days.

Top: *Bill Jung, holding a piece of shrapnel, and Tom Newton. Courtesy of Bill Jung.*

Bottom: *Road marker on Highway #1. Courtesy of Bill Jung.*

Then on we went to Da Nang. The day after, I boarded a C-47 and flew down to Chu Lai where I joined the 9th Engineers.

"Chu Lai is about 60 miles south of Da Nang and is also along the edge of the South China Sea. The only Marine outfits here are our battalion and some flying or wing outfits at the air strip. There are some Seabees here, but most of the people are Army, members of the Americal Division. Our area is about four miles from the sea. The land is sandy with scrub pine and scattered rice paddies. To the west not too far off are the mountains, always looking down on us. The coastal strip is not too wide.

"The battalion compound is large and flat, and of course surrounded by the usual berm line, bunkers, barbed wire, and concertina. We share the camp with an Army engineering outfit. It's a good camp with plenty of facilities: beer hall, barber shop, Korean laundry, outdoor movie, a small PX, even a boxing ring. Of course I'm in the usual Vietnam hootch, a 16' × 32' wood structure on legs and covered with a tin roof. We have outhouses and a shower shack, but since the guys are a long ways from the shack, we use a hose. I've again been issued an M-16 for my T.O. weapon. I've been assigned to the drafting and surveying section in the battalion S-3 shop. This of course means I'll be a surveyor. This seems to be a good outfit. I think I'll like it here.

"Please start sending the Advance and the Beaver Dam paper. This time I have plenty of socks, skivvies, clothes, and cleaning gear. The only thing I'd really like is some canned goods and Stateside reading material.

"I hope you were able to take some kind of vacation. You both could use a break. I'll be watching for the kid's (my little brother) name in the Advance. Thanks for everything during my three leaves. I had a great time, especially during the last one. Johnny's gas sale totals will go down now that I'm gone.

"The weather is hot as usual. The monsoons won't start in earnest for a couple of months yet. As for me, don't worry. I'm in a good outfit and spot. I'm quite happy here.

"Love,
"Bill
"P.S. We're about 55 miles from Laos."

SEPTEMBER

**George E. Ballard, Sgt., A Company, 1965–1967,
SSgt., C Company, 1969–1970**

I rejoined the 9th Engineer Battalion after a two year tour in the States, on September 25, 1969 and was assigned to C Company, Equipment Platoon. The Company and the Battalion was still located in the 9th Engineer Compound in Chu Lai. The compound was across the road from MAG 12 near a small hamlet whose name I have forgotten. The compound was made up of Headquarters and Service Co., C Company and I believe one more Marine support Company. Our living quarters were plywood strong-back buildings with metal roofs. The sides were made with plywood halfway up and the rest was wire screen. Most buildings had sandbags stacked up to the beginning of the screen wire to protect the occupants from sniper and mortar fragments. The compound was either ankle deep in dust or mud. We had a Battalion Mess Hall, Battalion Aid Station, Battalion shower and laundry.

There were things to do after work when you were in the compound. There was an Enlisted Club and NCO Club where you could get beer or soda for ten cents but no hard drinks. It was a place to get away and relax. You could go and see a movie or get sack time.

The Commanding Officer of C Company was 1st Lt. Nolenburger, the Company 1st Sgt. was 1st Sgt. Robert Stepp, the Senior enlisted man Lt. Maxwell. I was assigned as the Engineer Equipment Officer

Bill Jung at the end of the day in Tam Ky. Courtesy of Bill Jung.

and Engineer Equipment Chief. The platoon contained Equipment Operators, Equipment Mechanics, Welders and Motor Transport Drivers and Mechanics. We had twelve M51 dump trucks, three M54 cargo trucks, two M52 tractor trailer low beds to haul construction equipment and the full compliment of Heavy Equipment.

The mission of the Company and the Heavy Equipment platoon was to keep Highway One open for the movement of personnel and supplies. The normal work schedule was six and a half days per week and ten to twelve hours per day. We were normally given Sunday morning off, if possible. Our main function was to concentrate on that section of road from Chu Lai to Da Nang. It had to remain open to traffic. We conducted mine sweeping operations, filled in holes, graded the unpaved sections, repaired culverts and bridges, and any other repair work that was assigned. Sometimes our lowbed trucks and cargo trucks would be tasked to join other truck convoys to haul supplies south from Red Beach in Da Nang. This kept us real busy most of the time. A lot of the previous construction jobs that we got the first time I was in-country were gone. Now we were only doing maintenance upkeep type of work. We were also tasked with engineer support for the Americal Division.

The Company was responsible for providing its own security along the protective berm and barbed wire fences. It was made up of personnel drawn from all the platoons within the compound. During full alert everyone was assigned a position on the berm. We would go to an alert status every time the Air Base was hit with rockets or mortars because we seemed to be under their flight path. We would get probing action from time to time. They liked to get between us and an Army Counter Mortar Radar Unit located on a hill next to us. This sometimes caused us to shoot at each other.

Edwin J. Raley, PFC, D Company, 1969–1970

A few days after I reported to D Co., I was placed on inner perimeter guard duty. Once in the early morning, when everything is so quiet and I am manning my post in a proper military manner, overlooking this rice field with lots of water, I heard what I thought was a man walking through the water in front of me. I thought, this is one bold SOB and shot. Well, here came a couple of the old timers and advised me that it was a rat that I shot at and don't do it again. Well, I said OK, but knew rats can't make the kind of noise I heard. Before long the sloshing and stomping started again and I shot again, feeling good and bad about killing my first Cong. That didn't last long. The old man himself got up and came to my position, highly upset about being woke up by his newest rat killer. Cussing, he said he was going to stand there with me and we were going to watch this huge rat walk out and make his way to the mess hall. Well, shortly, the beaver sized rat walked out, shook himself off and went to the mess hall, just as he said. My face glowed red, even in the dark.

Another funny thing was when this Marine, Lowman, got himself a good case of crabs. He decided he would treat this himself instead of seeing the doctor. Well, he went to the gas drum and doused himself in the crotch with gasoline. The river was half a mile down the hill and the only source of water. Lowman starts to run around the bunker about to die and, of course, nobody would give him a ride to the river. In the end, the crabs survived, Lowman had to see the doctor, and we all got a good laugh at his expense.

William C. Jung, Sgt., August 1969–July 1970

These pages were copied from a green squad book of mine regarding notes for (2) patrols on 1 and 2 September, 1969. During my (2) tours in Vietnam I probably ran a couple hundred patrols while in the infantry and engineers in Vietnam. These pages are typical of my patrol notes.

Day and Night Patrols 1 and 2 September, respectively PERSONNEL ROSTER

1. Patrol leader Sgt. Wm. C. Jung 2248620 O+ 2. Asst. patrol leader Cpl. S. G. Feldhausen 2315196 A 3. Grenadier Cpl. Buchanan, R.B. 2474676 B+ 4. Radioman Pvt. Potter, M. T. 2443925 5. Corpsman D. R. Mower HM3 8430347 O- 6. Tail end "Charlie" Pfc. Prattas, C. J. 2443394 B+ 7. Pfc. Hill, R. L. 2537525 O- 8. L/Cpl. Hall, D. 2429293 9. Cpl. Jager, J. J. 2412094

ORDER OF MARCH:

1. Jung 2. Buchanan 3. Potter 4. Hall 5. Jager 6. Feldhausen 7. Williams

DAY PATROL, 1 September, '69 Call Sign: Yankee 1 1300 —? Starting Point: An Tan Bridge 498066 Check Point #1 Fishing Weirs 496056 Check Point #2 Pine Lane 498059300 meters, 25 az. Check Point #3 500045 Along edge of tree line facing center of paddies Check Point #4 495043 Dam along dike Check Point #5 494041 Work along base of Hill 49 and road to C.P. #5, Zorba rock Then work back toward C.P.

1 SEPT. DAY PATROL: Six man patrol was a day recon. It rained during the entire patrol. Covered a lot of ground, a lot of it off the regular route in order to confuse anyone following or watching us. This way they won't know our exact route tomorrow night. I took point. All went well. The men tended to bunch up too much though.

NIGHT PATROL 2 September, '69 2300 – 0300 "Yankee 1" S.P. AnTan Bridge 498066 C.P.#1 Fishing Weirs 496056 C.P.#2 Pine Grove 499061 C.P.#3 Edge of Paddy 500045 C.P.#4 South of Dam 49650400 C.P.#5 Zorba Rock 505039 Skip #1 O.P. at #3 Pass Words: Primary BACK WILD Secondary NATIVE FIGHT come in gate #4 by bunker #10

Order of March: 1. Jung, Point, P. Ldr 2. Buchanan, M-79 3. Potter, Radioman Williams 4. Mower, Corpsman 5. Hall 6. Feldhausen, Tail End Asst. P. Ldr.

2 SEPT., NIGHT PATROL: Long patrol, about 6000 meters. First half was very dark since it was a dark overcast night, finally the moon came out and helped some. No rain.

Clyde Ricks, PFC, D Company, August 1969–February 1970

My best day in-country was my first mine sweep. When I first reported they put me in the office. We didn't do any mine sweeps for a few weeks. They kind of liked to protect your headquarters personnel, but one day they were shorthanded for some reason and I got to do a mine sweep. I thought this is what it's all about. I get to do one.

One other time was the closest I ever saw the Vietnamese civilians being brutalized. We stopped for a break and a gal was selling sodas or something. This guy starts to feel her up, just a little, and push her

Harvesting rice. Courtesy of Bill Jung.

around, and I'm sitting here thinking ... hey, my mom didn't raise me to watch something like this. Then a sergeant made him stop. I remember feeling so relieved because I thought if you do anything, you're a dead man. You'll be on that guy's list and you'll probably end up dead. I couldn't let him do anything real brutal and still live with myself. But the sergeant can just say, "hey knock it off" and then that was cool.

OCTOBER

George E. Ballard, Sgt., A Company, 1965–1967,
SSgt., C Company, 1969–1970

There were a few times when we hit the berm for practice and then gathered on the Company street and conducted a hootch by hootch search for illegal weapons and drugs. At times we would confiscate a jeep trailer full of weapons. The Company CO would log all weapon serial numbers and types, and I would take them to my welding shop and cut into them with a torch. But the troops were very resourceful and could somehow get more.

Another form of security was the squad-size patrols that we performed. The assignment was on a rotating basis between all the Companies in the compound. If you had patrol duty on Wednesday night, you would take out a daylight patrol on Monday or Tuesday. You would coordinate your activities through the S2 section. There you mapped out the route and check-in points along the way. It was a very good idea for them to know where you were if something hit the fan. Most NCO's in the Company made it a point to go out with their troops at least once a month. Most of the time nothing happened and all you lost was sleep. But the VC knew what we were doing and sometimes put trip mines or other obstacles in the way.

This was also a time when racial tension within the compound and throughout I Corp was at a high point. The black troops, or brothers, the name they preferred, were becoming very militant, aggressive and unproductive. The number of fights, drug sales and unrest within the Division was bad. A new phase of tactics was developed by the radicals called "fragging." Let me tell you that this act scared the hell out of me. I could accept facing danger and possible death from the outside enemy. This kind of terror and disobedient acts did not keep me or the other Staff NCO's from doing our job. I grew to be more aware about all things happening around me and unusual acts inside the compound. Sometimes I felt safer outside the compound with the real enemy than inside with the racial hate and bigotry.

The tension mounted even more when an Army group of Engineers moved into the compound. This is when I saw, first hand, how bad things could get. There was this group of black soldiers, and a few Marines, who desired not to go back to the bush and fight and die for their white honkey leaders, their words, not mine. They barricaded themselves inside their living quarters and threatened to kill any white person who stuck his head inside. It was something to watch as the Army tried to talk them out. All the Army wanted was for them to just do the job they were sent to do. This conflict led to someone throwing a hand grenade at the Army Company 1st Sgt., wounding him in the foot. A CS (tear gas) grenade was thrown in the Staff NCO quarters and others thrown in different parts of the compound. These acts finally led to the day that a few of the defensive positions on the berm turned their guns on the compound. Can you imagine how this feels?

The Commanding Officer of C Company went to the berm and told the Marines that they had to lay down their weapons or he would come up and take them. They threatened him with death if he tried. He told them that they would have to shoot him because he was on his way up there and that they were coming off the berm one way or another. I thought this was a brave thing to do and showed real leadership. He reminded me of John Wayne the way he took control of the situation and brought the matter to a conclusion. These were some of the things that happened over a three to four month period while we lived with the Army. Once we separated from the Army, things quieted down. They were not gone, but came back under control. Most of the troops were too busy to get involved with any of this because of our work schedule.

The first thing each day the mine sweep teams would sweep the road for mines. They would leave from different locations. One team from the 9th Engineer compound, one from A Company located halfway from Chu Lai to Tam Ky, and another from LZ Baldy, outside of Tam Ky.

This was a long, boring and thankless job that had to be completed each and every day prior to allowing traffic on the road. The VC took note of how the sweep was conducted and what patterns we were setting. It was the mine sweep leaders job to not set a pattern. They had to walk the road looking for signs of digging or other unusual activity. About 80 percent of the road was paved with asphalt so you had to look close at all culvert and bridges as a possible mine site. Most of our culverts were metal and the mine detector did them no good. They also dragged grappling hooks to catch any electrical detonating wires. Like I said, long and boring.

Edwin J. Raley, PFC, D Company, 1969–1970

We lost some people during that time if I remember correctly, two Corpsmen and one Marine. One Corpsman was killed by a sniper, the other I don't remember. The Marine, a black man from Harlem, got on a booby trap left in a road barricade by the ARVN. He died at the north end of the Ba Ren river bridge in my arms as I was clearing trash from his mouth in an attempt to save him. My first encounter with death and I never will forget.

William C. Jung, Sgt., August 1969–July 1970

"29 October, 1969

"Dear folks,

"I'm at the rock crusher now. Four of us have been here a week already. The day is a rainy one, so I thought I'd take the opportunity to write and tell about this place.

"This is a small outpost on a knoll near the base of Hill #167 (meters). They call it a hill, but we call it a mountain, since it's so large. The mountain of course towers above us. The rock crusher facilities are below us. At the base of knoll south of us is Route 535, a 1½ lane road, very muddy now. There's a company of infantry, a pla-

East-west road from rock crusher. Courtesy of Bill Jung.

toon of engineers, and of course, our little band living here. The camp consists of a few bunkers. It reminds one of an old stagecoach way station. About two miles to the east is Hill #63, home of the 7th Marines.

"The view from the mountain top, once you make it up there, is fantastic. One can see 30 miles north to Da Nang, 40 miles southeast to Chu Lai and all the lowlands and coastline in-between. The highlands begin below us and the mountains stretch behind us to the west and Laos. I took some great pictures up there. The mountain itself is steep and covered with huge boulders, elephant grass, trees, thorns, and masses of tangled underbrush. It's beautiful, but a mess.

"Our job is to map the camp, the rock crusher and quarry basin, and the mountain. The first two are no sweat, but the latter will take many long hot days of work. We've spent two days on the mountain already, and it wasn't easy. We have to set our instrument up on the boulders. The rodman and shotgunner have to cut their way across the slopes with a hatchet

Temple outside of Tam Ky. Courtesy of Bill Jung.

and a machete. Most of our work is done outside the perimeter, so we have to carry our weapons, ammunition, food, and a day's supply of water with us. With the terrain, heat, and the fact we're in unfriendly 'Indian country,' it's hard work.

The weather was hot and clear the first 4½ days, so we got a lot done. It has rained almost steadily for the past 2½ days, so we've been holed up. We spent all of yesterday filling sand bags. First we dug a trench bunker outside our tent and sandbagged it. Now we've got a fighting trench to jump in if we get in-coming. Then we built a sand bag wall half way around the tent to stop any sniper fire that may come from the country on the other side of 535. It took us the whole day to build both of them, and that was between rainy spells.

"I've got to tell about our tent. It's big enough for the four of us and our gear & surveying equipment. The place is cozy and pretty dry. We only have a few leaks. To make sure I stay dry, I've got a poncho over my cot. The tent is on a slight slope, so water doesn't collect in the tent, it keeps right on going. We use ammo boxes to keep our gear in, an ammo box for garbage, and a table made of ammo boxes. We use it for card playing and cooking. Our main diet is C-rations. We've got plenty of rations. Ski here is always eating. It never fails he has a can in his hand unless he's sleeping. Of course gear is hanging from all loose strings. It's home to us. Our main activity is card playing, hearts is the game.

"The war is very real around here. Since we're on high ground, we can see for quite aways. The days and especially the nights are alive with artillery and fighting. Our neighbors next to our tent are two mortars and their crews. They're firing right now. The people back home can talk peace all they want; the Paris farce talks can continue; but here the war is still very real.

"At any rate the kid is all right. Life here is busy and harder, but all goes well. The rain has stopped, so we're going to try and get some work done.

"Hope all goes well at home. Keep the flag flying.

"Love,

"Bill

"P.S. Please excuse the paper and damp ink."

Clyde Ricks, PFC, D Company, August 1969–February 1970

People think the Marines are so callous and cruel. But the Marines taught me that you try to rescue the people that were hurt, even ... even if it might cost you your life. They didn't want it to be sheer suicide, but they wanted you to try.

My mom wrote me almost every day. Quite a few other people wrote me too. Mail meant a lot. When I first got there, I think I went about two weeks without mail before it started catching up with me again. And when it caught up, it was just like Christmas or something.

I had things good. I was in an office

most of the time. Just before I got there a guy named Chavarie got killed in an ambush. And after I'd been there a couple of months we had a convoy ambushed and a couple of guys got killed, a corpsman named Welch and a guy named Mehaffey. [pause] But I barely knew 'em.

Mehaffey and Steven Martin Welch, a Navy Corpsman, got killed at the same time. Oh, it was a terrible deal. Our Captain threw a fit because this one truck stayed too long up at our compound one night. It was after curfew, so he should never have let them go. But he sent them back ... I don't remember if they were going out to the rock crusher or to stay with the Koreans. We'd have a platoon go with them and they got ambushed and those two guys got killed. It happened October 21st 1969. I can remember that. Keith had only been there for awhile. But that Corpsman, Welch, everybody thought that the sun rose and set on him. The "Doc," everybody just thought he was the greatest. I think Keith and I only got there within a couple weeks of each other. I noticed in my directory of the Wall that it was only five days after his twenty-first birthday that he died. His mom said there's a church named after him back in North Carolina.

NOVEMBER

Edwin J. Raley, PFC, D Company, 1969–1970

I visited Capt. J. K. Nagazana's office pretty regularly for minor infractions, mostly speeding and being off limits. Capt. Nagazana was a mustanger, an L.D.O., one fine leader of Marines and just a good man. He was the Company commander during most of my tour. He understood the non rate. For the first few speeding tickets I got he chewed my butt. Then when they kept showing up, he took to slapping me on the hands and asking if I knew what that was for. For being off limits, he understood that Marines must reproduce and let it go.

I drank beer every day. One day I had too much and let dark catch me not in the compound. He came looking for me and found me, truck and bulldozer creeping up Highway One, drunk, singing and having a good time, all by myself. He put me in the jeep with his driver and drove the truck back. I then got an invitation to dine with him in his mess. I reluctantly tried to eat tuna, got sick and took that opportunity to disappear from his presence. Never heard anymore about that either, but that's the kind of man he was.

I questioned his judgment once on the Ba Ren bridge when we finished unloading timbers for the bridge after dark. We normally did not move after dark and he wanted to return to Baldy after dark. He quickly informed me that he would lead me back, not the other way around.

When his regular driver went on R&R, I was called to his office, told to get in full uniform and report back. I figured one too many speeding tickets, pay up time. When I returned, he told me that I was his driver for the next two weeks, check out the jeep and get ready to go. This was odd. I had the most speeding tickets of anyone in the country. As it turned out, he liked to ride just like I liked to drive. It was a good two weeks.

Clyde Ricks, PFC, D Company, August 1969–February 1970

Even though I live in the section of the country where the winters are very hard, it gets 30 to 40 Fahrenheit below here sometimes in the winters, the coldest that I ever remember being in my life was when the wind was blowing and I was wet in the monsoons. I used to get teased about being a virgin.

DECEMBER

**George E. Ballard, Sgt., A Company, 1965–1967,
SSgt., C Company, 1969–1970**

I remember leaving the compound one day and heading north on Highway One looking for the mine sweep team. After driving about fifteen miles and not running into them, I had the driver pull off and see what was going on. After gaining radio contact with them, I discovered that we were ahead of them by about eight miles. They had a late start and I had an early one. Now that makes a believer out of you.

One of my responsibilities was to drive the distance from the main compound at Chu Lai to LZ Baldy, north of Tam Ky, a distance of about 45 to 50 miles. I was to look for road damage and any vehicle that needed help. A main problem was flat tires and maybe mines and snipers. One of my favorite things was finding a truck with a front flat, and the driver just sitting there waiting for someone to bring him another tire. I would tell him that he had four spares, so what was he waiting on. His typical response was that his spare was flat, too. I would remind him of the four outside tires on the rear of the truck. Just pick one and change the flat.

On several occasions my driver and I were caught on the road after dusk and had to remain on the road by finding some secure place to wait out the night. There was a detachment of South Korean Marines just south of Hoa An and we could stay just outside their compound. The VC activity near their compound was almost nil. They worked with a different set of rules when it came to dealing with the locals and the enemy.

Edwin J. Raley, PFC, D Company, 1969–1970

The worst day of my life, to date, was Christmas Day, 1969. I was at D Company's rock crusher just west of Baldy. Christmas morning we were taking a break and noticed a small Vietnamese child, 4 or 5 years old, picking through the garbage for something to eat. We had all received care packages from home and decided that since it was Christmas day, we should go down and make this a good day for this child. We brought him to our bunker and gave him some of everything we had. We really made his and our day. Later, everyone dispersed and I was in the bunker with this child. This Lieutenant, can't remember his name, came in, saw the child and proceeded to make this out to be a firing squad offense. He told me to get rid of the kid and report to him at his bunker. This I did, casually, and he then told me to go get in the proper uniform and report to him as I was taught in boot camp, very unusual for Vietnam.

When I returned and reported as I was told, I was a little upset. He then began to raise all manner of hell over this in the presence of all the staff NCO's. This caused me to lose all respect for this man and I went into a "want to kill you" mode. When he finished, I had decided that he must die to satisfy me. He had humiliated me in front of all those people. I told him, in front of all those people, that his life belonged to me and that I, in fact, was going to kill him for what he did. I don't know why nothing was ever said about this. Of course I didn't kill him, but every Christmas this comes to mind. To this very day I have no respect for a military officer unless he first earns it.

Clyde Ricks, PFC, D Company, August 1969–February 1970

The monsoons closed our mess hall. It just got so muddy and messy and everything they closed our mess hall for a couple of months. We had two meals of C rats a day. That lasted for a couple of months

... and I can remember the helicopter supply drops. When we'd be out on perimeter, they'd be dropping these big nets full of supplies and you'd have to hunch up like a turtle with your helmet and flak jacket to keep the stuff from blowing in your face. That's how we got a lot of our supplies. Then we got a lot from convoys too.

I decided I didn't want to go on R&R because [pause] when you came back from R & R you were expected to [pause] tell all these explicit things about how we'd done sexually. I couldn't have done it, I just wouldn't. I was extremely shy and I'd been raised with a sexual morality. Probably because I was a Mormon you just didn't have sexual relations until you were married. That was my excuse for not going on R&R.

Thomas P. Carras, 2nd Lt.,
A Company, B Company, Hdqtrs. Co.,
December 1969–September 1970

My first taste of the "real" Vietnam came my first night at about 1:00 a.m. when the airfield was rocketed. Although the explosions were far off, I no longer felt as nonchalant about my pending tour.

My first days in Vietnam were spent checking-in at the 1st Marine Division Headquarters in Da Nang. After meeting with the Division Engineer, I was assigned to the 9th Engineer Battalion that was headquartered in Chu Lai. So, with orders in-hand, I caught a C-130 on Teeny Weeny Airlines down to Chu Lai. Travel in Vietnam was on a catch-as-catch-can basis, and Teeny Weeny Airlines was really a shuttle service run by the Air Force to move troops as well as Vietnamese military, civilians and dependents associated with the U.S. up and down the coast. During my tenure in Vietnam I became quite adept in hitching rides with anybody going my way from a Vietnamese scooter driver to an Army CWO Loch (two seater) helicopter pilot.

Finally on December 11, 1969 I joined the 9th Engineer Battalion. Arriving at 1900, I was dropped off at a nondescript SEA (Southeast Asian) hut on the compound and told this was an officer's hootch. I found my way to the Officer's Club named the Red Fox and met some of the Battalion's leadership — Maj. Al Bernotas, XO (retired as Col.), Capt. Ted Shower, S-1 (reverted and retired as a M Gy Sgt), 1st Lt. Ed Wages, CO Land Clearing Company (retired as a Major) and 2nd Lt. Mac MacElroy, Platoon Commander. It wasn't until the next morning that I met two of my hootch mates, but the incident stands out in memory. As I was putting away my gear, two 1st Lt.'s (names will be protected to prevent embarrassment) were down at the other end of the hut. One was showing the other a .45 cal. pistol that he had found in a Viet Cong cache. Suddenly, there was a loud bang and the two officers who later became my good friends stood there shocked. They both sheepishly looked my way, but all I could say was, "I didn't hear anything." It didn't dawn on me till later that I could have been shot by accident on my first day.

I recount this story as metaphor for my experiences in Vietnam since my greatest fear was not that I would be shot or wounded by the NVA or Viet Cong, but rather by my own troops. When I arrived in Vietnam the anti-war sentiment coupled with the insurgency of black power was at its height in the United States. This is the environment that enveloped the military in Vietnam during '69 and '70. Throughout my tour there were frequent "fraggings," which is the term given to a fragmentation hand grenade being thrown by one of our troops to kill or injure other American troops. The 9th Engineer Battalion was not protected from these occurrences and I can recall three specific instances where I and fellow officers were targets.

The mission of the 9th Engineer Battalion, Fleet Marine Forces, was to provide engineering support for combat operations, and civic action programs throughout Quang Nam province (I Corp). This support translated into constructing bridges, extending and improving the road network and erecting living and working spaces. My first job as a Platoon Commander was repairing the road and culverts along QL-1 which was the main transportation corridor from Chu Lai to points North. My fondest memory was taking out the visible road sweep team on Christmas morning. All along the way the village kids would come out to wave and beg, so we brought an ample supply of Christmas candy to distribute. Another historic memory for me was having a chance to see Bob Hope perform on Christmas Day in Chu Lai. Bob and his entourage, Teresa Graves and Neil Armstrong of those I've remembered, did their best to inspire/entertain the troops.

JANUARY–JUNE 1970

Kissinger begins secret talks in Paris with Le Duc Tho, February 20. Sihanouk overthrown in Cambodia by Lon Nol and Sisowath Sirik Matak, March 18. Nixon announces, April 30, that American and South Vietnamese forces have attacked Communist sanctuaries in Cambodia.

Large antiwar protests spread across the United States. National guardsmen kill four students at Kent State University in Ohio on May 4.

Nixon proposes "standstill cease-fire," October 7, but repeats mutual-withdrawal formula next day. American combat deaths in Vietnam during the last week in October numbered twenty-four, lowest toll since October 1965.

On November 12 Lieutenant William Calley goes on trial at Fort Benning, Georgia, for his part in the My Lai massacre.

American troop strength in Vietnam down to 280,000 men at year-end.

JANUARY

George E. Ballard, Sgt., A Company, 1965–1967,
SSgt., C Company, 1969–1970

Life in a combat zone was both hard and interesting at the same time. Each day started with its own problems and you just had to work them out. Take the case of the extra jeep, for instance. We had a limited amount of Motor Transport vehicles around. I had three jeeps, one PC (personnel carrier), two M54 trucks. They were divided up as follows, one jeep to Company Co., one jeep to XO and 1st. Sgt. and one for myself. The PC was used by the Motor Transport/Heavy Equipment Maintenance NCO's. Each Construction platoon had a M54 truck. The Construction platoon assigned to LZ Baldy needed an extra vehicle. How was I going to get them one? In my possession was an extra Lm62 welding machine that my predecessor had gotten somewhere. I knew that I could make a great deal somewhere. There was an Army vehicle maintenance unit that I had a good relation with. I got things for them that they needed and they helped me out when I needed help. I talked them into trading one jeep for one welding machine. One evening we attached the Trailer mounted welder to a truck and hauled it to them. In return, we loaded the jeep in the back of the truck and hauled it back to the shop, under the cover of darkness.

Now it is not easy to conceal an extra vehicle when every one is looking for a ride. Also, that white star on the hood of the Army jeep was difficult to remove. We repainted the jeep Marine Corp green and put new ID numbers on the hood. Now this jeep was to remain at LZ Baldy most of the time. The answer was to give it the same numbers as an existing jeep so that all maintenance work could be completed on either jeep. The only problem was not to let the two jeeps be seen at the same time. This feat was carried out for four or five months until the Lt. from LZ Baldy came down for a meeting with the Co. His driver parked the vehicle next to the dispatchers office during an inspection by Hq & Serv. Co. Someone noted that we had two jeeps with the same vehicle numbers. I was asked a lot of questions and finally decided to give the questionable vehicle to Service Company who were short three or four jeeps due to accidents and combat action losses. There are more stories where you need to improvise to get the job done.

It became quite a problem to keep all of your Motor transport assets on the road each day. Each evening during the Commanding Officers meeting I had to tell him how many vehicles I could get on the road the next day. It was my goal to keep a minimum of ten of my twelve M51 dump trucks available. To do this, I started a night shift of mechanics to fix any broken trucks. We went well beyond our level of maintenance to include replacing engines and transmissions. We would trade with the Army vehicle maintenance, which we were not supposed to do, to get any parts that we could not get from our own supply group. This ability to make friends with other units served me well during that tour.

Charlie Company maintained the highest rate of vehicles per day to support the upkeep of Highway One. The 9th Engineer Bn. was awarded the Army Meritorious Unit Commendation for their work supporting the Americal Division.

The road that ran between LZ Baldy and LZ Ross was one of the most hazardous sections of road in I Corp area. The road was littered with blown up vehicles of all types. There was a burned out fuel tanker, numerous jeeps and cargo trucks, armored personnel carrier and a couple crashed and burned aircraft. Trying to mine sweep the road was next to impossible because of all the metal fragments imbedded in the road. It was here that I lost a friend of mine. We were at Baldy to look at a Bailey bridge that needed to be removed and a wooden bridge built in its place.

An M60 tank had been drug across the metal bridge and severely damaged it. He was riding in the back of a M37 PC truck when it hit a command detonated mine. It threw all the Marines riding in the back out, killing two and severely injuring three others. The loss of life would have been higher had not a passing helicopter landed and took the wounded to Charlie Med at Da Nang.

Clyde Ricks, PFC, D Company, August 1969–February 1970

I was raised in a real strongly religious culture and a strongly agricultural culture. You get in the Marines and you meet all kinds of people.

You're around Blacks. You're around Italians. You're around Spanish. The Spanish in my city are generally looked down on and they'd do the more menial labor

Remains of church going into Baldy. Courtesy of Bill Jung.

type job. In the military they're your equals or your superiors. That was real good for me to examine another culture. I probably had the hardest time with Southerners. They seemed like know-it-alls to me. But you get to experience all these other people. They come from their cultures and to me it's real healthy. People that grow up in one area and live there all their lives miss so much of the world.

One night when I was on perimeter, somebody fragged the Staff NCO. It got their hut and left one guy, Staff Sergeant Holm, a vegetable for life. They brought up the CID guys, and only the 16 of us on perimeter that night weren't suspects. I was glad I was on perimeter.

Thomas P. Carras, 2nd Lt.,
A Company, B Company, Hdqtrs. Co., December 1969–September 1970

On one occasion a buddy was working late in the company hut when he heard something land on the metal roof. Luckily, he dove for the floor boards just as the grenade went off. The next morning the hut was well ventilated and the young 2nd Lt. was a few years older. Then there was the morning I awoke to an explosion. The Battalion had just moved up to Da Nang and setup in the old Seabee compound that was in close proximity to a rock quarry. I didn't think much of the blast until I heard the commotion in the camp and discovered that someone had set off an explosive charge on the officer's side of the mess hall in an attempt to get the Battalion CO. I say this because the explosives were placed on a metal rack outside the back wall directly behind the place where the CO would normally sit. As fate would have it, the CO didn't go to chow that morning, but a few other officers were injured. Then there was the time one of my buddies found a hand grenade rigged with a trip wire between the "Lieutenant's" hut and the S-4 shop.

Now, I do not want to give the impression that everyone lived in fear of their own troops, but the climate of discontent and "why are we still here" pervaded the psyche. This was part of the Vietnam that I experienced but definitely not the entire story. The relationships and camaraderie formed during my tour with 9th Engineers endures today. Bob Miller, the "Cowboy Bob" of LZ Baldy who supervised the rock-crusher unit, is a close friend. Lloyd Prosser, Alpha Company CO and now retired Lt. Col., maintains contact. And Lt. Col. John P. Kraynak who became my mentor after Vietnam was an inspiration until his untimely death in 1973.

It was around this time that talk of redeployment back to CONUS was being rumored, so I was nominated to become the Battalion Embarkation Officer. This meant I had to be trained and on January 7, 1970, I had orders to the Officer Embarkation Course at Camp Hansen on Okinawa.

FEBRUARY

George E. Ballard, Sgt., A Company, 1965–1967,
SSgt., C Company, 1969–1970

There was a program started called Vietnamization. It began either before I returned or soon after my arrival back in-country. The Battalion was involved by providing Construction Equipment and Motor Transport vehicles to South Vietnam Engineer units. I believe that the equipment we gave them were older pieces of equipment that were approaching the end of its life cycle. These were the older gasoline engine and some diesel engine equipment. We were changing to multi-fuel vehicles and more modern equipment. As the newer equipment arrived in-country, the older pieces were turned over to the unit responsible for getting it to the South Vietnam Army. I believe one of the requirements for the program was that the cost of shipping the piece of gear back to the states was less than turning it over to the Vietnamese.

Most of this activity took place after we moved from Chu Lai to Hill 55 at Da Nang. This was during the early part of 1970 and we were located next to the ammo dump for Da Nang Air Base. We began to concentrate more on equipment maintenance and less on operational requirements. We were told to get as much of our equipment in tip top condition as we could. I believe we were in the very early stage of our withdrawal from Vietnam.

We then made the move to Freedom Hill, below Division Hq., next to the old Navy Construction Battalion Compound across the road from the Freedom Hill Exchange. It was at this stage of the withdrawal that we had to get the equipment and Motor Transport gear ready for redeployment to the United States. It was here that we traded all of our good equipment for equipment that needed extensive Depot repair. It was this equipment that we backloaded on ships for the trip home. The equipment had to be steam cleaned to pass export inspection at the shipping docks. This took a lot of man hours of work to complete the task in time.

During this time, all the troops with enough time remaining on their tour were transferred to other units in the battalion. After all the shuffling was completed, we were down to one officer and twenty-eight enlisted. Lt. Shoupe was in command and brought us back to the states. We were back loaded on two LPD ships. C Company was on the USS *Cleveland*. The ships were part of a Midshipman cruise and it was a tight fit for us Marines. We all lived in one small compartment. We started loading 31/06/70 and sailed on 10/07/70. We arrived in San Diego on 1/08/70 and moved all the equipment to Camp Pendleton. The Company was assigned to the 4th Marine Division and space in the 14 Area of Camp Pendleton with the 11th Engineer Bn. The equipment had to be gotten ready and turned over to the 11th Engineer Bn. Once all the equipment was accepted the Company folded its colors and was deactivated in August, 1970. We were all reassigned to other units and thus completed our tour.

Clyde Ricks, PFC, D Company, August 1969–February 1970

It was the left front tire of the MRS 100 tractor we were driving that set off the mine. At first all they did was sew up wounds. I had a cut under my right eye. I had my glasses on and it blew both the lenses out. I didn't know that for about 10 minutes. At first I was spitting out blood and that scared me because I thought, boy, you might have something internal. But as soon as I got to a mirror, there was a cut under my right eye and the blood was running in my mouth from it. They stitched that up and told me to take the rest of the day off. Then by the next morning I was bleeding out of my left ear.

There's another story, this will be spiritual or even religious. Within an hour or two of the time I was wounded, it would have been late morning in 'Nam, but it was Sunday evening in America. My folks were at church and the speaker promised them I'd come home okay. I asked him about it later and he said, "I didn't have any intention to do that. The spirit just told me I could make your folks that promise. It was a real sudden thing." That was real comforting to my mom.

Thomas P. Carras, 2nd Lt., A Company, B Company, Hdqtrs. Co., December 1969–September 1970

Upon return to the Battalion that was in the process of moving up to Da Nang, I was made the XO of Bravo Company that was positioned North of Tam Ky. My stint as XO under 1st Lt. Tim Turner was uneventful although I did take out my first patrol in search of hidden weapons. We didn't find anything, but we scared a lot of water buffalo.

MARCH

Thomas P. Carras, 2nd Lt.,
A Company, B Company, Hdqtrs. Co.,
December 1969–September 1970

In March, I was ordered up to Da Nang to assume duties as the Embarkation Officer under Major Doug Hibbs, the S-4. Our Battalion Commander, Lt. Col. John P. Kraynak, decided that he would get a jump on redeployment preparations so he had the four companies start to mobile load their gear and prepare to leave while maintaining operations. As we discovered, this preparation was a little presumptuous and we had to unload most of the gear. This exercise earned me a little song that my fellow Lieutenants Tom Peterson, Bob Miller, Lloyd Prosser, Bob Pruitt, Hugh Speed and Barry Smith loved to sing to me at the club. The lyrics were to the melody of "Alouette" and entitled "Carras' Embarkation." First you put it on the truck, then you take it off the truck. On the truck, off the truck — oh, Carras' Embarkation…'

JUNE

William C. Jung, Sgt.,
August 1969–July 1970

"24 June, 1970

"Dear folks,

"Happy birthday Dad! Here's hoping you'll celebrate 51 more in the years ahead!

"I sent two boxes and some film home today. The boxes contained books, clothes, my surveying course materials, and some souvenirs from Australia. There are two sets of salt and pepper shakers in there

Air strike seen from Highway #1. Courtesy of Bill Jung.

Mom. Take your pick. Pay day is only a week off, so a check will soon follow.

"Your package arrived in good shape. I thank you. I'm sitting tight on T-shirts again. The chow will come in handy down south.

"Tomorrow we head down south for a two to three week period. We have two jobs about 35 miles down the road and another about 25 miles from here. They're all road projects. We'll be staying at Hill #10, home of our B Company.

"We spent this morning greasing and generally preparing our truck and trailer for the road. They're in fine shape. Then we loaded all our gear. We would have left today, except Newt' had to go before the 'old man' for battalion office hours. The colonel busted him. So we'll head out in the morning as soon as the road is clear.

"Our trips on the road are actually quite involved, so I thought I'd take the time to explain how we've been working it.

"Here or when we were down at Chu Lai, we'd leave the compound in the morning and return around 5 in the aft; can't stay out too late on the roads over here. Sometimes as we will do in the next two weeks, we live in another compound and work out of it. Again we leave as soon as the roads are clear in the morning after the mine sweep, work all day, and return in the evening. Usually if we're a long way out, it calls for a lot of driving.

"You just don't hop in a truck and take off though. There's a war on and one has to be prepared for anything that might arise. When we're on the road there's only a few us. Our crew now is three men. Except for passing vehicles, we're by ourselves. So we carry enough gear to handle not only our work, but also fighting, the weather, or an accident, or any other situation that may arise. Our truck and trailer are loaded now. I'll list our gear we're taking south tomorrow to give you an idea of the situation we face and work in.

"1. ¾ ton load truck (Dodge) and trailer; 2. two spare tires; 3. extra gasoline; 4. tire changing gear; 5. ax, shovel, and pick; 6. fire extinguisher; 7. canvas and rope and tent; 8. tool kit; 9. surveying equipment and drafting equipment, which consisted of a lot of gear; 10. smoke grenades; 11. a radio for communication; 12. extra radio batteries; 13. chow and water; 14. a few hundred rounds of M-16 ammunition, extra; 15. first aid equipment, everything from battle dressings and band aids to malaria pills, water purification tablets, and tourniquets; 16. salt tablets; 17. an M-60 machine-gun with 600 rounds of ammo; 18. maps; 19. each man has a helmet, flak jacket, rifle, magazines and ammo, first aid gear, water, knife, and medical gear; 20. rain gear; 21. a compass.

"As you can see, we go prepared. It's always been this way with our crew. We're in the situation where we work but still have to be ready for anything else, primarily a fight. It's serious business, especially when you're on your own until help comes if necessary. All it is is a matter of not being caught with 'your pants down.' That's true in any war.

"I really enjoy the life on the road: the work, the excitement, the danger, the feeling of really being involved. You're always traveling, moving on and seeing new situations. Never a dull moment.

"Anyhow, this should give you an insight to what it's like. Then there's the heat and dust or rain and mud. There's the convoys, traffic, and civilians to contend with also.

"The work of course is shorter. 37 days about as of tomorrow. My orders aren't in yet, so I can't tell you what my next assignment is.

"All is well though, so don't worry. Maybe now that you see how organized we are in a field situation, you won't worry any.

"Hope all is well at home —
"Love,
"Bill"

HOMECOMINGS

Walter Hayes, Platoon Sgt., B Company, 1965–November 1967

I really believe that Americans feel guilty about the way Vietnam veterans were treated when they came back. I don't know if I was at the right place at the wrong time, or the wrong time at the right place. I went home just once and I was treated like a king. I went up to Milwaukee to see my brother. I wore my uniform the whole time I think. I'd get into a bar and I couldn't get out until I was drunk. [laughs]

Ted Zealley, Lt., D Company, 1 November 1965–June 1967

The real memorable feature of our departure from Vietnam was our arrival at Kadena Air Force Base in Okinawa. As 165 combat veterans departed the plane, we were greeted by newspaper headlines of the start of the 1967 Arab-Israeli War. We all wondered if we would be heading east or west from Okinawa. Our stay there was extended to five days which seemed like an eternity.

Larry P. Howell, PFC, H & S Company, May 1966–November 1966

I was Medevaced to the states with a gunshot wound to the head, so that wasn't too good. When I finally got to go to town, I was spit on, called baby killer, etc. Not what I call a good homecoming.

Fred H. Scheuter, PFC, B Company, May 1966–1967

Around March 1967 I was notified by the Red Cross that my mother was ill. I got on an airplane in Chu Lai and landed in Da Nang at three in the morning. No sooner than one minute after I got off the airplane the Viet Cong were rocketing and mortaring the area. I noticed the rockets were landing between the planes. They killed forty-one people that day. I had to wait twenty-four hours before they could send any planes in the air. I reached Okinawa the next day and I got my dress uniform out of storage. I must have built up my chest doing all that work because my uniform would not button. The next day I flew to Alaska, then to South Carolina and to New York City to meet my father. At the airport in South Carolina there was a Marine Officer who came up to me and told me that I was a disgrace to the Marines. My uniform did not button and I had no shave and haircut! I got to see my mother that day. She died that night. Before the funeral I got my uniform fixed. After about two weeks I flew back to Vietnam.

Raymond Joseph Simonetti, LCpl., Service Company, May 1966–January 1967

I was surprised to see what was going on back here in the states. When I landed and was being processed out at El Toro, there were people demonstrating at the gates. There were people trying to spit on us and calling us baby killers. It's sad when you don't have the backing and your country is not committed behind your efforts.

A lot of people put out a lot of good effort and paid the ultimate price. I developed an attitude when I saw that kind of stuff back here. It was really, really sad. When I got home I didn't have anything. I didn't have any old clothes. It was just like they didn't expect me to come home.

**Lawrence Stephen Roberge, LCpl.,
Service Company,
June 1966–January 1968**

There was nothing. When I came home my family was happy to see me, but besides that I was invisible. I left Da Nang by civilian airline. That was so great, comfortable seats, air conditioning, real food, and best of all "round-eyed" girls. We spent a couple of days in Okinawa where all my money was stolen. I never understood how a fellow Marine could steal from another. No scruples I guess. Welcome back, right? When we landed in California, I had $3.00 in my pocket and I had to get to New Hampshire. I hitched a ride to Treasure Island and got an advancement on my travel pay. It got me home and I paid my own way. It was great being home and seeing my family and friends, but there was no one to talk to. How could you talk to someone about 'Nam unless they'd been there? But it was great being home.

**Jim O'Kelley, 2 Lt.–1 Lt.–Capt.,
HQ & D Company,
August 1966–1968**

My first trip back home was in September, 1967 — a thirty day leave because I signed up for a second tour in order to insure that my two brothers did not have to serve in Vietnam and also so that I could get a Company. The first trip home was uneventful, but very nice. It sure was tough going back! I made it back, eventually got the Company after some hassle and completed my extension period primarily at Ca Lu and at Hill 63 (LZ Baldy).

My second trip home was a different story. After leaving Chu Lai we flew directly to Da Nang, spent one night there and flew via a Continental 707 to El Toro, Calif. We arrived at El Toro at "zero dark thirty" which is USMC time for somewhere between 0300 and first light of day. The USMC bussed us up to LA International. At about 0700, myself and another Marine officer were eating breakfast in a shop at the airport. We had stored our seabags in lockers and were sitting there in our summer khakis. Five "war protesters" came up and said, "You been to Vietnam?" Of course it was obvious we had. They then dumped my breakfast all over me and we got into a serious fight. To make a long story short, myself and the other Marine officer got arrested. As the police officer took us in handcuffs to the car, the paramedics were policing up the war protesters — four stretchers with IV's, etc., and one unconscious individual against the wall. The officer took us out and as we drove off he said, "Damn, guys, I'm sorry I had to arrest you, but I had to get you out of there before you killed those guys!" He turned out to be a former Marine — he didn't arrest us, but took us under the terminal to a One Hour Martinizing cleaner where we got our uniforms cleaned of food and blood, etc. He took our keys and went back and got our seabags and then took us discreetly to our airline — American Airlines. We went into the VIP lounge — he talked to someone — next thing we knew we have personal attention fit for a King and upgrades to First Class on the flight home!

So that experience conditioned me to the hate and anger so many of the "cowards" and "protesters" exhibited in 1968 and after that. The difference between my coming home in September, 1967 and May, 1968 was night and day. Frankly, I wasn't sure where the real enemy was, in Vietnam or in the U.S., and I felt in danger often in the U.S. because of my USMC haircut, etc.

As I look back now, almost thirty years later, I feel sure that we did our very best while we were there, but the politicians had already sold us out as was so evident with McNamara's book [*In Retrospect: The Tragedy and Lessons of Vietnam*]. As the quote states in Harry Summers' book [*On Strategy: A Critical Analysis of the Vietnam War*]:

"You know you never defeated us on the battlefield," said the American Colonel.

The North Vietnamese Colonel pondered this remark a moment. "That may be so," he replied, "but it is also irrelevant." (Conversation in Hanoi, April 1975)

**Ed Whitaker, PFC,
Headquarters Company,
December 1966–October 1967**

I came home and waited for orders to catch up with me because I was on emergency leave. I will say this much, when you are on an emergency leave, nobody gives you any flack. You have those little papers in your hand that say emergency leave and you go to the front of every line. Everywhere. My dad never got out of the hospital until April of the following year. He was 40 years old at the time and I thought that was old. Now I'm 47. He drove a semi-truck and for whatever reason he blacked out and ran into the back of another one, and the steering wheel caught him right in the midsection and totally destructed his midsection.

When I came home from Vietnam, I couldn't get use to how quiet it was. I didn't notice Vietnam being so noisy. It just kind of grew on me. Less than half mile from our camp they had these big holister guns. You couldn't have a shelf and have stuff sitting on it because the ground would shake so much it would fall off. It just shook the whole ground.

**Robert Terry Sperling, LCpl.,
Service Company,
December 1966–December 1967**

Spicer, Schickel, and Sperling took a small plane from Chu Lai to Da Nang. As we waited for a flight to Okinawa, the flight was canceled for about the 4th time, perhaps due to the Marine Corps trying to send too many people home for Christmas all at once. There were several hundred Marines waiting in a huge building and a very drunk Marine, upon hearing the 4th cancellation of the plane, yelled out several times very loudly, "Fuck the Marine Corps." Without hesitation another Marine knocked him out with one uppercut. It did not seem that unusual back in 1967.

In San Francisco International Airport, a civilian in charge of the U.S.O. Center informs us that we would have to leave due to the fact that they had received a bomb threat. I moved out immediately. I can still hear the Army Sergeant behind me saying, in a loud voice, "I didn't spend two tours in 'Nam to be blown up by a bunch of ********** hippies!"

I had told my family that I would be home in mid–January, not knowing if I would make it by Christmas. When my brother saw me at the door, he yelled, "Mom, Bob is home!" Mom cussed out Terry like a Drill Instructor until she heard me say, "It's me, Mom!" My mom sent me a photo when I was in Vietnam which contained our front steps and a rubber mat with the large letters *Welcome*. She was way ahead of her time. *Welcome Home*.

Myself and other Vietnam Veterans have often not spoken of our Vietnam experiences due to an unspoken taboo from society, friends, our own families and even ourselves. Only a few days after my return from Vietnam in late 1967, my mother complimented me on my never complaining about Vietnam.

When I was stationed in Iceland in 1968, the experiences of my Infantry (grunt) friends were so horrific in comparison to mine, I felt that my Vietnam experience was hardly worth mentioning. However, my experience is more similar to a higher percent of the Veterans that served in Vietnam than those of my friends from Iceland.

Ron Rainer, PFC, A Company, January 1967–October 1967

I spent about 16 straight months in Portsmith Naval Hospital. Then they retired me from the Marine Corps and sent me to Washington D.C. Veterans Hospital. That's where they fitted me for a prosthetic limb and they let me come and go everyday. I got a little apartment in Prince George, Maryland. I would come in every day for physical therapy and then I started doing radio. Then I figured things were changing with the anti-war movement going on. Even though I grew up around that particular area and would go over and visit a lot of my friends in Virginia, they weren't the same kind of people. A lot of them were into drugs and the anti-war movements. I didn't feel every comfortable around them at all. I decided to just shelf it as far as that particular part of my life was concerned.

Paul E. Virtue, LCpl., D Company, March 1967–March 1968

Friday, 15 March, 1968 Clear
Was flown out this morning from Da Nang N.A.S. (Naval Aid Station) and stayed one night.
Tuesday, 19 March Clear
Arrived at Japan in the late noon.
Wednesday, 20 March, 1968 Clear
Sat on the best seat in the house for the first time in a long time. Being restrained on a stretcher while being Medevaced, I could not use regular toilet facilities.
21 March, 1968
Left for Andrews Air Force Base, Maryland. First we have to fly to Alaska, stop then to Scott AFB, Illinois, then to Andrews. It was 02:30 when I got to bed. I left around 11:00 for Newport. With all the stops the plane made on the way, I finally got there at 17:30.

Friday, 22 March, 1968 Cloudy
The wind is really whipping up a storm outside with a few snow flurries.
Saturday, 23 March, 1968 Cloudy
The wind is cold and seems to come right on through the windows. I could look out and see the new toll-bridge being constructed in Narragansett Bay.
Monday, 25 March, 1968 Cloudy
Had some regular X-rays taken of knee and chest.
Friday, 29 March, 1968 Cloudy
Was in operating room at 11:00. Took spinal injection. I was awake during the operation, but wasn't allowed to watch (per Dr. Izzi).

Edward L. Casper, Cpl., Headquarters Company, August 1967–August 1968

When my time to rotate came, I went home alone and felt I had left a part of me there. I still have flashbacks monthly in my sleep where I will wake up in a sweat after seeing faces of Vietnam and the base. Other times I will thrash around violently and then go awful stiff as I visualize the alerts and other Vietnam sounds and sights. This is what my wife tells me.

Peter Allon, PFC, Service Company, November 1967–December 1968

When I got medevaced, they stole my seabag [laughs] and everything. I was kept in a barracks in Hansen, in Okinawa. I had to pick up a uniform out of Bremerton. They stole everything. I wasn't the only one. A lot of guys had their gear stolen, personal and whatever.

When I come out of the hospital, I was on thirty days leave. I came home and was wearing my uniform. I think I took a train. Right in the train station I got my ass whipped. [laughs] Three guys jumped me. So that wasn't a very good day when I come home.

Eric Kenney, PFC, Service Company, November 1967–December 1968

I got home close to Thanksgiving and was able to celebrate with my family. When I left, the monsoon was coming in. It was pretty bad and they kept saying, "you can't go, you can't go." So we waited a day. Nothing was flying anywhere.

There were some new guys that had just come in-country. That night the hospital area around Chu Lai got rocketed. They were scared shitless. I said, "Oh, hell, don't worry. They're shooting over there." They were really scared. There were three or four of us. I was going home and they were coming in. The only thing I can remember about that night is the damn rats kept coming up from under the pallets. A lot of guys had been through there and they'd eaten snacks. Potato chips and crackers dropping down in those pallets so it was easy pickings for those rats. They're feasting on what they could get. When they got tired of feasting on what was there, then they'd jump from the floorboards and try and get our legs. I was worried that I'd get bitten by a rat and probably have to go down and take rabies shots. That's what they would do to you. Needless to say I don't think I slept a wink that night.

I do remember flushing the toilets in Okinawa because we hadn't seen a flush toilet for over a year. A couple of us just laughed and giggled for about ten minutes, flushing the damn toilets.

We were on American Airlines on the flight from Los Angeles airport to Chicago. They had a couple of young stewardesses on there that were just absolutely beautiful. We were just overwhelmed by the fact that they had round eyes.

Dan Diridoni, LCpl., Service Company, December 1967–December 1968

Memorable silence. That would be the way I would describe my homecoming. There was so many things that I wanted to say. There was so many things that I wanted to be able to tell. My parents were not rude to me, but they didn't want to know. I think the reason they didn't want to know is because now that I'm a parent, I probably wouldn't want to know what my kid went through either. I can understand that. It was everybody else. Nobody wanted to know anything. They didn't want to talk about it. I think that's one of the reasons why there have been so many veterans that have had problems. If you hold things inside of you for too long, it will affect you.

Robert Handley, LCpl., D Company, January 1968–February 1969

I went to Pendleton to Schools Battalion, Headquarters. I was there until August of '71 when I was discharged. I got attached to Motor Transport Schools Battalion. I did some time driving for Colonel Hall. When Nixon was in office, I went to Temporary Additional Duty with the Provost Marshal's office. I was on Nixon's security up at San Clemente for awhile. It was just like guard duty. I never saw him. Nixon's compound was on the south side of San Clemente and bordered Pendleton's boundary. We weren't in the compound itself. We were on Pendleton, but right on the border there. Whenever he was in the state, we'd be called up and have to pack things up and go up there. We stayed up there on duty until he left.

I liked Nixon. [laughs] I thought he was a consummate foreign policy strategist. I didn't care for his lying, but overall I'd have to say that I liked him. Would I vote for him again? Yeah, I would. I didn't like Agnew. I wouldn't trust anyone with the first name of Spiro to begin with. [laughs] I even have an autographed picture of Nixon. When Henry Kissinger and Al Haig went to China for Nixon to open up the ties with China, I was with the MP's in that office with the secretaries. They were at the typing machines and stuff and we were guards. We were trying to get a conversation going to find out what the hell they were doing because everyone was running around with their heads cut off. We got to know the secretaries pretty well, both male and female. I just asked one if they could get me a picture. I never did meet him. But when I got separated from the service, it was like eight months later, this package came. It was a brown envelope and had his picture in it. It doesn't say "Bob" or anything. It just says "Best Wishes, Richard Nixon." It's probably an autopen. [laughs] It broke the next day that they had been negotiating with the Chinese. That was a pretty big moment. That was done at San Clemente, at the western White House.

Dave Nichols, LCpl., B Company, January 1968–February 1969

I had both a negative and a positive experience when I returned from Vietnam. Our flight landed at Travis Air Force Base, which was okay because there was a group of military dependents to greet us. I was traveling in my dress green uniform so I could get a "stand-by" ticket for half price. When we got to San Francisco Airport, to fly home, we were booed and spit at by the hippies. Then to top it off we found out that student stand-by had priority over military stand-by, so we had to stand there and wait while the hippies got on the plane. Fortunately, we did get on. The positive experience happened when I arrived at my parents' home. I got home in February 1969. As we pulled in the driveway, I saw a Christmas tree in the front window. My folks had one of the first green artificial trees, and my family decided to hold Christmas off until I got home. They put the tree up at Christmas, but only opened a few presents for the benefit of my little brother and sister who wouldn't understand. They took the tree down after Christmas, and set it up the day before I got home. I just couldn't believe it!

Brian Althouse, PFC, A Company, March 1968–October 1969

Five days before you leave the hill, you don't have to go out on the sweep. But I went out until three days before I left. The Vietnamese kids would sell you stuff and they found a Mark 5. It was in a rice paddy. It was on the inside of a dike, in other words, if you were going to step up on the dike, you'd take one step and then step up on the dike. And if you stepped on that, it would blow your leg off. So I paid them money for that and they showed me where it was. I'm not going to disarm anything. I'm going to blow it right there in place. I was setting the charge, but my hands were shaking so bad when I was capping the fuse with the blasting cap. I was crimping it and my hands were shaking so bad I thought, shit. I set it to a little piece of C4, put it around the cap, took it down, lit it with a cigarette, ran back and blew it. Then I said, that's it. I'm going in today. So I stayed in the last two days. At Da Nang I looked like the guys I saw when we first got off the plane. I felt sorry for the new guys coming in. I felt bad for them because they didn't even know what they were in for.

Bill Spadafora, Cpl., C Company, A Company, June 1968–July 1969

I volunteered to go to Vietnam. I felt it was my duty. I love the Marine Corps. I love my country. I thought my country loved me until I came home. I remember coming home after we came back from Okinawa and landing in the United States. The Receiving Officer told us that, "If you can, get into civilian clothes, and travel in civilian clothes because military people are really not welcomed, or you may incite some problems. People may look down on you." I really couldn't believe that so I wore my uniform home, all the way home to New York. I got into New York about 4:00 in the morning. My parents were waiting for me. But I wouldn't trade my uniform for anything. I wouldn't trade my experience for anything. [pause] I know we didn't have any parades, but we do have the Vietnam Memorial which I think is important because I've got a lot of friends on that wall. As much as I don't go and see them as often as I should, when I do go I can feel them. I touch that wall and I feel the compassion of all the families, of all the suffering that's occurred. Hopefully this country has learned from this mistake. Whether it's a mistake or not, I don't know.

Martin L. Brown, PFC, D Company, August 1968–August 1969

Two weeks after I left Vietnam, they gave me a five month early out. What they were trying to pull was to have us sign waivers, that if we took an early out, we would give up our GI bill rights. We were stupid. I don't remember signing the thing. I sent away and got my 201 file and I found that form in there. They made them illegal immediately. Once they found out, they just made them illegal. So I got out five months free and still had all my benefits. They knew eventually most of us were going to have some stress reaction. For a year or more after I got back I was homesick to go back to Vietnam.

My mother never really said anything. My father couldn't accept the fact that I got a five-month early out. I had only done a year and a few months. I was home probably four or five weeks and one day he just started yelling at me. He told me I was AWOL and to get the hell out of his house. [laughs] I never really had much to do with him after that.

Jim Tagye, PFC, D Company, August 1968–February 1969

After I was wounded, I spent nine-and-a-half months in a hospital. I was discharged from the hospital November 16th. I went home and just lived a normal existence until February the 12th 1970 when I was officially discharged. Six and a half of those months in the hospital I couldn't walk. I have a lot of heavy damage to my legs and my feet. My spleen was taken out and my stomach was blown open. I was hit pretty bad. Maybe that's why I'm more bitter. I feel the pain every day.

I'm from Philadelphia and it's a different feeling. Maybe that's why I hide it. My family, naturally, gave me a big celebration when I got home, but that was it. No one ever wanted to talk about Vietnam. Even my family didn't want to talk about it. None of my friends in Philadelphia wanted to talk about it.

I can remember my trip home. I was on a stretcher and I was coming home from Japan. They routed me from Japan to Alaska, to Michigan, to Washington. I had my own nurse taking care of me. We got to Alaska and she said, "What do you want?" I said, "I want some snow." It was so hot in Vietnam, even though it was about twenty-five days between the time I left Vietnam before I actually made it home. I said, "I'd like to have some snow." She went out and got me some snow. I can still remember that. From Washington they put me on a private jet and sent me to Philadelphia. Then they picked me up and took me to a VA hospital. That's how I came back.

Clyde Ricks, PFC, D Company, August 1969–February 1970

When I got medevaced, they flew us to Travis Air Force Base and then I was a patient at the Oakland Naval Hospital for just over two months. I was euphoric. I just stayed euphoric for the first few months after I got home from 'Nam. It was just so nice. It was so safe and nice. I had a former baby-sitter and her husband was working construction in that area. One Sunday afternoon they came up and got me and took me on a picnic with them. Afterwards they took me to their apartment. I can remember being stunned at how nice and clean it was. After all those months you almost forget what real homes are like.

**Thomas P. Carras, 2nd Lt.,
A Company, B Company, Hdqtrs. Co.,
December 1969–September 1970**

Needless to say, the 9th Engineer Battalion was ordered to stand down on 19 July, 1970 for preparation to redeploy to Camp Pendleton as part of President Nixon's Phase IV redeployment schedule. My job as the Battalion Embarkation Officer took on a whole new meaning as ships were being scheduled to Da Nang to embark, not only the 9th's redeployment, but the 7th Engineer Battalion and the 1st Bridge Company. The first ship that I developed embarkation plans for was the USS *Cleveland*. This turned out to be an exercise in frustration due to the mission the Captain of the ship had in mind. I had planned to load the ship with a large amount of bridge bulk as well as rolling stock. Unbeknownst to me until they arrived was that there was a contingent of midshipmen aboard from the Naval Academy for their summer cruise. So, while the middies enjoyed a day of sun and fun at China Beach, I had to load the ship.

My first problem arose when the loading started to bog down. The U.S. Army ran the Port of Da Nang and I couldn't get exclusive use of the loading craft. The Combat Cargo Officer of the ship, under pressure from the skipper, kept fretting about the amount of "junk" we were putting on his ship and the time it was taking. Well, when the middies staggered back to the ship, I had only loaded about half of the staged equipment. I then heard the announcement over the ship's intercom ordering all non-party personnel to return to shore. Although my boss, as well as the 1st Marine Division representative, tried to intercede, I found myself standing on the dock as the USS *Cleveland* steamed away. I later heard that when the ship arrived in Hawaii, the Captain was censured and that a new policy requiring all ships to be fully loaded upon departing Yankee Station was issued.

I must report that all further embarkation plans went well as we started redeployment. In support of the Army of Vietnam (ARVN) we were ordered to display our best 5 ton trucks, PRC-77 radio's and M-16's for their selection. Additionally, every compound we pulled out of had to be left immaculate before they would accept it back. Numerous hours were spent cleaning and restoring facilities for the ARVN takeover. One of the biggest jobs to be accomplished prior to embarking any equipment was the environmental cleaning. Every unit begged, borrowed or stole a steam generator to complete this onerous task. The environmental inspectors took their job very seriously and caused great heartache when they continually failed pieces of equipment due to minute specks of Vietnamese earth found in unaccessible places. Finally, on August 23, 1970 I, along with most officers, staff NCO's and some key equipment operators started loading the USS Juneau (LPD-10). The Battalion had sent most of the troops home by way of Pan Am, so working around the clock we crammed bulldozers, trucks, jeeps, trailers, scrapers with pans, cranes and the rockcrusher units all loaded with gear aboard this Landing Platform Dock. Even the flight deck was covered with 9th Engineer equipment. On September 10, 1970 after eighteen days of devising ways to annoy the Navy officers (eating all their popcorn before the evening movie worked well) and suntanning, we pulled into Long Beach Harbor with the last contingent of the 9th Engineer Battalion. Accompanying Lt. Col. Kraynak was Capt. Brad West, 1st Lts. Mike Harris, Harris Lancaster, Chuck Atwater, Jack Nance, Barry Smith and yours truly. We were home!

The official deactivation of the 9th Engineer Battalion, 5th Marine Amphibious Brigade took place on 20 October, 1970 in the 14 area, Camp Pendleton, California.

YESTERDAY AND TODAY

Walter Hayes, Platoon Sgt., B Company, 1965–November 1967

I stayed four years overseas. In 1960 I went to Japan and didn't come back to the states until '64. I went all over the Far East. As far as the culture, it didn't bother me at all, but it was a shock to the younger guys to see how people lived overseas. I had been through it and I had no hate for anybody. I got to admit that but I can't understand why I just didn't like the Vietnamese people. I loved every place I went. Japan, Thailand, Okinawa, Korea, anywhere I went I just fell in love with the people. I think seeing Americans hurt might have played a part in it, but deep down in my heart I can't say that. I don't hate them, I just have a feeling a lot of it has to do with hygiene. We built bathrooms for so many of the villages and taught them hygiene. Then we'd come back and they'd never been used. Feces would be all around outside rather than them go in and use them.

I got to admit I was a little disappointed in Saudi. I was one of these guys, probably, when I seen all these homecoming and all that, at first I didn't even give it a second thought. That's great for these young boys. Then I got to thinking, that's sort of shitty. When they did that, they put all the Vietnam veterans down. I don't even hold a grudge. I don't see what they did in Saudi. As a matter of fact, I've got a couple of kids working for me right here who were in the Marine Corps and went to Saudi. They'd be the first to tell you that they really didn't do anything. The Air Force did everything. Then they get the welcome back.

Robert F. Goins, Captain, A Company, November 1965–May 1966

My overall feeling about our commitment in Vietnam is that we should have had the full support of our country behind us. Any shortcoming in victory was due to the protests of cowards who showed a divided country and therefore strengthened our enemy.

Larry P. Howell, PFC, H & S Company, May 1966–November 1966

My experience in Vietnam wasn't easy. It was hard not knowing who the enemy was or who was friendly. A lot of people were killed for nothing. I think it was a money maker, a political ball game. Our government stuck their nose where it didn't belong and used us for their gain. There are 58,196 names on the Wall in Washington, D.C. that shouldn't be there and that is not counting the men and women who took their own life or died of Agent Orange. They will never be on the Wall and that number is over 130,000.

I no longer can work because of problems from Vietnam. I drank heavy for 23 years trying to bury the hurt. Now I don't drink, but I am troubled by PTSD and other problems related to Vietnam and our government. The Veterans Administration doesn't give a shit about us or doing anything for us. It is hard when you can't provide for your family the way you need to, with pride and dignity, and have to fight for everything you need or should have. I wished it could have been different and I think the Government *sucks* 'cause of what they ain't doing for the POW/MIA's.

Fred H. Scheuter, PFC, B Company, May 1966–1967

I feel it was wrong now that we were over there. I still think it was wrong about how we were treated when we came back home from 'Nam. I would like to see my son join the Marines, but not to fight in a war like Vietnam.

Raymond Joseph Simonetti, LCpl., Service Company, May 1966–January 1967

The only thing I would like to tell the world is simply before you go ahead and commit combat troops into a combat situation they need to have the resolve and the backing of the country and the politicians and all concerned. This halfhearted type thing or piecemeal type thing just doesn't get it. Something like that should not take place unless there is a firm commitment and 58,000 people weren't wasted in vain for no reason whatsoever other than to show the communists that we were willing to fight and die.

I felt the politicians basically drove the troops over there without the commitments and simply sold us out. Also, I felt that there was not only a political type deal, but I think a lot of big people in the country made a lot of bucks. Officer Bly and people like myself were the tools of war, so to say, but a lot of people were getting rich while a lot of guys like myself were getting killed. I don't think that's changed. I think the country has learned a lot of lessons. Anytime you want to go play war you always take all your tools and play with them to the full extent.

I volunteered the first time around and I'd probably volunteer the second time around. The only thing I would say is don't tie our hands behind our backs the second time around. If you want to send me to do a job, then let's rock and roll and go. It has a lot to do with advice and dealing with my son. My son was looking to go in the service and he asked me my opinion. I told him the service is a good place to get a start. If you are thinking about the Marine Corps because I was in it, he couldn't serve with a bunch of better guys. They are all number one. However, this country will find some asshole place in the world to drop you off and you will find yourself in a fox hole waiting for some gook son of a bitch to come up and slit your throat. You'll be looking at the same moon as the people back home and the difference is they are in a peaceful situation and you are in a hostile situation. So, if you want that type of thing, I suggest that you join the Army or the Marine Corps and they will definitely find someplace for you to experience that.

I recommended the Navy to my son and he went for the education. He is in electronics, serving on the nuclear sub Holland. I guess I'm getting paid back for what I put my parents through, volunteering to go to a war zone and all this other stuff. It's hard. I know he is not in any imminent danger. I don't think there are any gooks running around on his ship looking to slice his throat. I just tried to give him a shot of reality that this will definitely happen and this is what you are asking for if you volunteer for it. It will definitely come to pass and so far I haven't missed my call. There has been Somalia. We have our Bosnia.

I believe when you are ready to send boys off to war and enter them in combat zones, I don't think you ought to be going around dumping chemicals on them and in the areas that they are working in. If you are going to send people into combat, you've got to back them then, you've got to back them when they come home and you've got to back them throughout the rest of their lives. What they are ultimately doing is putting their all on the line. You ought to be right when you send them because they are right in what they are doing and they are trying to do what is being asked of them by their country.

When I watched Desert Storm, I thought those people never, never, never could possibly touch what went on in Vietnam. They tried to piecemeal Vietnam, a little here, a little there, and they never made the full commitment. In Desert Storm they were committed. It's what I've been saying all along. They kicked some butt. They did their thing, but they were prepared and they were given the authority to go ahead and do that. I think they pulled up a little short and I don't understand why they cut them off. I guess that's where the politics came in. The guys deserved everything they had coming.

Lawrence Stephen Roberge, LCpl., Service Company, June 1966–January 1968

The world only saw the killing, the destruction, and a country being destroyed. Most of the world never saw the good things being done. I know that only the bad news makes good movies, news and television, but a lot of good was done by a lot of good and proud men.

Being a Marine in 'Nam is probably what made me who I am today. I grew up very fast. Being from a small town in New Hampshire, I had no idea what was out there in the world, never mind the 'Nam. I found out that things that I used to take for granted here at home were nonexistent in 'Nam. I matured fast in 'Nam, and I learned that it is not the valuables you put in the bank or put in your pocket that make you someone. It is the people you touch, the friends, the memories, and yes, some were good. Today, 28 years later, I still don't have a bank account, but I have a great family that's like gold and many friends that I cherish very much.

I'd say everything about 'Nam was interesting. A culture I knew nothing about, a land that was so primitive, a way of life that was strange and foreign to me. Here is a people that work from sun up to sun down just to exist. There was no pay, no vacation, no weekends, no retirement, no way out. If they were lucky, they would survive to be 30 or 40 years old. Why? Why work so hard to end up with nothing? Their way of life, their religion, their culture, that was interesting.

Would I go back to 'Nam knowing what I do now? Yes, in a minute. Knowing what I know now I'd be more serious about my job as a Marine, but I wouldn't hesitate at all about going back. 'Nam was a very important part of my past. Some of it I'd love to forget, but some of it is so meaningful and has made me the person I am today. There was a lot of suffering in 'Nam, but also a lot of learning and growing up for me. Every vet from 'Nam comes back with a different feeling in his or her heart, different memories. Some want to forget, some can't, I don't want to forget. Those 19 months were and still are too damn important to me. I don't want to live and dwell in them, but I don't want to forget them.

I hate wars, but I do think they are necessary. I can't imagine the horror if we would have stayed out of World War II. Just think of Hitler controlling the world! The only sad part of the 'Nam war was that it was fought by politicians, not by the generals. Too many hands tied. Too many rules. When you let the generals do their job, as in Desert Storm, things get done.

It was scary to think we were going to war again, but it was great the way the military handled it. We went in, finished it, and got out. It's too bad Saddam wasn't finished, but the men and women of Desert Storm did a great job. Their homecoming was great. Maybe 'Nam vets should be jealous, they have a right to be, but we have to live on. We can't take away from what they did and deserve. Great job to Desert Storm.

Ed Whitaker, PFC,
Headquarters Company,
December 1966–October 1967

One thing I was surprised about in Vietnam was that it was never a war. According to our United States Constitution, it was never declared a war. It was a conflict. If it had been a war, there's a different set of rules that are implemented. Over there you just can't start shooting. One day we had a patrol out and were getting shot at. The first thing we had to do was have the radioman call back to our headquarters and then they have to call over to division headquarters to see if they could return fire. Meantime, you could get shot up or whatever. You just can't start shooting.

I just have some real mixed feelings because of how the whole conflict went over there. It was too much of a political thing. These Vietnamese that were hauling this rock, they had a French war over there in the 50s, and they had these old trucks that they had fixed up. They also had brand new Ford dump trucks and brand new International dump trucks over there. How did these Vietnamese have enough money to have them imported from the United States, clear to Vietnam, just to haul this rock? There was people in Vietnam that had the right influence with the right people. My neighbor bought a truck just identical to one in Vietnam and he paid $4,000 for it here. In Vietnam it cost $8,000.

A lot of guys that I went to school with went to Canada. I have a lack of respect for them because they did that. I can't believe I would go to Canada. I know the VFW had a hard time with Jimmy Carter when he pardoned them. I remember his speech enough as to where he says "now there is a difference here men." Well, it's either right or wrong, nothing in between. All the people who went to Canada have now come back. I don't know of anyone that is still gone. I know of one man in particular. He was quite an athlete in school, quite popular and so forth. "We're all going to Vietnam." "I don't think so," and he was gone in a flash. He works for the county now in parks and recreation. I can't say that I really hold it against him. I can't say I'm bitter towards him, I will be polite to him. But I guess I will always feel he didn't do right and I can't respect him.

On the other side of the coin maybe neither one of us want to be in a war situation, but I don't want that person to be a flake either. He is going to have to do his best while he is there. I'm going to save his life or he's going to save mine. If a guy is just not with it, he might be better off in Canada because he's not going to do us any good.

The biggest thing with the Persian Gulf thing was it was on the news. With today's technology we knew within just a matter of minutes after some target was hit. In Vietnam it wasn't like that. It was more of a delayed reaction to the different events and happenings.

I had mixed feelings about the homecoming for the Desert Storm troops and I'm probably not going to explain them or express them in the manner that I'm going to say them. The country felt so bad that they messed up with the Vietnam Vets that we're going to really do something for this group of people. I don't know if that's right or not, but you know they got recognition right away, where with the Vietnam Vets it took forever.

Ron Rainer, PFC, A Company,
January 1967–October 1967

I have suffered some pretty bad injuries

from Vietnam and I came back home. I was able to get my undergraduate schooling and graduate schooling on the GI Bill. Even though I lost one limb and lost the use of the other limb and had eye damage in one eye, I was still able to get my education. I was still able to work a good 20 years. I had my own business for about nine years in the timber business. I was able to do most of the things I wanted.

You have to either quit or go on. That's the way it is. I think the Marine Corps training had a lot to do with my perspective on life. No matter what your situation you have to try to reach your goal. I think the self discipline in the Marine Corps had a lot to do with me being able to overcome my injuries and not worrying about so much what anybody else thought about my injuries. I was able to put a lot of things behind me regardless of discrimination in some places. I don't think it will ever change. I think things have gotten better for disabled people, but it's still there.

I'm a little bit confused about what's happened to some of the veterans that have come home. I know that I went through college and graduate school during the anti-war days and I had some very negative experiences, but I had some very positive experiences. You have to weigh them out and go on.

I would think if you got into a situation where you were consistently down on yourself and consistently made your own negative daily experiences, then you could very well end up with post traumatic stress. But, again I think a lot of it goes back to your roots and to religion. I have always been a church-goer and I continued that through the Marine Corps. I continued that even when I was in the hospital recuperating. Faith has a lot to do with those things, too. I think I have been very fortunate in life.

My wife was killed in a car wreck in 1983 and I have a little girl that just turned twelve. I have been raising her ever since my wife was killed. She is doing quite well in school and wants to go to Auburn.

Us little ones, we're not in control of the political atmosphere or the business atmosphere as far as wars are concerned. It's sad that so many people were used up because I think we have a lot of people on that wall, and a lot of people with severe mental injuries that would have made excellent politicians and businessmen and everything else.

Robert Terry Sperling, LCpl, Service Company, December 1966–December 1967

Just before Desert Storm I was very worried about the possibility of hundreds of Marines being killed in an Amphibious Attack of Kuwait City. I was also *very* worried about the possibility of a chemical war. I felt very uncomfortable watching Desert Storm on television, however I watched everything I could. After returning from Vietnam I unconsciously chose to never watch it on television.

Edward L. Casper, Cpl., Headquarters Company, August 1967–August 1968

I am not a believer in war or against war. I feel that there are times when if all else fails, military strength may be needed. I believe no one has the right to force people into submission by murder, threats and so on. I am proud of my service and did not do anything to bring discredit to myself, comrades or country. I wear my Purple Heart proudly in honor of those other wounded and the ones that lost their lives.

I thought it was great that the servicemen and women received a wonderful homecoming after Desert Storm as they deserved it for a job well done. Again, there were sacrifices. This was a welcome home that all Vietnam veterans should have gotten. My Air Force Reserve unit,

52nd APSS Squadron, was activated and sent to Saudi Arabia to support Desert Storm. Our job was to evacuate wounded back away from the combat zone. We were attached to the 3rd Marine Air Wing Marine Corps.

This was my second war and I almost got emotional when we stepped off the plane coming home at Kennedy Airport in New York and hundreds of people that we did not know rushed to meet us shook our hands, and even gave us a hug. It was especially gratifying to see the children do it. We received free phone calls home, free pizza and beer or soft drinks. I received my coming home now and for 20 years ago.

Anonymous

The POW/MIA issue is something that really bothers me. I'd give anything to help the MIA and their family. In front of my home I fly the flag, on my car I have the stickers, on both my wrists I wear bracelets and I have a POW/MIA dog tag. Why? I don't want to forget. I don't want anyone else to forget. Just the thought of having one of my sons missing in action brings tears to my eyes. Not knowing whether they were alive or dead would drive me crazy. When they die, you bury them, and you grieve, but missing in action and never knowing is a real nightmare.

I keep having this dream where a hooded figure comes to me and tells me "it's time." It's time for me to trade places with him. He's a POW who wants to go back to his family and I have to take his place. The real scary thing is that as I take his place, my three kids fade away and my family is gone. Some nights I wake up with big tears in my eyes.

I came home from 'Nam after 19 months without a scratch. Seeing all those who died, those who came home with so many things wrong with them has always made me feel somewhat guilty. It feels like I haven't done my best, like I owe something to all those guys.

I don't think the hurt will ever go away. I don't want it to. While I feel the hurt, it makes me feel like I'm giving back to all those who gave so much.

Would I let my sons go? It would hurt me very much to see them go, but if it was their decision to go I wouldn't try to stop them. I pray to God I never have to make that decision.

Charles King, Sgt., B Company, September 1967–September 1968

I was a career Marine. The biggest thing was that I missed my family. To me it was a job to do, and it had to be done, but that was just it. I thought we were there for a reason, and I have different thoughts on it now. At that time it was a job to be done and we should have done it and got out.

Politically, we were held back. That's my personal opinion. But, all the guys were great and I enjoyed serving with them.

Peter Allon, PFC, Service Company, November 1967–December 1968

I didn't think very much of the draft dodgers who came to Canada. [laughs] They wouldn't fight for the States, and Canada opened the door. If Canada ever went to war, they sure as hell wouldn't fight for Canada. They were king of the castle in Canada and took all the jobs. A lot of them were educated in the peace movement, so they were taking the jobs of the guys that joined. They still got draft dodgers up there now that wouldn't go back to the States. They got it made in Canada now. [laughs]

There were 26,000 of us Canadians that joined the service and served in Vietnam. 26,000 of us from the time it started until the time it ended, and most of them were in the Marine Corps. We still have three

MIA's ... somewhere. A lot of us came back all screwed up. We still are, aye. We were treated the same way as the Americans were. The draft dodgers were very much an agitator, especially in the Universities. Before the draft dodgers came up there was no dissension in Canada about the Vietnam War.

They say a lot about the Americans being over there, but there were a lot of Australians, Koreans and Turks. There were a whole bunch of people there that haven't gotten recognized.

Canada made nothing but money from the war. They had a lot of CIL ammunition over there. [laughs] DuPont, out of Montreal, which made all that Agent Orange defoliant. But they were never involved because it was sort of hid under the table and this is a very bad point with a lot of us guys. They supplied millions and millions of dollars but Canada never supported the war.

Eric Kenney, PFC, Service Company, November 1967–December 1968

The world has really changed a lot since 1968 both dramatically and drastically. The things that we did, or we didn't do in 'Nam are now being recorded in history books. The true nature and understanding of our presence will continue to be debated for decades. I know that we gave the full measure of our talents in body, in mind and in spirit while a majority of our nation looked on with confusion, disbelief and mostly silence. I remember Nixon's "silent majority." I truly feel you ought never commit soldiers to the ultimate sacrifice unless we first decide the ultimate goal or ideal that we must accomplish. There is no honor without courage, and no courage without honor. I know that I personally went to Vietnam for honorable reasons and returned courageous. But I was in it for both. "A dirty little war that nobody really wanted to win." I ask you, is that a legacy to die for? Is that our legacy? You can see your own reflection if you stand in just the right place when you visit the wall. So God bless Malloy and Williams and Clark from Platoon 2219. And God bless "Heavy" Savare and the forty-two other 9th Engineers that we know of, because there's nothing left but Semper Fidelis.

John Vasarab, PFC, Service Company, 1967–1968

Their biggest mistake was letting the press and other media in there to film our men in body bags and on the ground bleeding while waiting for a chopper ride to a hospital. You cannot show *Mom* and *Dad* Public their son being medevaced while they are eating supper. The people of this country do not have the mentality to comprehend war. The men in uniform know they might die, but not the public. War is death and destruction, pure and simple. The only sad part is that some innocent civilians must also die. You cannot be the nice guy in the war and try to win the people over with soap and first aid stations. You must sink to the same level as your enemy to show you are just as determined to win as he is.

When you have people in your country trying to undermine your military and their actions, you have already lost and might as well pick up your ball and go home. When I returned, I was not the same "boy" that left thirteen months before. My attitude changed towards most things. What people in this country think is important doesn't mean much in places like Vietnam. The people that ran to Canada or hid out in college because they didn't approve of the war don't deserve this country. They will always be runners and wimps. They take everyday life for granted and won't do anything to protect it. The everyday life of the young in this country is more than most kids in the world could ever hope for. If they don't have running water, heat, prepared food, great clothes or any other of life's must-haves, they would be lost. They could not survive on their own for two days. The country they live in is the best thing going and they are blind to that fact. What they need is to be exposed to an alternate lifestyle for a year. Then, and only then, will they know what they have.

As far as I am concerned the war in Vietnam didn't seriously screw up my mind. The only thing that I have a habit of doing is to tell people to quit their sniveling and keep going. Life doesn't end with one set-back. I also tell them what I think of them or their ideas. Sometimes it gets me the dirty end of the stick, but the world didn't end because of it. What I had seen and done over there had changed me. I cannot stand people who have this idea of self importance. They are no better than me or you. They might have more than me, but that doesn't make them better. I am by no means a radical or a nut case, but if I don't like something, I say so. Honesty is very hard for people to handle. I will not lie about anything because I don't know who would change my life that much, that a lie would help. There are stupid things that people do that I cannot handle very well either.

I am by no means anti-war. If somebody needs their clock cleaned, and it will serve the most people by doing so, then let it happen. Desert Storm was a good way to fight a war. Have at it but don't stop until you are completely done. Make them know that you will put them on the endangered species list if they try anything again.

Dan Diridoni, LCpl., Service Company, December 1967–December 1968

It seems like people started opening up about ten years ago. In the last four or five years it has become acceptable to say that you are a veteran.

I feel I was cheated out of my youth for no reason. I feel very strongly about what I did. At the time I thought it was the proper thing. The guys that went to Canada, not to avoid the draft but to make a statement, are people that I respect just as much as people that went to Vietnam with me. They believed in what they were doing at the time. I believe they had their childhood robbed from them, too. I know I am very bitter about it actually to be quite honest with you.

I wish I had those years back. One thing I'm a bit testy about, when the conversation comes up, "you boys lost that war." That is the most absurd statement I have ever heard in my entire life. If you look and read anything you want about this war, we never ever lost any major battles in that country. We never lost Tet. We inflicted more casualties.

I had mixed feelings on Desert Storm. First of all, I was very, very happy with the way that they conducted the war. I was really fearful for the guys going there, first of all. I would much rather be in the jungle than I would be in the damn desert with open ground like that. But, second of all, I liked the way they went in there with the air power and minimized casualties. I thought that was terrific, the way it should of been. But I think there was a lot of political things falling into that, too. There was a lot of things underneath the surface of why we were there.

I felt very jealous, but I was proud of them, too. I met quite a few of those fellows, and I thought it was terrific but I think a lot of it was guilt. I think that maybe a lot of people didn't want to have the same stigma attached to these boys as the last group of boys. I think they might have overdone it a bit. At least if we are in a situation that the majority, and I say that loosely, the majority of the people feel that a situation is correct to be in, then let's get behind it.

Robert Handley, LCpl., D Company, January 1968–February 1969

There is no way I would go again knowing what I know now about why we were there and who was pushing the buttons. The President and the Secretary of Defense were telling our strike aircraft where to bomb from a desk in Washington, D.C.

I was 100 percent behind Desert Storm because it was led right and there was planning. They knew when they were going in and when they were coming out. They had goals. They could see what they were doing. Bush let them do it and they did it. They were successful. I'm sorry about the casualties. Aside from friendly fire we would have gotten out of there relatively unscathed.

Their homecoming was pretty good. I thought it was great. It didn't bother me at all. The only people that I hear that are really bugged by that are the ones who are down and out, alcoholics or drug addicts, people that probably would have had a problem in life anyway. They have Vietnam to blame it on. I know a lot of vets that you don't hear about. They are successful businessmen and are participating citizens in their communities. They don't gripe about anything. They aren't on welfare. They have good jobs and have had them for years.

Dave Nichols, LCpl, B Company, January 1968–February 1969

The thing we did wrong in Vietnam was the way we fought the war. The politicians back in Washington, D.C. should have kept their noses out of it. We had the skill and technology to wipe North Vietnam off the face of the Earth but were never allowed to use it. There were important targets in North Vietnam that couldn't be touched because some civilians might be killed. Fighter jets could not be attacked while they were on the ground. What kind of way is that to fight a war? You certainly won't win a war this way. We had similar problems in South Vietnam. In some cases, while we were on guard duty, we had to get permission before we could shoot at someone. I remember that once, after we had moved back to Chu Lai, we had a guy taking pictures of our guard bunkers. I requested permission to shoot, but the Officer of the Day said no. He decided that because the man was not in uniform he was probably a tourist. Yeah, right!

If I was in the Marines again, I would go wherever they sent me, no questions asked. I would not desert. If there was a draft, I would not flee to Canada. This brings me to another point. I don't think we should have pardoned the draft dodgers who fled to Canada. They violated federal laws and should have been prosecuted for it. I know the President was trying to heal wounds, but I don't think it helped. If anything, I think it made things worse. Those of us who went to 'Nam couldn't help but wonder how these cowards could run to Canada to save their own skin, and now could come back home and face no penalty. It is a slap in the face to those who served and especially those who are now handicapped as a result of injuries sustained in the 'Nam. Of course, I guess I must now be in the minority with this opinion because we now have a draft dodger as Commander in Chief. I refer to Clinton as the "Coward in Chief."

I guess I would still be considered pro–war. To me the term anti–war means we never would be involved in a war. I still think there are times when war is necessary. The gulf war is one example. We need a large military might to keep this country safe. I don't think we would have seen the fall of Communism if we had been militarily weak. I just think that before we commit troops, we need to know the purpose and goals and how long we expect them to remain there. We also need to let the military run the war and keep the civilian politicians out of it.

I was wishing I was there when I watched Desert Storm. It looked like this was going to be a war we could win, and the public was in support of it which was something we didn't see much of during 'Nam. Also, the young men had very few actual combat veterans they could talk to about what to expect. I cried like a baby during the homecoming they had. They stepped off the plane to thousands of cheering people. They were greeted by their family members, right there at the airport, another advantage of moving whole units in and out of combat together, instead of as individuals like they did with Vietnam. It was very emotional to see them hugging their wives and children, but there were other emotions as well. They came home heroes. Bands were playing, people were cheering, there were even parades in some cities. We came home to boos and were called baby killers. We fought just as hard and under conditions just as bad, and we were in Vietnam for thirteen months, but we were rejected by our own country when we returned home. I guess I was jealous. I was glad they had the whole country supporting them. I am one of those supporters. It was good to see a war fought the way it should be with the military leaders running it. It was just hard to think back to what we endured when we came home.

**Bill Spadafora, Cpl.,
C Company, A Company,
June 1968–July 1969**

If I had to do it all over again, I think I'd do it again. I don't think I would do it for my government as much as I would do it for the people that are oppressed, whether it be the people of South Vietnam or people who are oppressed in other countries. I think it is important that the United States use its military power to alleviate suffering and hunger and prosecution and persecution and murder by other countries and their government. I would certainly lay down my life again for my country anytime. Whenever I mention I was in the Marine Corps, the 9th Engineer Battalion is the first thing that I mention because of the fact that I served with them.

I think that it's important that people understand, especially the younger generation, about what the Vietnam Era meant to this country and some of the consequences that we suffered. Also what happened to our men and women that served over there, and how they were treated when they came home. I really can't tell you how much I appreciate you giving us the opportunity to tell our story.

**Jim Tagye, PFC, D Company,
August 1968–February 1969**

The way I feel about it now, after doing a lot of reading of history, I really feel that it was an unjust war. I don't think we should have been there. I'm very bitter at the fact that the Johnson Administration, Johnson himself, would not let us fight the war the way we should have fought it. I think a lot of men were killed for no reason at all. I'm very bitter against it.

I started to gather information regarding our involvement in the war. As I was doing this, McNamara's book [*In Retrospect: The Tragedy and Lessons of Vietnam*] came out. The information I had was leading me to the same conclusion about the involvement that McNamara wrote about. The more I researched, the more angry I got. In my opinion, the people who got us into the war should have been tried as war criminals. It's a shame we can't lock them up now. There was no reason to be in this war. All the misery it caused so many people is not fair.

I'm proud that I served there, but I'm also bitter that we lost 58,000 men for nothing. I really feel that we went there for no reason at all except so Johnson could get some extra votes in the election, and some other reasons, but that weren't justified. I just don't think we should have been there in the first place. But I'm proud to have served though.

I thought the country was beautiful. I would like to go back as a civilian to see where I was. I think that would be interesting. I'm a pacifist today. I don't believe in war, I guess because I've experienced it. I see what happened to a lot of guys. I spent nine and a half months in the hospital. I saw a lot of guys come back without legs, without eyes, without arms. I was next to them in the hospital, and I just don't believe in war at all.

Up until recently I hadn't fired a rifle for twenty-six years. I am an anti–gun person although I'm not against people that go hunting. I believe they should have that. But now I'm starting to change my mind. I'm thinking about even possibly buying a gun myself. I may never do it, but I see the crime wave happening out there and it's scary.

One of the reasons why our war was so different from the Second World War and the Korean War was that it was a seven-day war, twenty-four hours a day, three-hundred-sixty-five days a year, three-hundred-sixty degree war. It was all around us. If you take the First Marine Division in the Second World War, after they got through with Guadalcanal, which was a six-month campaign, they were sent back to Melbourne, Australia for a year before they hit the next campaign. This is basically the concept of the Second World War with the Marines and the Army. They would get in the big campaigns, but they might only last two weeks. Then they might have a six-month R&R before they had to go replenish it. We were constantly surrounded by it. We were always in a war, for twelve months, or thirteen months, whatever you had to stay. That is one of the significant differences between our war and their war.

I have run into discrimination from World War II vets. Maybe it was more perception than anything. When I was out at Camp Pendleton, in February, the World War II vets wanted to get a picture. They all were getting together. Then the China Marines said, "Can we join you?" The World War II vets said, "Come on." Then the Korean vets said, "Can we join you?" They said, "Sure." There were only a few Vietnam vets there, so we asked if we could join. They said, "No." I don't know why that was. I never did ask my uncle, but I really felt very slighted. I felt very hurt inside that they didn't consider us as part of the warriors like they were. We did just as much, if not more, than they did. I felt so sad inside. That's the first time I felt the hostility from the Second World War vets. Otherwise, I've been hanging around a lot of them, and they're really great guys. Maybe it was more my perception than anything else. Maybe they didn't really feel that way.

Given the status quo, I would not go. Knowing what I do know today about the war, about the history of it, I would not go at all. I mean, if it was a justifiable war, I would definitely be proud to serve my country. And I am proud I went, but I don't think I'd go back. Because of the fact that I'm in pain every day from the wounds I suffered. I can't do a lot of walking. I can't do a lot of standing. I was a jock before I joined the service. I came back and I couldn't play any sports again. It really has disturbed my life a lot, and a lot more than I think I know.

My first reaction when I saw that we first bombed Iraq ... I got sick to my stomach for two hours. I was visibly shaky just thinking about our boys were going over there. Initially I was against it. After a while I got in the mood to watch and I was watching it all the time. I did support the guys. It was really a small police action. I'm glad that we didn't lose a whole lot of guys over there. You have to realize that they were fighting a paper tiger as opposed to who we fought against. They had the firepower and Bush let the generals do what they were supposed to do.

I think watching Desert Storm is probably what started me thinking about what went wrong with the Vietnam war. I started doing more research into it, and the more research I did into the reasons why we got into it, the angrier I got and the more bitter I got against the Vietnam War. It made me very angry. If we would have been able to do our job, we would have definitely gone into North Vietnam and we could have wiped them out. We could have won that war but we weren't allowed to. According to a Marine Historian, it would have taken 500,000 combat troops to do that.

Martin L. Brown, PFC, D Company, August 1968–August 1969

I feel that by us being there, even though we pulled out, basically we left some sort of a foundation in there so that eventually it's going to come around. It's already started to. I read on this stuff all the time. I hang out on the Vet link, computer systems. Fidonet, Internet, I read a lot of stuff on those. People who go over there now they say that a lot of the old people in the south that went to reeducation camps are now important people because they're the ones that know how to get this new capitalist movement going. I read stories about how these people sit in real plush restaurants now with jailers that used to beat the shit out of them. And they are just as important. Because they know how to run capitalist way of thinking. I don't think we lost. We did what we were supposed to do.

We never knew when it was going to hit us, that was the main thing. When it did hit us, we couldn't get even and that's where the stress comes from. It's kind of followed me all the years. Out of the blue I might hear a noise or something, and it just triggers something, and I'll just jump. There's a certain particular smell of diesel fuel that gets to you. You just kind of flashback. I don't have flashbacks like I'm in combat or something. I'll flashback for a split second to a point I was at in life or a memory. There was a lot of stress there. If it weren't for booze, I probably wouldn't have made it.

I watched Desert Storm continuously on TV. Part of me wanted to be there. Part of me envied those people because they were there doing their job. It made me realize I was getting old. [laughs] To me it wasn't even a war. It was just a chase-them-out-of-there thing.

I try to live my life where I don't get upset over things that I can't change. I actually felt a lot of relief when I knew he was doing the right thing. In fact there wasn't much anger at all, it was more on the relief side because I knew that he was doing the right thing. I kind of knew that they had gotten the message from the past. I was pretty happy about the weapons system that I saw them developing that they were using with perfection. That made me feel good. Vietnam was a big test ground, as far as I was concerned, for a lot of stuff.

Their homecoming kind of annoyed me a little. It was a lot different from what they gave us. I also saw it as a political cover-up for us. Okay, you Desert Storms guys, we'll give you a big hooray, and that makes all veterans look good in our eyes. They were trying to use them to appease us a lot.

Clyde Ricks, PFC, D Company, August 1969–February 1970

What I'd like the world to know is that the guys I served with in Vietnam as a group were the greatest people I'd ever known in my life. The good humor and resilience they showed in potentially fatal situations has served as a strengthening example for me all through the rest of my life.

The way I feel now is our government deliberately sacrificed the lives of the most disadvantaged and powerless young men in our society because our most powerful politicians didn't want to appear soft on communism, and yet they didn't want to offend the upper middle classes by asking their sons to die in the war. It tends to make you bitter.

My perception of what we were doing at the time was so good. I had the example of courage and sacrifice by so many great young men to sustain me through all the rest of the trials of my life. It seemed to me that small unit leaders had to have the wisdom and fairness of Solomon and the courage and kindness of King David and Jesus, too, to earn the respect of their men. I probably would go again because [laughs] I'm an American. It's hard for me to have Clinton for my commander-in-chief because he tried so hard not to go and yet now he wants to be the commander-in-chief.

I've been going to support groups since '82 and it's so good for me because I see these guys that have given up and I know they don't have to. You can live with almost anything. You can work again. You can have a family life again if you want it bad enough. There's a Jim Croce song, "It Doesn't Have to Be That Way."

There is a novel called *The Winter Marine*. This is a passage from it. "My boy was a Marine, too, just like his old dad. I used to sit him on my knee and tell him the biggest lies about the war. Played it up to him, told him about all the laughs I had with my buddies, made it seem like a great time." Well, I didn't ever want to be guilty of that. Even though that's the way I mainly remember it, I want them to know that there was sure a lot more to it than that. I want my son to know you could lose your legs, you could get captured and tortured or you could do things you might be ashamed of the rest of your life. You could make mistakes and get other guys killed.

Without my wife I'd probably have been dead by now. I would probably have gone to bars and got in fights with guys who were knocking the Marines or 'Nam vets or drove drunk and ended up dead. I just wasn't stable but I would do almost anything to make my wife happy. I've made myself into a fairly respectable citizen, partly because you don't want to embarrass your wife and kids. For 19 years I've believed God has a plan for me and I've wanted to fulfill that.

My thoughts on Desert Storm was that they did it so fast. They got in and they got out. They didn't waste lives for years and years. In 'Nam it was like they were playing with our lives. We gave them our lives and instead of being careful with them, they just played with them. They just played with us.

HIGHWAY ONE TO HEAVEN

Corporal **Robert Elmer Bryant** was an engineer equipment operator and died on 13 September 1966 when a 550 grader rolled over on him after he had moved it to the edge of the road so some civilians could pass by. Robert was 22 years old and had served his country for three years. He was married and from Washington, Pennsylvania. (Location on the "Wall" 10E L90)

Staff Sergeant **Kenneth Clayton Friddle** was the assistant mess sergeant. He died on 8 October 1966 while going down to check on an assistant cook assigned to the ROK Marines. Kenneth was ambushed on the road. He was 34 years old, married and had served his country for sixteen years. Kenneth was from Atlanta, Georgia. (11E L62)

Private First Class **Linza Norris** was a combat engineer and died on 30 October 1966. He was 20 years old, married and from Baltimore, Maryland. Linza drowned while swimming at Amtrac Beach. (11E L131)

Lance Corporal **Thomas Joseph Brooks** was an engineer equipment operator and died on 10 November 1966, three months before his twentieth birthday. He had served his country for one year. Thomas was from Weirton, West Virginia, and was killed in a vehicle accident. (12E L49)

Private **Jeffery Thomas Dines** was a field radio operator with Headquarters Company and died on 13 January 1967, two months after his nineteenth birthday. He was from Waterloo, Iowa, and had served his country for two years. Jeffery died along with five other men when the vehicle they were riding in hit a mine. (14E L20)

Lance Corporal **John Patrick Eads** was a motor vehicle operator and died on 13 January 1967, three months after he turned twenty-one. He was from St. Louis, Missouri, and had been in the service for one year. John died along with five other 9th Engineers when the vehicle they were riding in hit a mine. (14E L21)

Sergeant **Bobby Gene Jackson** was an engineer equipment operator and died on 13 January 1967. He was twenty-six years old, married, and came from Marshall, Missouri. Bobby had served his country for six years and died when the vehicle he was riding in hit a mine. He died with five of his buddies. (14E L22)

Private **Aaron Burr Jones, Jr.,** was an engineer equipment operator and died on 13 January 1967, three months before his nineteenth birthday. He was from Wilmington, North Carolina, and had served his country for one year. Aaron died with his buddies when their vehicle hit a mine. (14E L22)

Lance Corporal **Michael Joseph Kehoe** was a combat engineer with Delta Company and died on 13 January 1967. Hailing from New York City, he was twenty years old and had been in the service one year. Michael died with his buddies when their vehicle hit a mine. (14E L23)

Private First Class **Leroy Pierson** was a combat engineer and died on 13 January 1967. He was twenty years old, and came from Hamilton, Ohio. He had served his country for one year. Leroy died when the vehicle he was riding in hit a mine. He was killed along with five other 9th Engineers. (14E L23)

Staff Sergeant **James Rodney Moore** was a basic combat engineer and was listed as Missing In Action on 28 February 1967. He disappeared while on patrol and is believed to have been pulled down into a tunnel network by the enemy. A subsequent search of the area showed no sign of James. James has not been returned as of this date, nor has his body ever been recovered. He is unmarried, hails from Ontario, New York, and was nineteen years old on the date he disappeared. (15E L120)

Corporal **Howard Stanley Stevens** was a combat engineer and died on 28 March 1967 in a mine explosion. He was attending a 7th Engineer Battalion class in mine warfare in Da Nang when a land mine accidentally exploded. Twelve other Marines were also killed and one was wounded. Howard had turned twenty-two just two months before and had served his country for one year. He was from Baltimore, Maryland. A memorial to these thirteen Marines was dedicated in Valley Forge, Pennsylvania. It is a circle of thirteen trees. (17E L64)

Corporal **William Wesley Patterson** was a combat engineer and died on 30 March 1967 from small arms fire. He was twenty years old and came from Casa Grande, Arizona. William was single and had served his country for one year. (17E L74)

Private First Class **Joseph Everett Lavigne** was a combat engineer and died on 31 July 1967, from a mine explosion. He was twenty-one years old and came from New Britain, Connecticut. Joseph was single and had served his country for one year. (24E L55)

Lance Corporal **Ignacio Espinosa Sablan** was an electrician and died on 3 August 1967 from a fall. He was twenty-six years old and came from Santa Rita, Guam. Ignacio was single and had served his country for one year. (24E L75)

Staff Sergeant **James Robert Simmons** died on 14 October 1967 from a mine explosion. He had been in-country for five months and had served his country for twelve years. James was one month shy of his thirtieth birthday. He was married and came from Charleston, West Virginia. (28E L5)

Lance Corporal **Robert John Molossi** died on 13 January 1968 during a mortar attack. He had served his country for one year and had been in Vietnam for almost eight months. Robert was unmarried and was twenty-one years, two months old. He was a motor vehicle operator hailing from Daly City, California. (34E L43)

Hospital Corpsman **Jerry Lawayne Collier** died on 7 February 1968 from small arms fire. He had served his country for three years and had been in Vietnam for nine months. Jerry was single and came from Boaz, Alabama. He was twenty years old. (37E L80)

Sergeant **Peter Burr Hedlund** died on 9 February 1968 from wounds received when a mine exploded. He had served his country for four years and was unmarried. He came from Cedar, Minnesota. Peter arrived in Vietnam on 26 May 1967 and died one week before his twenty-fourth birthday. (38E L50)

Lance Corporal **Forbis Pipkin Durant, Jr.** was an engineer equipment operator and died on 10 March 1968 from a mine explosion. He was two months away from his twenty-third birthday and had been in-country four months. Forbis was single and hailed from Atoka, Oklahoma. He had served his country for one year. (44E L6)

Private First Class **Howard "Hard Heavy" Leroy Savare** was a field radio operator and died on 25 March 1968 during an enemy mortar attack on the Command Post. Sixteen men were wounded during the same attack. He was one week shy of his twenty-third birthday. Howard had served his country for four years and was married. He came from West Richland, Washington. (46E L23)

Lance Corporal **Carl Marion Mabe** was a combat engineer and died on 2 April 1968 from a mine explosion. He died two months after his twentieth birthday. Carl had served his country for one year and had been in Vietnam for over eight months. He was from Pembroke, Virginia, and was single. Two other 9th Engineers were killed in the same explosion. (47E L40)

Private **William George Wilkins** was a combat engineer and died on April 2, 1968 in a mine explosion. He was from Mt. Pleasant, Pennsylvania, and was single. William was eighteen years old and had arrived in Vietnam on 18 December 1967 with Charles Leonard Yates. (47E L44)

Private First Class **Charles Leonard Yates** was a combat engineer and died on 2 April 1968 in a mine explosion. He was twenty years old and came from Fairmont, West Virginia. He died along with two other men. Charles arrived in Vietnam on 18 December 1967 with William George Wilkins. (47E L45)

Lance Corporal **Stephen Thomas Sullivan** was a combat engineer and died on 28 May 1968 from small arms fire. He had served his country for three years and was killed five months after his twentieth birthday. Stephen was from Melrose, Massachusetts, and was single. He had been in-country for three months. (64W L16)

Corporal **William Michael Livingston** was a combat engineer and died on 25 July 1968 from a mine explosion. He had served his country for two years and died two days before his twenty-first birthday. William was from Columbus, Ohio, and was single. He had been in Vietnam for ten months. (50W L7)

Sergeant **Terry Charles Corson** died on 8 September 1968 in a mine explosion. He died one month before his twenty-first birthday. Terry had served his country for two years and was from Skowhegan, Maine. He was married and had been in Vietnam for almost ten months. (44W L2)

Corporal **George Allen Yarbrough** was a combat engineer and died on 17 September 1968 in a mine explosion at Bridge 35. He was from Jackson, Tennessee, and was single. George was twenty years old and had served his country for two years. He had been in Vietnam for over nine months. (43W L22)

Hospital Corpsman **Kurt William Duncan** died on 19 September 1968 when the truck he was riding in hit a land mine. He was from Princeton, Minnesota, and was single. Kurt had served his country for two years and had just turned twenty-one, eleven days before. He had been in-country for nine months. (43W L35)

Private First Class **Arlon Glenn Schaeffer** was a combat engineer and died on 24 September 1968. He was twenty-three years old and had served his country for two years. Arlon died when a mine exploded. He had been in Vietnam for over three months, was single, and was from Loveland, Colorado. (42W L7)

Private **David Alan Lanning** was a field radio operator and died on 1 February 1969 in an accident. He was from Gary, Indiana, and was single. David was eighteen years old and had served his country for one year. He had been in Vietnam for thirty-nine days. (33W L32)

Lance Corporal **Steven Lawrence Leach** was a combat engineer and died on 1 February 1969 in an accident. He was from Waynesville, Ohio, and was single. Steven died the day before his nineteenth birthday. He had served his country for one year and had been in Vietnam for over ten months. (33W L32)

Lance Corporal **Martin Robert Powers** was a combat engineer and died on 27 February 1969. He was from New York and was single. Martin had served his country for one year and had been in Vietnam for ten months. He died one week before his twenty-second birthday. (31W L84)

Corporal **Randy Warren Molkentine** was an engineer equipment mechanic and died on 5 March 1969 from malaria. He was from Milwaukee, Wisconsin, and was single. Randy had served his country for two years and was twenty-one years old. He had been in Vietnam for over two years. (30W L48)

Corporal **Norman "Frenchy" Joseph Chavarie** was a combat engineer and died on 21 July 1969 when the jeep he was riding in got hit with a grenade. He was from Augusta, Maine, and was single. He would often entertain the surrounding troops with the "Frenchy Show." Norman had served his country for two years and died one month before his twentieth birthday. He had been in Vietnam for over twenty-two months. (20W L27)

Private First Class **Keith Dale Mehaffey** was a combat engineer and died on 21 October 1969 from small arms fire on Landing Zone Baldy. He was from Waynesville, North Carolina, and was single. Keith died five days after his twenty-first birthday. He served with Delta Company and had been in Vietnam for seventy-eight days. (17W L102)

Hospital Corpsman **Stephen Martin Welch** died on 21 October 1969 from small arms fire on Landing Zone Baldy. He was from Syracuse, New York, and was single. Stephen had served his country for two years and was twenty-one years old. He served with Delta Company. (17W L101)

Lance Corporal **Steven Douglas Le Vesque** was a combat engineer and died on 5 December 1969 in a mine explosion that also killed two other 9th Engineers. He was from Barre, Vermont, and was single. Steven was twenty years old and had served his country for one year. He had been in Vietnam for eight months. (15W L28)

Lance Corporal **Ralph Lee Taylor** was a combat engineer and died on 5 December 1969 in a mine explosion with two other Marines. He was from Baltimore, Maryland, and was single. Ralph died eight days before his twentieth birthday. He had served his country for one year and had been in Vietnam for eight months. He arrived one day before Steven Douglas Le Vesque. (15W L30)

Sergeant **Richard Allen Watts** was a

combat engineer and died on 5 December 1969 in a mine explosion that also killed two other Marines. He was from Schenectady, New York, and was single. Richard was twenty-two years old and had served his country for three years. He had been in-country for eight months and had arrived the same day as Ralph Lee Taylor. (15W L30)

Private First Class **Charles David Newman** died on 18 December 1969 from multiple fragmentation wounds. He had served his country for one year and had been in Vietnam for just over five months. Charles was a combat engineer and was two months shy of his twenty-third birthday. He was single and came from Pittsburgh, Pennsylvania. (15W L70)

Lance Corporal **Terry Bruce Lund** was an engineer equipment operator and died on New Year's Eve, 1969. He was from Kenosha, Wisconsin, and was single. Terry had served his country for six years and was twenty-three years old. He had been in Vietnam for seven months. (15W L113)

Corporal **Alan Ross** was a basic combat engineer and died on 24 May 1970 on Landing Zone Baldy. He was from St. Louis, Missouri, and was single. Alan was nineteen years old and had served his country for two years. He served with Delta Company and had been in Vietnam for nine months. (10W L92)

CONTRIBUTOR BIOGRAPHIES

Peter Allon, PFC, Service Company, November 1967–December 1968
Taped interview 8-13-94

I ran into a guy who was in the Army. He was in 'Nam and asked me, "How much pension do you get?" "I don't get anything," I told him. "What? What's your card? Do you have a card?" He showed me a blue card, and I said no. "Well, you should have a purple card." This was about 1982 or something like that. "What do you mean a purple card? Is that service connected?" He said, "Yeah." So I got in touch with the American Legion in Helena, Montana and about six or seven months later, I get a check for $5,000. They took $2,000 back pay for the last ten years. But that's the card I get. They said you should have had that when you got discharged. Live and learn. There's a lot of vets up in Calgary that are still hurting.

I find civilian life really tough.

I got wounded mostly in the head. I just saw too much and have what they call PTSD. Over a long period of time you're tired of holding your buddies in your arms because they're dying and you're alive. I got sort of zapped up in Quang Tri, aye. I was with 7th Motors then. I got out of the VA hospitals and they warehouse you from here to here. Living in Canada you're sort of a treadmill number, aye.

I get benefits now, but being the VA, they can cut them or raise them. That's why a lot of guys who are drawing benefits now that should get 100 percent, are only getting 30 percent. They're scared of going in, because they can either raise it… or lower it. I don't think they can take mine away, now… it's been twenty years now. But if they did, I'd be completely lost. I was 100 percent for about eight months, then they came back and cut it to 60 percent. Finally, about five or six years ago, they cut it to 50 percent. Canada won't do anything for us. With my 50 percent I can get in a VA hospital in Canada strictly for what I'm service connected for, aye. Anything else and I've got to go to the States. But we're five hundred miles away from the nearest VA hospital [laughs]… in the States.

Brian Althouse, PFC, A Company, March 1968–October 1969
Taped interview 1994

I'm a member of the Marine Corps League and shoot on the rifle team. There's a competition every year. I'm still a Marine. I got married the first time while I was still in the Marines when I came home from Vietnam. It turned out to be a bad marriage. When I did get out of the Marine Corps, it even became a worse marriage. I came back in October of '69 and went overseas again in March of '70 on a Med cruise. I signed up for that because I didn't like being stateside. I hated stateside. I really did have a hard time with it.

Six months after I got out I was thinking about re-enlisting again. I couldn't adjust to civilian life. I really had a hard time with civilians. I really did. I just couldn't handle them. I didn't like people. I didn't like people around me. Everybody was cutting down the Vietnam war and that's what I stood for. That was part of my heritage now. That's what I did. I fought for our flag. I came home for my buddies. I lost buddies and now you tell me I'm a dirtball. I don't think so, dude. I had a hard time with that. I still do. So it took a long time, and plus, I had a bad marriage. So, finally I got a job. I worked in a deli that I worked for before I went into the Marine Corps. Then I got a job working in a steel mill. I worked there for six years and then I got fired. Deservedly so. You're supposed to be there at eight o'clock and I used to come in at 9 o'clock, and that don't work out too long. I had a hard time adjusting.

I have two boys by the first marriage and I have a daughter. She's ten. She's my sweetie-pie.

When I was over there, the Vietnam dream was to come home and have a house, a wife, a couple of kids, a boy and a girl and a dog. I haven't got my dog yet. I'm getting one this fall. This is what we used to talk about. You're sitting in the hole, either wet or dry or hot, and that's what you talk about. That's what it's all about. Then you get home and lose track of these guys. I got buddies named Harry Hammon and Jim Hoke. Both of them are from Philadelphia and I can't locate them. It's hard.

George E. Ballard,
Sgt., A Company, 1965–1967,
SSgt., C Company, 1969–1970
Phone call 4-8-94, letters received 7-6-95 and 7-22-95

After my first trip in '67, I came back to the states. I went back in '69 and came back home in '70. I was there at the beginning and the end.

Martin L. Brown, PFC, D Company,
August 1968–August 1969
Taped interview 8-12-94

Two months after I got back I went deer hunting. I was walking down through the woods and saw a rabbit about one hundred yards away and I just picked it off. To me it wasn't sporting anymore. I was too good a shot. So I just dropped it and didn't pick another gun up until five years ago. I went way over the top, anti-gun, anti-war for a few years. Then I got away from that and pretty much swung back to the middle politically. I don't like anti-gunners. I'm a member of the VFW and I've never been in the club. I like reading their magazine.

I was never in the closet. Never. I never tried to hide that fact. Nobody's ever given me any shit over it. I'm a big guy. They probably wouldn't anyway. [laughs] I've never had anybody get down on me for it. If anyone's ever objected to it, they never said anything to me about it. Politically I've discussed it with people over the years. Sometimes we've had the same views, other times we don't. I never get any crap over it. I'm from Northern Vermont and when I got back everybody up there was pro–Vietnam anyway. There were very few people that were anti, they were around, but not many.

I couldn't settle down for years. I got into drugs and booze pretty heavy. In 1981, I quit that. I'm on my third marriage. I married two VC first. They used the same tactics. They think like VC. The old hit-and-run, can't get even type stuff. They fight like them. That's what I used to tell them. I ended up in Massachusetts in '72 and met a woman in a barroom one night. We kind of fell in love with each other because we knew we could slowly kill each other over a long period of time. Nothing really violent, just mental torture. I had two kids with her. I got a job in a factory. Basically I was a tool and die maker. I went to school for it and got a job in a machine shop running machines for seven years.

I'd love to go back to visit. I wouldn't even mind staying there for awhile. I used to sit in there at night with the kids and the families. I didn't understand the language, but it was nice. It had a good feeling. I had a good time. I used to like the geography. I used to like the way their air smelled. Not always [laughs], but most of the time. I liked it early in the morning. Everything had kind of a heavy haze on it. It was that kind of air, when a bomb went off, you could see the shock waves go up from it. Real dense. It was cooler, but it was dense.

Thomas P. Carras, 2nd Lt.,
A Company, B Company, Hdqtrs. Co.,
December 1969–September 1970
Fax received 8-16-95

Tom lives and works in California as the Director of Academic Affairs for the Southern California campus of the University of Phoenix. He retired from the Marines as a Lt. Col.

Edward L. Casper, Cpl.,
Headquarters Company,
August 1967–August 1968
Tape received 4-8-94

I'm a two war veteran. I survived two wars now. I'm still in the Reserves. I've got about three or four years to go and I hope I may not have to see my third one, but you never know. The third time may be the charm.

I now work at Illinois Department of Corrections. I'm a 17 year veteran in corrections. I'm married almost 24 years to a wonderful woman named Lynn. I have an 18 year old son named James, a 20 year old daughter named Kim and now I have a wonderful little almost two year old granddaughter I adore. My wife is an 18 year veteran with the Postal Service.

Since Vietnam and now Desert Storm, I'm a lot different than I was before. I've changed a lot, but I survived and I make it all right. It's strange, but for 25 years I checked the VFW magazines, in the reunion section, to see if our battalion was going to have a reunion. After 25 years I saw it in the VFW and I contacted the people running it. They took my name and out of the clear blue sky I got this call one night from Freddy Wood, a dear friend from there, and we been corresponding ever since.

After Desert Storm I got one of the biggest honors of my life. They had the big victory parade in Washington, D.C. in honor of the Desert Storm vets. I was selected from my unit, the 52nd Air Patient Staging Squadron, to represent our unit in this parade and it was a deep honor. It was held in Washington, D.C. and I got to go see the Wall. It was a moving, [pause] solemn [pause] experience. I was afraid to walk on it because it was sacred ground, [pause] but I had to find my friend's name, Hard Savare. The other gentleman I was with had some of his friends that got killed when his base was overrun. It was very sobering. All Vietnam veterans should be able to get there and see the Wall. If it hadn't been for my unit selecting me, I'd probably never got the opportunity, but it was a great honor.

Mike Daly, PFC, Hdqtrs. Company,
July 1967–April 1969
Letter received 11-28-95

My name is Mike Daly, nicknamed "Groucho" because of physical appearance and the cigar. I served in Headquarters Co., Heavy Equipment Plt., 9th Engineer Battalion from July 1967 to April 1969. Serving in the Heavy Equipment platoon, I had the opportunity to serve with all the letter company's, the ARVN's, the Korean Marines, and the Army from the Americal Division. During my tour and extension, I earned the Vietnamese Cross of Gallantry with the gold star which was individually awarded, and the Navy Achievement with the combat V.

Dan Diridoni, LCpl., Service Company, December 1967–December 1968
Taped interview 9-2-94 and letters received 8-94 and 9-94

I read a book by this guy by the name of John Del Vecchio who was in the 101st Airborne. His book basically was about the A Shau Valley, the 13th Valley. I read the book and he mentioned several places where I was when I was there. The way he described it didn't sound right. So I took a chance and wrote him a letter. He answered me and was real curious about what I meant by how thick this area was. I sent him pictures of what it looked like when we were there in '68, and he was there in '70. What had happened though, was they had defoliated it with that Agent Orange. I took pictures of the planes dropping the defoliant. He said it was barren out there, in that short of a period of time. You know how things can change. I don't know how those people are living out there today. I mean I wonder how the country side has grown back.

One of my favorite books was *No Shining Armor*. That was great and another book that I read that I thought was excellent was *We Were Soldiers Once … and Young*. Boy, was that a sad story. I saw the show on television about it. I heard about that but I never really understood what it was all about, and then I saw that documentary. To find out the blunders of what happened there was sad. They were all disorganized. I think that was the essence of the early part of that war.

Of course, that was the first major confrontation of any size whatsoever, and I think there is a lot of valuable lessons learned by that, by both sides. First of all, be organized. Second of all, for the NVA or VC, we cannot defeat these people and their fire power and their air power. The only way we can stay close to them is by staying close to them. Then they can't use their fire power. They are very intelligent. They not only knew what they were doing, but they had a real cause. They were very, very dedicated people, let me tell you. Thinking back on it now, I have the utmost respect for those people. I don't care what anybody says about gook this or gook that, they were tough people. I think we might have learned a few lessons from that ourselves.

We are not invincible. We are not invincible especially when somebody has a cause like that. I don't care how much fire power you have. What if someone were to come to this country and try to colonize us or whatever, what do you think would happen?

After I got out I wanted to be a probation officer. I got about two quarters on a masters in counseling and then I got this job as a probation officer.

I lasted six months. There was so much red tape involved in it. They gave you a case load of one hundred kids. How were you supposed to deal with a hundred kids and their problems. You just didn't have enough time. If you wanted to take an extra step to try to help a kid and do something that you felt might help him, they wouldn't let you because it wasn't in the cards. It wasn't the proper way or this and that. I just couldn't do it. I just felt that I was going to be frustrated for the rest of my life doing that. I had already been frustrated. I didn't want to be frustrated anymore. So, I got out.

I was totally blown away. That was my whole goal in life. I had a probation officer help me out when I was young. He talked to me and kind of straightened me out. Of course, the Marine Corps straightened me out a little bit, too. So, I thought I could do the same maybe someday. When I got out of the service, that's what I wanted to be. That's what I went for. I became a very good student. I was dedicated and blown away, to say the least. Then I just walked away from that job and went home. I stayed at the house for three months or so and let my hair grow long. I didn't know what the hell I really wanted to do. I was just blown away.

I remember one day my father-in-law came over to the house before my wife came home from work and he basically said, "I really like you, Dan, but I will be God damned if my daughter's going to be married to a bum. You are going to get off your ass and go do something." He evidently had already talked to his boss, who had a big dealership, and he brought me down there the next morning and they hired me on as an apprentice body and paint man. I loved it. I absolutely loved every bit of it. I still do. I still enjoy working on cars. It has been very very good to me as far as my life and my livelihood.

One guy that I know of has skin cancer and is dying and he was one of the guys that hauled us around. His name is Elroy Schultz. I saw him three years ago. He dropped in here out of the blue. I hadn't seen him since he pulled me out of Bastogne, honest to God. He has skin cancer all over his body. He is dying. I don't know if that's Agent Orange. I could not say. I'm not a doctor, I don't know. I've heard a lot of things and I've read a lot of things about it. It's interesting when I went in there to the VA, they were sarcastic and obnoxious to me. They wanted to know how I knew I was exposed to it. I threw my picture at them. I said, "This is how I know, right here." "We would like to keep this picture for your file." I said, "Over my dead body you will. You're not keeping that picture." I took it in there on a fluke. I had heard stories about how they give you the third degree. That was one of the infamous drops of ranch hand in the A Shau Valley. They were dropping Agent Orange, Agent Purple and all kinds of crap out there. John Del Vecchio is a testament to that. There was nothing out there later. It was barren.

The physical they gave me was the most thorough physical I ever had in my life. It took two days. They did all these tests, I don't know what kind of tests they were doing and I don't know what they found. I just did that more or less to protect my family in case something does happen down the road. I mean at least they would have some kind of recourse.

I thought the documentary on HBO, *Dear America: Letters Home from Vietnam* was great. It made me very emotional. My mom keeps a lot of the letters at home that I wrote. My wife kept every one I wrote. It's kind of funny looking back on it. That was a terrific documentary. I couldn't imagine the parents watching that documentary that lost their kids. That would be horrible. That would destroy me. My dad and I were not the best of friends. The typical son father relationship where I got older and thought I knew all the answers. I was trying to become a man if you want to say that. Well, when I got out, we became a little bit closer, but I never realized how much it bothered him or affected him. He passed away about five or six years ago and I helped my mom sort through some of his stuff.

We found one of his old wallets that he had for years. She opened it up and inside of it were some pictures and one of the letters that I wrote to him. It was just to him during some hard times for me and I just ... it was like talking to him. It was the only way of getting certain things out of my mind and he kept it in his wallet all those years. It was nothing but tatters. I never knew this, I never knew this. He never told me this. He never talked to me about it or anything. Evidently, it was a very, very bad experience for him also as a parent. So it was not just us, it was the parents. The poor parents that had to go through all this crap. This is a testament to them, too.

Robert F. Goins, Captain, A Company, November 1965–May 1966
Letter received 4-6-94

Robert Handley, LCpl., D Company, January 1968–February 1969
Taped interview 9-10-94

I was really kind of surprised to see the casualty list after I left and I'm kind of surprised at the relatively short history of the battalion.

I got married three or four days before I went over. We were married on the 26th of January and the 29th of January was when we flew out. [laughs] Nice honeymoon. And all these years later we're still together.

My son's on a fast attack sub, the USS *Albany*. I told him not the Marine Corps. I didn't want him joining the Marine Corps unless he was an officer. We went and talked to the Navy Recruiter in Port Washington, which is north of here, and he got interested in the nuclear program so he signed up for six years. He's going to college when he gets back out. He's getting out in September '95.

I have three children. When they ask, I talk about it. When they were little, they would ask because I have a shadowbox with my ribbons and stuff on the bedroom wall. I'd tell them I didn't see anything horrific over there. I didn't care for the bodies but it's like never-never land when you're trying to remember it. They can pull out the pictures and ask questions when they want.

I got out in '71 and worked at a gas station and then sold insurance. Then I drove a semi for awhile and then I got a job in 1973 at a police department. I've been at it ever since. What's funny is, I got a job at the police department where I live and they knew me pretty well. It was always a joke. They couldn't beat me, so I had to join them. They never could catch me. In fact, the story goes that when I joined the department they cleared about eight reports. It was all juvenile stuff. It's kind of ironic, but the chief that hired me used to chase me and my brothers and sisters around. It's kind of ironic that I'm there. I'm second in command, a Captain. We're a small department and I don't go on the road anymore.

I did like it, but it's changed now. We're part of Milwaukee County and we just had an officer killed on Wednesday. He was a kid I knew from the neighboring department. He went to the city of Milwaukee Police Department and somebody sniped at him and shot him in the back. His wife is pregnant with twins. It's what the courts aren't doing and things like that are encouraging veteran police officers to get out. I look forward to the day I can retire. It shouldn't be too long. I've been here twenty-one years. It used to be a lot of fun. It was interesting. We weren't hamstrung by the courts. We could lock somebody up and expect that they would stay locked up instead of being released to commit more crime. It's just changed and there is nothing we can do about it.

I liked the reunion. I was a little touched. I'd get in an elevator and a World War II vet would say it's nice to see a Vietnam Vet here and I wish more of you guys would show up. Then I'd go and do what I had to do and get back in the elevator and there would be a Korean War vet. And he'd say it's nice to see the Vietnam Vets here and that went on. That was kind of nice. It was nice seeing the old faces if you could remember them. I couldn't remember all of them.

Wayne Hansen, PFC, A Company, May 1968–February 1969
Taped interview 4-7-94

I was a Combat Engineer with Alpha Company. I got there in May 1968 and I got medevaced out in February 1969.

I have PTSD. I have a rough time, in

fact it was a big effort for me to call you. I live in Pennsylvania now, but I lived in Florida for 17 years. I went to college in 1976 and graduated with a BA degree from the University of South Florida in 1980. I worked in social services mainly as a counselor. In 1986 I received a position in Protective Services for Children. I worked through the Florida Court System and was assigned by the court cases of abused and neglected children. I did that for five years and the stress exacerbated my PTSD. I developed heart and blood pressure problems. Part of the thing was that I had seen a lot of children maimed and stuff in Vietnam. And I was kind of replicating that. It got to the point where I had to check myself into the VA. Between 1989 and 1991 I spent a total of five months in the VA hospital down there. So I had to leave and I very rarely would go outside. So I moved to Pennsylvania and it's a lot easier going up here. It took a toll on me.

I'm glad that at least someone's taking an interest in it and I was just hoping that the real truth would come out. The 9th Engineers did a hell of a job there.

I had to call a friend of mine about six months ago. He lives on Long Island. Mike apparently blocked out everything. He told me on the phone that he couldn't remember too much. I didn't want to push him. I was a little afraid to call him because I don't want for him to have the problems I did. But he remembers all the funny things and there were a lot of funny things. We entertained ourselves.

The one thing about the Marines that I served with was the love they showed for the children in Vietnam. There was always children surrounding a 9th Engineer Marine. The children trusted the Marines and we tried to protect them.

I remember what my buddy Frenchy did on a minesweep. He had the mine detector and three or four little kids were following him. I was security that day. The VC opened fire, about six or seven rounds, then the VC ran. I tried to return fire but there was no target. I then looked to the side of the road and there was Frenchy, laying over the little kids. I think Frenchy should get the Silver Star for that heroic act. God bless him! He was one brave soul and I miss him. That one day he saved those little children while putting his own life at risk. Frenchy was a real hero, someone who will not be forgotten.

A MESSAGE TO MY FRIEND, FRENCHY

Rest Well Dear Brother, rest well,
rest in peace and rest in Honor,
you have served your tour in hell.
We were sent to Vietnam to fight,
God sent me home and he gave you
   the eternal light.
It could have been me asleep in that grave,
but it was you who died, while being Brave.
It was you who stayed and died,
it was me who came home and cried.
Rest well my brother, rest well,
in peace you shall remain,
you died with Honor, and not in vain.

Walter Hayes, Platoon Sgt., B Company, 1965–November 1967
Letter received 5-25-94, taped interview 7-25-94

I was born 22 May 1943 in Milwaukee, Wisconsin, joined the Marine Corps in June 1960 and retired in 1981. I had two tours in Vietnam, one with the 9th Engr. and then another with 1st Engr. Both were great tours and I'm proud of both. I went to boot camp in California and was a Drill Instructor twice at Parris Island, South Carolina.

I'm married 31 yrs and have a 17 yr. old daughter. I am the Security Chief for Moss Creek Plantation and have ten retired or former Marines working for me. After I retired I went to college for four years while working full time at a job I really enjoy, even after fourteen years with them. I have always lived for today and tomorrow, not the past. I think both Battalions did real good. They had nothing to be ashamed of. We worked hard. We had so many experiences. A lifetime experience in thirteen months is what it added up to.

When I got on the drill field, it gave me the capabilities of telling them stuff and reasoning it out. I didn't have to say, "Well, it could be this or it could happen." I could actually say it did happen. It helped me a tremendous amount to have gone through Vietnam twice, and come back and have all the experiences behind me and I could relate to the young men.

Mentally you could tell them why they had to be in such good shape. They'd have heart attacks when I'd tell them that they'd have "junk on the bunks." That is laying out all your equipment and being inspected. Here in the states you fold stuff and the creases and everything is in line. It's laid on the bed just a certain way and they are all uniform. Everything's inspected, from canteens to boot laces to you name it, for serviceability and things like that. They would have heart attacks and think you're in a combat zone and having "junk on the bunks." But yet, when you go on an operation and your boots fall apart because you didn't want to polish them, and then when you'd get out in the jungle and the doggone things would fall apart on you. It was something that really riled a lot of the troops. It was a necessity and they just couldn't believe it would happen.

Now I look back on my whole twenty-two years and I have no qualms. I had a lot of problems, but throughout my career there wasn't any problem really. If there was trouble, I could find it. Nowadays, if any of the Marines would do just one of what I did six times, they'd be booted out. Back in those days it was a different Marine Corps. I'd been busted twice and had six office hours and all of it was for fighting. Even my last day in Vietnam I got office hours. A Lance Corporal told me he wasn't going to stand Battalion guard. I had to prove he was going to stand it and I got caught with my hands in the cookie jar, around his neck. It cost me one hundred and fifty dollars, but he stood Battalion guard. And I got relieved. [laughs] I don't know. Maybe it was worth it and maybe it wasn't.

When I tell my employees now to go swab the deck, they don't ask me what a swab is. [laughs] I had that happen to me with a civilian. I feel more comfortable with them because they know leadership and making decisions without having to think about it for fifteen or twenty minutes. We carry firearms. You'd feel more comfortable knowing that man knows what to do with that pistol on his hip. Plus they look sharper in uniform and they got that military bearing. It reflects to the people around here. They see it and they appreciate it. They think it's neat. They make my job a lot easier when I chew them out, and they know I'm chewing them out for me and them. Not just being a asshole about it. Plus I don't have to tell them to get haircuts. We ain't got nobody running around here with long hair and earrings. It's a military atmosphere. It makes life easier on me.

If I could get away with it, which I can't, ex-Marines is all that I would hire. I had to go out and get me a 10 percent civilian and a 10 percent army guy. [laughs]

Larry P. Howell, PFC, H & S Company, May 1966–November 1966
Letter received 8-31-95

PFC Larry P. Howell, H & S Company, 9th Engr., Chu Lai & DaNang, 5-16-66/11-17-66

Then I went to 3rd Bn., 1st Marines, 1st Mar. Div. H&S Co., from 11-18-66 to 9-4-67 as a wire/radio operator F.O. I am Life member to the D.A.V. (Disabled American Veterans), Life member to the M.O.P.H. (Military Order of the Purple

Heart) and a member of the V.V.A. (Vietnam Veterans of America)

I am just a little in the "closet," but have been getting out more and more in the past three years. I stayed in a can and bottle for almost 23 years but quit that cold turkey. I'm on my 4th marriage. I drove 18 wheelers for thirteen and a half years on and off and brought up four children by myself. Now I am trying to help Vietnam Vets who are having problems with the V.A., as there is over one hundred Vietnam Vets in and around this town.

**William C. Jung, Sgt.,
August 1969–July 1970**
Letter and articles received 12-95

Letter to State Historical Society, which will be publishing two of my contributions.

"Dear Ms. Borkowski,

"I have read on several occasions that the State Historical Society is seeking material from Vietnam Veterans. I am therefore enclosing items for you to look at.

"I was born and raised in Dodge and Columbia Counties, having lived on five different farms and in both the Villages of Cambria and Randolph. I enlisted out of Randolph as 17 year old senior in high school. No one could change my mind, so after high school graduation I was gone!

"I served on active duty in the Marines for six years, from June of 1966 to June of 1972. During this time I served two tours in Vietnam in '68, '69, and '70. In Dec., 1974, I joined the Wisconsin Army National Guard and served with a Jomah unit for almost 17 years, retiring from the Guard in 1991. With the Guard I went to Germany three times and once to Korea.

"While in the Marines I kept a diary for all those years. My folks and wife also saved all my letters. I have many pictures too, also maps, squad books, hundreds of slides, etc. I was always a pack rat!

"I gave a slide presentation to a mixed audience of over 300 once at an institute in Stevens Point. I did it with mixed feelings, but it went over very well.

"While going to MATC in Madison in 1972-1974, I wrote up a 316 page manuscript about my days in the infantry in Vietnam. It remains in my study to this day, unpublished.

"I was stationed as a surveyor with the 13th Engineer Battalion of the 5th Marine Division at Camp Pendleton in California when reinforcements were needed in Vietnam during TET of 1968. I volunteered for the infantry and flew over to Vietnam with the 27th Marines. President Johnson himself saw us off!

"I served for over six months in the 3rd Platoon of K Company, 3rd Battalion, 27th Marine Regiment, attached to the 1st Marine Division. It was the best unit that I ever served with, but we suffered very heavy casualties for doing our job. The letter of 25 May 1968, was written during this time.

"When the 27th Marines were sent home, I was transferred to the 7th Engineer Battalion and finished my first tour with them as a surveyor. I was done with the infantry.

"My second tour in Vietnam was as a surveyor with the 9th Engineer Battalion of the 1st Marine Division. Two letters and my diary entry about Gorsuch (one of Wisconsin's MIA's) were from this period.

"William Dale Gorsuch and I were friends as boys, playing together long before we started 1st grade. We were confirmed together and even dated the same girl! Once I had moved to Randolph, we played football against each other. It seems like only yesterday that we were pitching rocks into the Cambria mill pond, but that was 40 years ago! I saw him last in 1969 when he was home on leave. I was between Vietnam tours. You can throw all my material away, but if you mention Dale, I would be grateful.

"I did not enclose the citations, DD-214, etc., to brag or be published. They are to prove who I am and what I did, so that you know that what I sent is up and up. Unfortunately, there are a very few wannabes who have posed as Vietnam vets nationally and in this state and have been shown to be liars. Some were never in the military. Others were, but never went to Vietnam. Some went to Vietnam, but never did what they say they did. I would therefore hope that you are screening everyone who gives you material. My neighbor, a Vietnam airborne veteran caught one of these pretenders at work. These people infuriate me. I hope that you won't come across any.

"You may do what you wish with my donation. If you want any pictures, just ask.

"Sincerely,
"William C. Jung"

Article in local paper, April 29, 1995

"When I think of Vietnam, I think first of the men that I served with. Those Marines were some of the best people I've known during my entire life. I will never forget them. They represented all types of creeds, religions, races and backgrounds. We shared everything together, not only suffering and misery, but also laughter and friendship. We never abandoned each other, especially in combat...

"As time went on, I came not only to like the country, but the people, too. Vietnam was a beautiful country, and its people hardworking and friendly. I learned as much as I could about their language, culture and history. They were so different from us, yet in so many ways alike.

"If anything has incensed me over the years, it's the image portrayed that we accomplished nothing in Vietnam. In my experience, nothing could be further from the truth. We drove the Viet Cong and North Vietnamese out of the populated areas. Farmers were allowed to return to their ancestral homes.

"Has anyone ever heard of the dispensary built near Chu Lai by Americans for the South Vietnamese? I doubt it. There are countless such examples.

"Certainly Vietnam had a negative impact on me, but this was far outweighed by the positive.

"To me, Vietnam was a good cause. I've never changed my mind. It's not the Vietnam vet's fault that in South Vietnam's greatest hour of need 20 years ago, the American government abandoned her in what to me was a monumental betrayal. Everything that we had fought, suffered and worked for was gone. I only have one regret about my days in Vietnam. I should have stayed longer. "

Eric Kenney, PFC, Service Company, November 1967–December 1968
Tape received 9-6-94

After my enlistment was up, which was September 12, 1969, I got out of the Marine Corps and journeyed back home and started back to college. I finished college and I can recall the Kent State Massacre. I was really overwhelmed by that whole mess and couldn't understand why a bunch of National Guardsmen who really were not in a great deal of trouble were issued live ammunition to protect a bunch of buildings that really were not in danger of being harmed. Then these guys shot some innocent kids. I never did understand that. I know we had been through that training, too, at Camp Pendleton. Nothing that we went through was anything like the way they handled it there. It was totally mishandled. I can recall that when we went through riot training at Camp Pendleton, they said under no uncertain terms would you be issued any live ammunition. That was the wrong thing to do. I don't know how it got into standard operating procedure for the National Guard to be issued live ammo. They weren't going to issue us live ammo there on the west coast.

CONTRIBUTOR BIOGRAPHIES

Charles King, Sgt., B Company, September 1967–September 1968
Taped interview 8-12-94

The bad things, most of them, you want to forget. That's normal. I'm a member of the VVA, a Vietnam Veterans group back home and most of the guys in that feel the same way.

I'm a mechanic. I worked heavy equipment for a couple of three years after I got out of the service, but the job I was working at in a small town finished up and I didn't want to travel anymore. I traveled enough with the Marine Corps. I picked up a job as a mechanic and I've been there for twenty-four years now. It's a small family-owned dealership.

Paul Kozak, PFC, D Company, September 1967–September 1968
Class assignments received 4-23-94 and taped interview 5-28-94

Wayne McGinnis, LCpl., D Company, June 1966–July 1967
Taped interview 9-26-94

My mother gave me maybe 150 to 200 letters, every letter that I wrote home from there. I've been going through them and it's almost like reading my own diary. They're all rubber banded together month by month and in dates. She won't throw anything away. My dad asked me before I went to not write home everything and to tone your letters down. Out of respect for my mother. But I am surprised at how much one will block out and you just tend to forget. That was the other good thing about the reunion, sitting around talking with the different fellows.

People ask me, why would you want to go back there? I think there's a part of me that's still over there. I don't know what part. But it's something that I really, really feel strongly about that I would like to do. I would love to take a tour of everywhere from Chu Lai all the way up to Hue. It was a beautiful country.

Dave Nichols, LCpl., B Company, January 1968–February 1969
Letter received 4-24-95

I have joined two veterans organizations. I belong to the Vietnam Veterans of America (St. Peters, MO) and the Marine Corps League (St. Peters, MO). I am very active in the Marine Corps League, but I haven't been real involved in the VVA. I have just been too busy to attend two meetings each month, but several VVA members are also League members, so they keep me up to date with what is going on. About once each month, lately, I've been selected to attend the National Fire Academy in Emittsburg, Maryland. I always visit the Vietnam Veteran's Memorial in Washington, D.C. I've been there five times, the most recent visit being last October, so I was able to see the new monument for the women who served over there. There is just something about the wall. I get choked up every time I stand in front of it. The last time I saw it was no easier than the first time I saw it. It's like you can feel the spirits of the people who were KIA and are listed there.

My life has been good since I got out. I have been in the fire service for fifteen years, the last six years as Fire Marshal in Chesterfield, Missouri. I just celebrated my twenty-fifth wedding anniversary (April 4). I have a daughter that will be twenty-one this summer and a son who will be eighteen this spring. He joined the Marines, in the delayed entry program, in June of 1994. He leaves for boot camp at San Diego (same place I went) on June 19, 1995. Obviously, if there is another war, I will let him go. At this point, I don't have much choice. I just hope we think about why we are sending troops into a country before we do it.

Jim O'Kelley, 2 Lt.–1 Lt.–Capt., HQ & D Company, August 1966–May 1968
Letter and diary entries received 1997

Ron Rainer, PFC, A Company, January 1967–October 1967
Taped interview 2-12-95

When I was able to get around a little bit better, I went on home to Georgia where my folks were living down in Albany. I did have a setback in '83 and '84. My left foot was turning in from the land mine explosion. They were supposed to have done an operation on it and they never did. I was out in the field doing forestry work in the heavy logging industry. I was covering 48 counties and it started turning in. It got to the point where I couldn't walk with a cane anymore.

So I went in the hospital and they did the surgery and fused the ankle on the left leg, cut the heel cord and set it at 90 degrees. Then of course you got the good old staff infection. Everybody and their brother gets it now-a-days when in the hospital. It took me a little while to get over that. Then I had to have surgery on my eye, to straighten my eye. I never had any more problems with that.

I went back another year in the forestry business, then I went as director of personnel and marketing for 11 Kentucky Fried Chicken Stores and two Burger Kings. Then I taught junior college and enjoyed that. That was the easiest way of making a living I think I've ever seen in my life. I mean set your time, your schedule and have plenty of opportunities for whatever you wanted to do. Then I went ahead and got my doctorate in management information systems. I knew that I was going to be raising my daughter, so I decided just to retire.

Then I did about 4,000 hours worth of volunteer work on the Lee County Four Wars Veterans Memorial. I had worked on the one in Albany, Georgia, for the Vietnam Veterans Memorial out of Veterans of the Vietnam War, Inc. out of Wilksboro, PA. I became a member. They were kind of radical in some of their approaches but I went ahead and worked with them and contributed to that. I did a little bit of the work on the Vietnam Memorial in Ufall, Alabama.

In this particular county, Lee County, Alabama, in World War I, World War II, Korea and Vietnam, we had per populace, more individuals killed in those four wars than any county in the state of Alabama. So if any area deserved a war memorial, it was this one. Then there were twenty-five from Vietnam that were killed from Lee County. We had about a two hour celebration for that. We had F16s fly over from Moody Air Force Base in Valdasta, Georgia and then we had the Marine Corps Band from Albany come up and we had the silent drill team. It was very nice. We also had special forces. They parachuted in with the American flag, Alabama State Flag and the POW/MIA Flag.

My daughter has met some people that have heard things from their parents. I'm sure that they were in the anti-war movement. Some of her friends said all those Vietnam guys were nothing but baby killers. She had them tell her that and she came home mad. She would come home and tell me some of those things and I would say, "Well, Laurel Ann, you were involved with the War Memorial and you helped raise funds for it. You know what I have told you about my experiences and you know what I was involved with." I told her, "You know there are things that happen in every war. They are isolated incidents. Sometimes people go off the deep end in everything. It is just human nature for people to make mistakes." I tried the best I could with Ann and she's never mentioned that to me again. But she doesn't listen to any of that anymore and I think she goes her own way. She is kind of like I was when I was in school during the anti-war days. She just kind of laughs at it and walks on. Because you know better. She is not harassed or anything like that, these are just isolated things. Little children are very cruel. She may have picked some of that up from television somewhere, too. You never know. That sometimes happens, too.

Edwin J. Raley, PFC, D Company, 1969–1970
Letter received 2-15-95

I served with Delta Co. of the 9th Engineer Bn from 1969 till 1970.

Clyde Ricks, PFC, D Company, August 1969–February 1970
Taped interview 4-2-94

In 'Nam I was a PFC and a Lance Corporal with Delta Company, 9th Engineering Battalion. We were on the LZ Baldy and the rest of the battalion was down at Chu Lai. I came in-country on the 9th of August of '69 and left on the 28th of February of '70.

My wife was extremely good for me because she taught me how to live. I got introduced to her on a blind date. Within weeks I fell in love and she has so much common sense. The way I was raised, nowadays they'd term it as abusive. My dad would knock me around, kick me in the butt once in a while, shake me... and curse me out. I started to be like that once with my son when he was in the Cub Scouts and she came in and said you're not gonna treat my kids like this or it'll be over my dead body.

Well, my mom wasn't like that. It was always just keep trying harder, just keep trying harder. [laughs] It just meant a lot to me that my wife wasn't that way. She has so many friends. People all over call her with their personal problems and she's always so helpful. She got cancer last year and she's had chemo the last few months. That chemo's tough. She grew up real poor and there's just something in her that always looks for the good. She can always figure out how to be happy no matter what is going on, and she taught that to me.

I was raised to react to whatever the situation was. Every little thing that could go wrong in our family, I usually got blamed for it because I was the oldest. We were taught to react by screaming and shouting and jumping up and down. It dawned on me one day, my wife has the same qualities I admired most in the best leaders in 'Nam. They would be extremely fair, extremely valiant. In tight situations, they'd stay calm. They'd be cheerful, but they wouldn't be so happy that you couldn't stand to be around them. She's got that.

We have five children and they've been great children. We have a son, 21; a daughter who'll be 20 next month; a son who'll be 17 next month and looks like he'll be one of the best milers in the state. Then a seventh grader and a daughter who is a third grader.

I'm a farmer. I think it's fun and enjoy it most of the time. With irrigated farming, you're pretty labor intensive, and that keeps you thinking and going pretty much all the time in the summer. Winter's pretty easy, unless it's a hard winter and you're pushing a lot of snow and shoveling your buildings off so they don't collapse. [laughs]

One support group I was in got the idea of a memorial. They asked nine of us to read the names at the dedication and on my list there were 27 names. But one guy who came to the dedication wanted to read his best friend's name, so I ended up just reading 26 names. I'd been a marathoner and got the idea of running a marathon and dedicating a mile to every name I read. I never ran at all in 'Nam. When I was in the states, I practiced and did real good in the three mile. If you did it in 'Nam, everybody teased you about being gung ho. I could run around the compound but I felt stupid.

Lawrence Stephen Roberge, LCpl., Service Company, June 1966–January 1968
Manuscript received 7-27-94

I got out of the Marines September 13th, 1969. A Great day. I started working for a small paper company here in Berlin on September 15th. That only lasted a couple of years, and I went back to school at N.H. Vo-Tech here in Berlin, and got an associates degree in automotive. Then I worked in a garage a couple of years. Then I got in the Berlin Post Office as a janitor, and I'm still doing that. Janitor doesn't sound like much, but it's got great advantages. 1. the pay is great, 2. the hours are good, 3. vacations are great, and 4. time off any time I need it, schedule change any time, all this with Saturday and Sunday off. Clerks and carriers have to work Saturday, they're locked into a schedule, and their vacations are hard to get during prime time. I love the flexibility of my job and not having to worry about getting time off.

It took me about 10 years to get off my "the world owes me something." I finally realized no one owes me anything. I owe, I owe all the guys that gave the ultimate sacrifice, their life. I owe all the guys that are still missing. I got to come home a better man, they never got to live their life.

My greatest moment in my life was meeting Susan A. Boucher, who is now my wife, best friend, and the mother of my three boys, Keith, 21, Ben, 18, and Steve, 13. This is what makes my life so complete, so full, my family. Now I know why I came home.

Another big part of the my life is "Boy Scouts of America." My wife and I became scout leaders in 1981, and it's been really great. I can't begin to count how many hours we've spent in scouting, or how much money we've spent, but knowing how many lives we've touched and how many boys we've helped makes it worthwhile.

I often wonder why so many men were killed in 'Nam, and why I came home without a scratch. I guess the good Lord has plans for all of us. Seeing all those kids living in the misery of 'Nam, made me realize no children should have to go through anything like that, and that helping a child get the fullest enjoyment out of his childhood and youth is one of the best things I could do with my life.

My life here at home has been great, good job, the greatest of marriages and family, and many, many friends who care about the important things in this world, the kids. They are our future.

The only veterans organization I've joined is the V.F.W. I pay my dues, and I support the V.F.W., but I'm not an active member in the club. My time is devoted to my family and to scouting. To the youth. The V.F.W. is great and I'm supportive of what it's doing for the vets.

I've never been in the "closet" about being a 'Nam vet. Berlin is a small town and most everyone is friendly here. I don't think I could sit and discuss 'Nam with just anyone, most just don't seem to understand.

Robert A. Schaefer, Bn. Medical Officer, January 1965–January 1966
Letter received 6-5-94

I was the Battalion Medical Officer from its formation at Camp Pendleton in January, 1965, and remained with the Battalion until I was transferred to 1st Hospital Company in January, 1966.

Fred H. Scheuter, PFC, B Company, May 1966–1967
Letter received 1-10-94

Raymond Joseph Simonetti, LCpl., Service Company, May 1966–January 1967
Tape received 1-29-96

Being a Marine helped me become a survivor. I switched to a heavy equipment operator while in-country, and I'm doing that same type of work today, as a crane operator, employed by the Department of the Army at Aberdeen Proving Grounds. We do the whole bit, the cranes, bulldozers, live fire vehicles. I also feel more comfortable working at APG because I am working with a lot of Vietnam vets than I did when I was on the outside. Working on the outside, I was a thirty-seven year old, working with people who tried to stay away from Vietnam. It's nice to be home and with guys that are the same... the same breed, so to speak. So, I think being a Marine in Vietnam definitely had a direction. Also, it made me feel, "What the hell, you survived this, you can survive pretty much anything." What are they going to do, send me back to Vietnam?

Basically the only type of music I enjoy is all the 60's and stuff. I listen to it every day. I listened to it in Vietnam. I listened to it wherever I could, whenever I could. I learned one thing. As far as I am concerned, I'm on borrowed time anyway. I've been blessed to be able to be here this long and be able to have a family, a fine son, my health and my job, just like the big guys do. So, music was definitely a comfort to me and still is.

My life since I left Vietnam ... I found a nice girl, got married, tried to make a living, tried to live the American dream. I bought a house, the whole bit and got my trade as a heavy equipment operator and crane operator. I went to college and acquired a Bachelor of Arts degree in Labor Studies. I find that my skills as a trades person, and a crane operator, certainly put more food on my table than my degree in Labor Studies. I've had a good life. We have a fine son, my wife and I. He is our lives basically. I was married in Vietnam, divorced in Vietnam. I got married to a lady back in the States and got my divorce papers when I arrived in Vietnam and an officer witnessed the signatures and I sent them back.

My contributions to society are just trying to be a good guy. Sometime or other, I was president of a community association, trying to do right by the community.

One fellow, Mr. Sullivan, a close friend, decided to extend in-country. I sort of told him it was bad for his health record and advised him to go on home when he served his time. He elected to extend and I wrote a letter to his house after I had been back here. His mother was kind enough to write and tell me a sniper had taken Sullivan out. I wished I had known what to do for him. I never knew what to do, so I did nothing. Finally, after some counseling, I went over to the Wall and visited his place. Basically, I didn't know who had made it. A lot of times we were there and people were being killed in one way or the other. You heard about it but you didn't know about it in a way. We had guys killed from industrial accidents with road graders rolling over on top of them, pans rolling over on top of them, being cut in half by servicing a front-end loader. One of the guys had the bucket up in the air and hit the wrong lever, and the bucket wasn't supported, came down, took him out. Shit happens.

As far as the closet... I came out of the closet several years ago. It certainly had a lot to do with a lot of hostilities that I was carrying around for a long time and they called it post stress syndrome. But I did attend some counseling and I also find comfort while I work with Vietnam Vets. But they had the same questions as I had. Why not just let the guys go and do what they're getting paid to do, win the damn war. I had a lot of respect for my first Sergeant and for everybody that was in-country. I had a decision to make about extending and I decided to go home because I felt it was bad for my health record. Before I made that decision, I asked the first Sergeant, "Are we going to head north, are we going to go for the victory, are we going to liberate these people?" And he was honest with me. He doubted that that was ever going to take place. And that if I elected to extend, it would be more of the same thing. It is very possible that I am talking to you today because of the decision I made to leave the country.

My friend Sullivan wrote me after I had left and told me that I was the luckiest son of a bitch in the world because a bunch of our guys got wasted on a dump truck that hit a land mine. He said he got to take the bulldozer out and leveled the village where they planted the mine. The road had been swept but the gooks did the mine after the road was swept. He wound up getting wasted with a sniper. Of course, I had lived for twenty some years with a little bit of a guilty feeling that maybe it would have been different had I stayed. Maybe I was supposed to have been in that dump truck? Through people like Bob Sterling and Eric Kenney and through being in contact, I found I had no reason to feel guilty. I found out that I wouldn't have been there with that particular dump truck anyway. But it was something that I lived with for twenty some years. And talking with guys like Bob and Eric, it was a vehicle to help alleviate that sense of guilt that had stayed with me for many years. You can't say enough about their efforts to bring things full circle. I guess I just wanted to tell somebody. Thank you.

Donald K. Snyder, LCpl., C Company, April 1967–May 1968
Letter received 12-24-94

Donald K. Snyder, lance corporal, Charlie Company, 1st platoon, located at Chu Lai and Hill 10. Honorable discharge 27 Feb. '67 USMCR 6th Engineer Battalion. South Bend, Ind. Reenlist at Chicago, Ill., Feb. 28, 1967

Bill Spadafora, Cpl., C Company, A Company, June 1968–July 1969
Tape received 8-18-94 and 9-21-94

Before I start telling you about some of my experiences in Vietnam, I'd just like to say that some of the stories that you are about to hear, you're probably one of the very few people that I've ever spoken to about some of my experiences in Vietnam. Not too many people, aside from veterans that have been there, appreciate some of the stories, some of the hardships and some of the good times. So, if I seem to hesitate, or I seem to not bring the right words out, I apologize because sometimes I feel a little uncomfortable talking about it. There were some good times and there were some bad times, sometimes it just gets to me, that's all. [pause] So just be a little patient.

I recently saw a movie *Forrest Gump* and if you haven't had the opportunity to see it, it's really a good heart-warming movie. But there is one scene in the movie where Forrest Gump is in the Army in Vietnam and his Company gets ambushed by the VC or NVA. It's funny how the mind works because there's bad experiences that you have, that you kind of push them aside or put them in the back of your mind. When I think about Vietnam, I think about the fellows that I served with and some of the good things that we did and some of the places that I went and some of the things that I saw in the service. I kind of stay away from some of the bad things that happened to me or some of the things that I'd rather not think about. This movie kind of brought out one incident on one of the patrols that I was on, where the CO and myself and seven other Marines and twenty-five South Vietnamese soldiers were in an ambush with between twenty-five to forty NVA soldiers. [pause] The incident just escalated to a firefight that was [pause] unbelievable. Again, I mentioned to you earlier in the tape that it was so dark there that you couldn't see your hand when you walked. I remember laying in the rice paddy and watching the tracers go back and forth between each other and wondering what was going to happen.

Again, I guess I could talk about Vietnam for a long time. I think, all in all, I went there as a boy, and came back as a man, and I don't think that will ever be taken away from me.

I am an Assistant Vice-President with Chemical Bank and I'm sort of like a trouble-shooter. I represent an area that supports the branches. When they get a problem, I go out and resolve that problem. We do investigations, we do hardware maintenance, software, facility work for the branches. That all comes under my division. I worked seventeen years for Nynex before I went over to the Chemical Bank.

I'm married and have five children. Two in college and three in high school. We have a dog, two cats, and we had a rabbit at one time.

I belong to the Marine Corps League now and the First Marine Division. Sometimes I run the house like the Marine Corps. My kids don't like it and sometimes my wife doesn't like it either. She says, "What do you think? You're back in the Marine Corps?" I get ribbed about it at work. I feel proud about it myself, to be truthful. It's a pretty good fraternity. We have a couple of Senior Vice-Presidents in the bank and whenever we're at a function, they'll come right over to me and talk because they're former Marines, also. People will drop their mouths and think that someone at that level would come down to my level and talk to me. There's no level there when one Marine talks to another. The President of Chemical Bank was in the Marine Corps, and one of the Executive Vice-Presidents was in the Third Marines in Vietnam, the same time as I was there. So it's quite interesting when we go to staff meetings.

That's why I joined the Marine Corps League, because at least once a month I can sit down and talk with fellows that have the same experiences, whether they be Vietnam or Korea or wherever. It's pretty nice.

Robert Terry Sperling, LCpl., Service Company, December 1966– December 1967
Manuscript received 1996

When I returned from Vietnam, I spent about two to three weeks at home, and then was assigned to 2nd Shore Party Battalion at Camp Lejeune, the same Battalion that I had left in October of 1966 to go to Vietnam. I was very uncertain. Should I leave the Marine Corps for college? Should I stay in for twenty years? I felt very uncomfortable in civilian life, it was like I was a foreigner there. I did not like Camp Lejeune and I sure did not want to go back to Vietnam! I extended two years to be a Security Guard in Iceland.

There was a variety of posts: some were single, some double, only one required three men, and some were with the Icelandic Police. During the first four months, I stood about every post possible. The posts that I liked best were the two main gates to the NATO Base which contained Iceland's International Airport. My very first time on one of these posts, the Icelandic Policeman on the gate with me, walked over and pushed extremely hard on one of my ribbons and said, "How many Vietnamese did you kill to get this ribbon?" Please understand that this is Iceland and the Police do not carry pistols or nightsticks, therefore they are very big dudes. I explained to him that it was my "Good Conduct Ribbon." They just wanted us to know that they were in charge of the gate because it was their country.

On the gates, our orders said that we were to search every third car, at minimum, for contraband which could be about anything which could be sold on the black-market for profit. Cars passing through the gate were not to have more that one pack of cigarettes which were unopened, a maximum of five cigars, only one camera and that only with a special pass. The only cars we were not allowed to stop were those of about eight high ranking officers, Colonel and above. The rules when stopping a car were to have the driver open all doors, the trunk, the glove compartment, and have every one step out of the car. We loved stopping Officers, Air Force and Navy, never Marine. If they ever gave us a hard time, seeing how we were Corporals, we just said, "Sir, would you like me to have your car searched by the Icelandic Policemen?"

Iceland averages about 30 degrees Fahrenheit in the winter due to the influence of the Gulf Stream. The winds, however, were very fierce! We even had to hang on to ropes on our way to the mess hall on rare occasions! The Northern Lights were very beautiful! It could be very green in the summer. I truly enjoyed Iceland until I became Sergeant, then it was a lot of work and responsibility.

Corporal of the Guard was the most difficult post by far. However, the Sergeant of the Guard was very good duty. Twenty-four hours on, twenty-four hours off. When I made Sergeant of the Guard, I had my own truck and would drive all around the base checking posts and talking to all the Marines.

Another job of the Sergeant of the Guard was to raise the Base Flags at 0800 and lower them at sunset, which was at a very early hour during the winter. It was serious business. People would look out their windows, cars stopped, military personnel on foot would stand and salute. There were three flags: American, Icelandic and N.A.T.O. There were three Marines, three Sailors and three Airmen for each flag respectively, the Sergeant of the Guard and a Marine Bugler.

One morning, a group of Cub Scouts observed our Flag raising. Afterwards, one of the scouts asked why I carried a pistol (M191A1 .45 Caliber). I said, "I hate to say it, but I am supposed to shoot anyone who drops a flag or does anything wrong." Their eyes got pretty big before I told them that I was just kidding.

All three flags were supposed to reach their zeniths simultaneously. However, the Marine Sergeant of the Guard would always enforce an unwritten rule that the American Flag would reach the top of its pole a split-second before the other two flags.

In April of 1968, the 1st Platoon of the Marine Barracks, Iceland, had an inspection by a Two Star Admiral. He never took a single Marine's Rifle. He just smiled and walked by as we snapped our M-1 Rifles to Inspection Arms. After giving the platoon, At Ease, the Lieutenant and the Admiral moved a distance away to talk. The Admiral kept wiping his eyes as he spoke to the Lieutenant.

The Admiral left and the Lieutenant called the platoon to Attention. The Lieutenant explained to us that the Admiral said that we were the most highly decorated Platoon that he had ever had the honor to inspect.

In March of 1993, after twenty-six years of forgetting about Vietnam, I found out about the 1st Reunion and Memorial Service of the 9th Engineer Battalion, 1st Marine Division. When I got out all of my military photos and papers from the attic, I noticed a set of return orders to the United States from Iceland, dated February 19, 1968. These orders were unique in that they give the address of each man's home. I located and called one of the men listed, a Michael Bednar. Mike said that a few friends from Vietnam had kept in touch over the years, but I was the only Marine from Iceland that had contacted him. If I had known who he was, I never would have called him.

Mike spoke fondly of Iceland and talked of trying to extend there since he had an Icelandic girlfriend, but they would not let him. We had a nice talk and were about to hang up when I told Mike that I did not remember him, but his name sounded so very familiar. I just had to ask him, even though it was a slim chance, was he one of three Corporals all up for Sergeant, who went into the Icelandic countryside with the Lt. Col., the Major, 2 SSgts. and about 30–40 members of the Icelandic Search and Rescue Team?

Mike said, "YES! YES! I was the guy with the funny hat, you were the guy with the 35mm Camera. You gave me the negatives of your photos. We have the same pictures. We spent the night in that Sheep Cave!" I then remembered about his unique and terrible experience in Vietnam. How could I have forgotten his story for all these years?

We did not talk about his experience at all, but I mentioned that I had always felt bad about being the one to get Sergeant and move to the other platoon. I felt a little better when he said that he heard I made a good Sergeant. We could not figure out the 3rd Corporal's name, but we remember he had an unusual amount of scrap metal in his leg and he was medically discharged a few months later. We talked a little bit about climbing the glacier.

There is a pause, Mike says, "Bob, about two months ago I joined the 1st Marine Division Association." I immediately butt in and say, "Mike, I joined the 1st Marine Division Association two days ago, because my Battalion Reunion is in conjunction with theirs." Mike replies, "Bob, I joined because I want to shake the hand of Richard Pittman." I butt in again with, "Richard Pittman, the Medal of Honor winner?" I explained to Mike that my in-laws had purchased a coffee table type book for me entitled, *Marines*. Only one Medal of Honor winner was presented in a two page story and a full page picture. Richard Pittman was the only Medal of Honor winner from the Vietnam war that I knew anything about. We talked a little more and in closing we both said "Bless" simultaneously, laughed and hung up. "Bless" is Icelandic for good-bye.

Only the 1st and 3rd Marine Divisions served in Vietnam, the 2nd stayed at Camp Lejeune in North Carolina. The 1st Marine Division had 28 Medal of Honor winners in Vietnam. Only three of them lived.

I was very glad that I could find Mike's experience mentioned in a book, since it is so incredible that perhaps no one would believe it if I alone wrote about it. Mike's article is from the series of books entitled, "The Vietnam Experience," in the book *America Takes Over*. The following is taken from pages 94 and 95:

> It was a harrowing night for Company I as NVA (North Vietnamese Army) soldiers probed to within fifteen to twenty feet of the Marine's perimeter. For Private First Class Michael Bednar, it was hell. Struck by a bullet, he fell near another wounded Marine just as some NVA soldiers emerged from a clump of trees. Both Marines played dead, but the NVA wanted to make sure. After the soldiers plunged a bayonet into the Marine beside Bednar and he groaned, they shot him through the head.
>
> On three separate occasions the soldiers jabbed Bednar several times with bayonets but he refused to cry out. Leaving him for dead, the soldiers snatched Bednar's cigarettes and watch and moved on to other wounded Marines.
>
> The next day, U.S. Artillery struck at NVA emplacements. Helicopters whirred in to remove the wounded, including Private Bednar, who had managed to crawl back to his lines "with his guts hanging out."

How could I have blocked out this man and his experience? I was the one that was chosen Sergeant...

I feel uncomfortable writing about it, but I did not pay much attention to the fall of Saigon in 1975, perhaps because I was in the process of hunting for a job since I was a Senior at Ohio State, nor did I pay attention to the dedication of The Wall in 1982. That was the year Jacque and I were married. I had never joined any veteran's organizations.

I remember sitting outside our home and being very thankful that I had not been killed in Vietnam. Today is Thanksgiving. I have no regrets. I have been bell to bell. I have been the Wolf Cop. I have been a graduate cum laude at Ohio State University in Mathematics Education with a Physics Minor. I have attended two reunions relating to Vietnam. I have known several Marines that were not only in the Marine Corps, but were the Marine Corps: Micheal J. Bednar, Terry Leist, Michael J. Padula, Jack Zelenak, George Cabunac, Casey Jones, Tim Kemp and Drew Martensen.

My oldest son, Scott, and I purchased a model of the Vietnam Veterans Memorial Statue and we put it together. As I tried to explain a little about it, I remember feeling especially good about this. However, I still say that the M-60 rounds should be pointing outward! I am taking a break now since I am so tired due to the radiation and chemotherapy. Jacque says that I need my rest. She is most correct. Good night.

Jim Tagye, PFC, D Company, August 1968–February 1969
Taped interview 8-12-94

I'm a member of the DAV and the VFW. They have a magazine of a lot of little battles that you never heard of which I think is very interesting.

I have kind of separated my life from that war as much as I can until this year. I don't remember a lot about what happened only because this is the first time I've talked to anybody. For twenty-six years I haven't discussed it with any of the 9th Engineers until this Reunion. So I don't have much recollection of what took place until talking to Marty. He's filling me in on a lot of stuff. For twenty-six years I've hid it. I don't broadcast that I'm a Vietnam vet. I don't say anything. I just wanted to hide it, I guess, until this year. I think I need to talk about it. I think I need to get it out. I think there are a lot of these hidden things in your head, like Marty said, that you've got to get out. You don't know what they are, but they got to get out. I think that's one of my problems.

I believe that there are no more POW's. I don't think there have been any POW's since the late 70's. I'd like to know where the proof is and where it's documented at. I don't believe that there are, and maybe that's because I don't want to know. I don't want to believe that there are any more men over there suffering. But I truly believe that there are no more POW's. There haven't been for a long time. If they're there, I hope to God they're not. I don't want to believe it. I don't want to believe it. Because I can just imagine the suffering those guys have been going through.

When I got out of Vietnam, I went back to the place I was working before. I was an apprentice Tool and Die maker. Afterwards, because of being wounded and I can't stand, I had to go back and take an office job. I worked as a sales correspondent, then I didn't like that. Then I went to another company as a sales correspondent and didn't like that. I drove a cab for about a month and didn't like that. I went to work for the fire department in Philadelphia as a dispatcher and didn't like that. I went to the police department as a dispatcher and didn't like that at all.

This time I'm about twenty-five and decided to go back to college and get my degree. I got a degree in Computer Science and a degree in Business Management, and am currently working on a degree in History. I got a job, first as a computer programmer working for the government. Then I went through different steps in the computer field, systems analyst, program analyst, systems programmer, computer specialist. I'm still working for the government. It's been eighteen years. I went to different government agencies. I worked for the VA first, Department of Navy, Department of Defense, and now I work for the Federal Aviation Administration in the computer field. My basic job is to tune and do trouble-shooting on mainframe computers and things of that nature. Right now I'm involved in a project where we are going to upgrade new hardware for the air system that we fly around in today. I'm involved in that. The computers today are rather ancient and we need to upgrade them.

It would be quite an experience to retrace my steps. It would be quite an experience to go back. I'd really love to go back. The temperatures ranged from about 80 to 120 degrees with high humidity. Once they open the country up, we'll be able to go back. I'd like to go back to where I was. I mean, LZ Baldy, what's there now? I think it would be interesting to find out. I'd like to walk along that road again. I'd like to see the bridge that we built. Those kinds of things. Even though I can't walk it, I would do it. I could sit down along the road. Sit down, get up, walk, sit down.. that's all I could do. I think it'd be neat.

**Bill Turner, GSgt., D Company,
May 1966–June 1967,
November 1968–June 1969**
Taped interview 8-13-94

**John Vasarab, PFC, Service Company,
1967–1968**
Letter and taped interview 8-94

Presently, I am working as a transportation construction inspector. Up until this time, I built bridges in the state of Pennsylvania. I pretty much stayed with the engineering field. I am not housebroken yet. I was married once before this one, and that ended because I guess she didn't think I was flexible enough in my ideas about what is important or needed. My new wife of eight years is the greatest thing to happen to me, ever. She is more mature than most women and she also did not have everything handed to her. We can talk and she tried to understand my mood swings. I am not an ogre, but sometimes I can be a Pill.

I do not offer to talk about my class trip to Vietnam because most people don't care that it happened and I do not want some clown to hold it against me and hold me back from a job or something. There are some real jerks out there who don't need much of an excuse to hold you back. I have enough trouble with my weight. I picked up a lot in twenty-eight years and I find that a lot of people can't handle being around fat people like me. I discovered last year that I have high blood sugar and mega blood pressure. This is also part of a heredity weight problem, and even though I am seeing a doctor, it will take time to lose some of this mass. I know I will never be the same as when I went to the Marines, but I will try anyway.

There are times that I just feel like I have dishonored the Corps by getting fat. It's not like I set out to do it on purpose. I want to attend the reunion in August very much and have booked a room already. The only thing that nags me is, will the other men that I was with hold my weight against me and ignore me because of it, or will they just accept me as is. You see that their opinion of me matters because they are the only people that I can say I have respect for. I would feel as though I let them down. The everyday people that I meet, I can handle. Their opinion of me doesn't matter because they don't know what is important in life. If the clothes, fat, or car are, and not the person themselves, then they are not worth knowing as far as I am concerned. This is the only thing that could keep me away from the reunion.

I mentioned that I thought my father would be proud of me for joining the Corps, I was wrong. It didn't make any difference. He was not happy about that or for that matter, my return. No matter what I did the man never appreciated any of my efforts to make him proud to have a son. I never did anything right or good enough for him. I still don't.

Paul E. Virtue, LCpl., D Company, March 1967–March 1968
Letter and diary entries received 1-5-96

P. E. Virtue, 2303059, USMC, 9th Engr. Btn., Chu Lai (March, 1967–March, 1968)

Paul E. Virtue, born January 24, 1947, in Cambridge, N.Y. After enlisting in June, I was activated on September 21, 1966, to Parris Island, SC for basic training. I was appointed as a 1371, Combat Engineer and completed my Engineer schooling on January 26, 1967, at Camp Lejeune, NC. I was deployed with D Company, 9th Engr. Bn., 1st Mar. Div. based at Chu Lai, Vietnam from March, 1967, to March, 1968. I was medivaced to Newport, RI Naval Hospital at that time for injury to my right knee, received at firebase Ca Lu (DMZ) on or about January 7 under hostile enemy fire.

My last duty station, January to August, 1969, was Guantanamo Bay, Cuba, with the minefield maintenance team. During this period of time, I was TDA (Temporary Duty Assignment) to the All-Marine Corps Wrestling Team at Norfolk, Va. in the 160 lb. weight class.

I have been married to Priscilla for fifteen years, and have two children, Paul Jr., age 14 and Patience Joy, 12 years of age. I am the sole proprietor of the family business, established in 1955. I am the family historian and genealogist of 7 lines of this family—Akin, Burch, Cornell, Deuel, Dodds, Morgan and Virtue.

Ed Whitaker, PFC, Headquarters Company, December 1966–October 1967
Taped interview 8-27-94

I have a son that is in the Navy in Norfolk, Virginia. One time when we went to visit him a few years ago, we stopped by the Vietnam Memorial Wall in Washington, D.C. It was of very significant importance to me. They also have moving walls, the portable ones. They had one here in Michigan a year ago last April. It's getting easier to go. The first one I went to, a couple years ago, they even erected a building just like the ones we slept in. I had a neighbor that lived a mile away and then another guy I went to school with, they both lost their lives over there. I always look up their names on the wall.

It really got to me when I walked in that building. Boy, did that bring back memories. It made me think and feel things that I didn't even ... know were there. It's got its importance and value to me. One thing that bothered me ... is that when we came back from Vietnam, it was like, where you been for two years, Ed? It was like we never had our own day. We never got recognized for what we were doing. It took a long time for that to happen. It was a war like no other war.

My son joining the Navy was his decision. I'm thankful he's in there. In fact, he just re-enlisted for the third tour of duty. There was a time when he was in his middle to late teens where he was hard to deal with. I'm very thankful he went into the service. Mainly because he was running with the wrong group and he was going to get into a lot of trouble. He was getting into enough trouble as it was... He's married now and he's got three lovely kids. In fact, he was just home here a month ago and that's the first time he has been home in two years. We live in a real heavily agricultural area and there are not many secure jobs, if there is such a thing.

I came home without a scratch on me, which I am very, very thankful for. It was a real experience and as long as I came home okay, I'm not sorry that I went. I feel real bad for the people that lost their lives because I know it wasn't ... it shouldn't have happened like it did. I feel real bad for that. I know there are people that, even though they came home okay, from a mental standpoint, they may never be the same. I just have a lot of mixed feelings and emotions about all the things that transpired down there in Vietnam.

I never had any children of my own. I got four adopted Korean children. I'm divorced now. I was married for eighteen years. I farmed full time up until the last couple of years. Because of the farm economy, I don't farm as much but I have another farm related business. What I do is I haul farm machinery or farm products. I just work by myself. It's a different company. I run a lot in Michigan, and a little bit in Ohio, Indiana, quite a bit of Illinois and Iowa. Of course, I never remarried or anything else. I just got myself, so sometime I'm gone for a couple of days or something. I'm not real big on that. I'm kind of a homebody. I live in an area here that is small, farming community. My local town is about 3,000 people and I've lived within a mile radius of my present location all my life. I don't stray too far from home.

I went through a lot of therapy when we were going through the marriage crisis and between that and my belief in God, it has really helped me to become a better person. We all have different levels of being able to cope with adversities, but I'm one of these people that just never give up.

Ted Zealley, Lt., D Company,
1 November 1965–June 1967
Letter received 5-17-94

APPENDIX A: "TODAY I WENT TO HEAR DR. GRAHAM"

(*Editor's note:* Lt. James T. O'Kelley, Jr., son of Mr. and Mrs. J. T. O'Kelley, Sr., of 158 Brucemont Circle, Asheville, N.C., wrote the following account of Evangelist Billy Graham's Christmas visit to Da Nang).

Today I went to Da Nang to hear the Rev. Dr. Billy Graham deliver his Christmas message to the troops of the III Marine Amphibious Force. Two planeloads of Marines left from Chu Lai. We arrived three hours before the service and ate a free lunch at Hill 137 USO.

After lunch, Lt. Darracott and I went over to Da Nang Amphitheater and got seats on the second level. At 1130 the seats were already being filled. I met a Lt. Col. Brown, from FLC, a chaplain whom I talked with at length. He was extremely nice to me and later helped me get a chance to talk with Dr. Graham and Lt. Gen. Walt.

There was a mixed choir of about 100 men from all branches of the services. I also was surprised to see many civilians including women and children. I later learned that many of the men, women and children were missionaries. There were also a couple of dozen Vietnamese. But the majority of people were U.S. Marines.

Even in the amphitheater the war was ever-present — on the hills to our flanks and rear I watched the "Grunts" trudge to take up security positions and occasionally during the service I looked up to see their silhouettes against the misty skyline.

The weather was typical Vietnam — rain, a light drizzle up until Dr. Graham arrived — then the sun shone until he left. This is not symbolism — it actually happened.

Dr. Graham's advance party arrived around 1340. We sang "O Come All Ye Faithful," "Joy to the World," and "God Rest Ye Merry Gentlemen" prior to Dr. Graham's arrival at 1350.

At 1400 the service began with the invocation by Capt. E. V. Lyons, the III MAF chaplain. People were still coming in and the Marines were taking pictures. Gen. Walt read the Christmas Story from Luke and then spoke to us briefly and concluded by introducing Dr. Graham. Gen. Walt said that although this was not the way we usually picture Christmas (without home and family, etc.) it would probably be one of our most meaningful ones. He is probably right.

After Gen. Walt the choir sang an anthem, "Praise Ye the Lord." They did a good job and it looked good to see all services, all ranks and all colors together

---

First published in the *Asheville Citizen-Times*, January 15, 1967. Used by permission of James T. O'Kelley, Jr.

singing. I especially remember a distinguished, graying full bird colonel singing base in the rear of the choir and a robust U.S. Army Negro sergeant major who wore glasses and sang baritone. You could also see berets, insignia patches, and faces of many different people brought together in Christian fellowship in a strange land during a familiar time.

After the choir, Rear Admiral J. W. Kelly, chief of chaplains, Washington, D.C., gave the Christmas prayer. Then George Beverly Shea sang "Go Tell It on the Mountain" and "How Great Thou Art." After Shea, Dr. Graham rose to speak.

As he approached the podium there was a tumultuous click-click of thousands of cameras. Dr. Graham began by saying he was privileged to be with us on Christmas. He said Americans at home knew what a job we had, how we were doing it, and were behind us 100 percent. He said that he'd received 5,000 letters from people who had sons over here wanting him to tell them "Hello." He knew he'd never see them all so he said "hello, everyone!"

Just as Dr. Graham was settling into his sermon, Chaplain Lyons had to interrupt him and asked members of the 3rd AT Bn. to report behind the speakers' platform immediately. As they were coming down Dr. Graham told a joke about a North Carolina boy hunting bears in Canada, "barehanded." Also a joke about the Civil War. After the AT people left, Dr. Graham spoke to us from the text of John 3:16—"For God so loved the world that He gave his only begotten son, that whosoever believeth in him should not perish but have everlasting life." He spoke of the promise and fulfillment of Christ and of the demands of being a Christian. He gave us three ways to find Christ: (1) Acknowledge and repent of our sins, (2) Receive Christ and (3) follow Christ's example. He spoke of the two ways to lose life, (1) physically by death or (2) spiritually while alive. Dr. Graham then asked us all to bow our head and close our eyes and any wishing to accept Christ and begin a new life to raise his hand. I peered and saw many hands raised. Dr. Graham then concluded with a prayer, and thanked us again for letting him come speak to us. He left us with the message "My prayers will be for you."

At the conclusion of the service I met Chaplain Brown at the rear of the platform and he took me up to Dr. Graham. He had a mob around him seeking his autograph. I managed to get to him just as one young Marine gave him a personal check "for his crusade." I gave him my program for his autograph and told him I was from Asheville. He immediately said, "Yes, Yes, very enthusiastically and then started questioning me. He said he had my name and address and was hoping to look me up but his itinerary hadn't carried him to Chu Lai. He took my name, address, and phone number and said he would call my parents and tell them he had seen me.

He also introduced me to another Ashevillian—Tommy Burrell—who it turned out lived five blocks from me. (He was a corpsman with 3rd Marines.) After getting my address and all, Dr. Graham wished me a Merry Christmas and I turned to leave and almost ran over Lt. Gen. Walt! He shook my hand and wished me a Merry Christmas. He talked to me about 10–15 minutes; we parted and returned to the trucks, to air freight and to Chu Lai.

I found this experience especially meaningful to me. It helped me to renew my perspective and outlook on life. It made my Christmas most memorable. I think many men were very impressed by Dr. Graham and his message. It gave them an extra something to carry back into the New Year. I am sure all the 9th Engineers enjoyed and benefited from the trip. Many of the men with us will no doubt remember Dr. Graham for many years to come.

APPENDIX B: FAMILYGRAM

HEADQUARTERS
9th Engineer Battalion, FMF
FPO San Francisco, California 96602

4 April 1967

Dear 9th Engineer Battalion Family:

This is the third in our series of "Familygrams" designed to keep the wives and parents of members of this battalion informed of what is generally taking place over here. Some have received the previous editions but for those whose Marine or Sailor has recently joined us, we warmly welcome you as we did him.

Since our last epistle of December 14, 1966, many things have happened and much progress has been made in meeting our objective. Christmas was observed through church services, a fine dinner, a holiday routine to relax and, in every living area were the expressions of the men's deep feeling for Christmas through unique decorations. The New Year was greeted by a full work day in spite of bad weather.

The monsoons draped its wrath upon the Chu Lai area during January by spilling 22½ inches of rain. The men accepted the misery that accompanies that amount of rain with the resulting mud without complaining. They did a tremendous job of maintaining the main supply roads and bridges in condition to allow a continuous flow of traffic which is vital to both the military effort and the economic life of the Vietnamese people. While the Da Nang area, where our Company "A" is located, didn't receive as much rainfall, there was plenty and they continued to perform at their usual high rate of proficiency doing the same type work as we here at Chu Lai. The battalion enjoys a fine reputation for its "gung ho" attitude and the professionalism of its completed work projects. This is a direct reflection on each and every man in the organization.

On February 6, 1967, Lieutenant Colonel Crispen, the former Battalion Commander, was ordered to duty with the 3rd Marine Division and on that date presented the Battalion Colors to me. I can honestly say that I felt privileged to assume command of the 9th and have dedicated myself to further building on the firm foundation established by my predecessor. I am continually impressed and amazed at the talents and spirit of each man in this battalion.

The constant rain lessened to occasional rain during February, and March brought further improvement which permitted more permanent results in the road building program. Other construction projects such as upgrading bridges, building underground bunkers, water towers, equipment maintenance structures, culverts, artillery gun positions, continued to provide support to the many other combat units in the area. The officers and men work long, hard hours but enjoyed this never ending business of construction. They need only to look around them each day to see the fruits of their labors.

I might point out that no construction project is accomplished by construction men alone. For instance, the Motor Transport Section with their multi-purpose vehicles haul men, materials and equipment to the jobs; the engineer equipment operators prepare the job sites and the motor transport and engineer equipment mechanics keep it all in an operating condition; the communications platoon maintains contact with all jobs through radios and field telephones. After the long hard day's work draws to a close there is a good hot meal and hot water showers for all hands to enjoy, thanks to the cooks and utilities section personnel.

The support rendered by you through letters and packages is an invaluable part of this operation so please continue to send them. As has been pointed out in previous familygrams, if you have an emergency, get in touch with the nearest American Red Cross representative. The Red Cross is the agency used by the Armed Forces to provide official notification so that we can take prompt action to assist in solving the problem.

I'm extremely proud to be associated with every man in this battalion. Its capabilities as an engineer unit leave nothing to be desired. You too can be proud of your man's work here.

Sincerely,
G BABE
Lieutenant Colonel, U.S. Marine Corps
Commanding

APPENDIX C: THE LONGEST BRIDGE

FORCE INFORMATION CENTER
III Marine Amphibious Force
Military Assistance Command, Vietnam
FPO San Francisco 96602

Release no: 4620
CIB
By Sgt. J. S. Addington
song ba ren bridge

Da Nang Press Center
Da Nang, Vietnam
Tel: III MAF 5532

DA NANG, Vietnam, Jan. 6 — What is believed to be the longest bridge ever constructed by Marine Corps engineers was opened today across the Song Ba Ren River, 29 miles south of Da Nang. The 722-foot span is an important link between Da Nang and military units operating at scattered outposts and operating bases south of the Song Ba Ren River.

Members of the 1st Marine Division's 9th Engineer Bn., headquartered at Chu Lai, began construction of the bridge in July. Enemy snipers, monsoon rains and mined roads continually hampered construction efforts.

"The earliest we could begin construction on any morning was around 10 o'clock," explained Marine 1st Lt. Jack Hawkins Jr. (Mobile, Ala.). "To reach the bridge each morning, our minesweeping team had to sweep the road from our compound to the construction site thoroughly."

Hawkins commands the 3rd Platoon of "D" Co., 9th Engineer Bn. During the construction of the bridge his platoon lived in a compound two miles northeast of the bridge with units of the Second Republic of Korea Marine Brigade.

Two members of the platoon were killed and four others seriously wounded during the sweeping operations over the road to the bridge.

"This was our first bridge," said Hawkins, a graduate of Alabama College. "None of my men have ever constructed a bridge before and my own experience was very limited."

The newly constructed bridge sits beside a swaying, sinking hodgepodge bridge originally constructed by the French.

"The old Song Ba Ren bridge is a patchwork job consisting of Army trusses, Marine steel stringers and sinking French concrete foundations," explained Marine Maj. Sven A. Johnson (White Plains, N. Y.), 9th Engineer Bn. operations officer and a graduate of the Columbia School of Engineering.

Approximately 300 yards from the

southern approach to the bridge, there is an abandoned church.

"Most of our sniper fire has come from the church," continued Hawkins.

The young lieutenant was knocked off the bridge a month earlier by sniper fire. Despite minor injuries suffered from the 30-foot fall into rocky shoals, Hawkins stayed on the job at the bridge to supervise the completion of the project.

"For several weeks snipers were opening up on my engineers at least every other day," continued Hawkins. "The men would exchange their building tools for a rifle and return fire."

As Hawkins spoke, a mortar barrage was hitting enemy positions a few hundred yards away from the bridge. Some of his Marines were using a surveyor's scope to watch enemy activity as Marine jets dropped explosives on Viet Cong and North Vietnamese Army positions.

"Building in the middle of 'Indian country' gave us some unique problems," continued Hawkins.

The initial problem was getting materials for the project. The bridge required over 100 forty-foot steel stringers, 178 wood pilings, over 20,000 four-by-eights and over 380,000 two-by-sixes.

The first two loads of materials arrived from Chu Lai.

"The materials were here and we had the blueprints," said Marine Cpl. Richard C. Hoffman (Chicago, Ill). "It was a little shaky at first, but we were all learning as we built and now we're ready to build another bridge anywhere, anytime."

After the arrival of the first two loads of materials, plans were revised and the source of supply was shifted to Da Nang.

"They were waiting for our first convoy from Da Nang," said Hawkins. "About five miles north of the bridge they ambushed the convoy and really went after trucks loaded with bridge materials."

During October and November heavy monsoon rains hampered construction efforts.

"To seat the pilings, we had to place our pile-driver on a barge sitting in the middle of the river," continued Hawkins. "We didn't have a power boat so the men would swim out to the pile-driver and physically pull the piles out to the barge."

As the rains continued, the task became more dangerous. During the height of the rains, the river was 12 feet higher than normal. Fighting against deadlines set because of the dangerous, deteriorating condition of the old Song Ba Ren bridge, the men continued to work despite the adverse weather.

"The rain completely washed out the road," said Hawkins. "We couldn't get to the bridge but could get to the river a few miles upstream."

To continue work on schedule, Hawkins and his men hired Vietnamese sampans and rowed downriver to their bridge.

In early November, the men were seating the last of the pilings. The rain had just stopped. Most of the men were eating lunch and Lance Cpl. Alan Farmer (Montgomery, Ala.) was standing radio watch on the bridge.

"I looked down into the water and saw Miller floating helplessly downstream," related Farmer.

Farmer leaped from the 30-foot bridge into the shallow water and swam to Miller's position. He kept the Marine afloat until the remainder of the platoon floated down the river to save the exhausted Marine.

"These men have all worked together tirelessly," said Hawkins, with obvious pride. "Three of them have been recommended for achievement medals."

The construction of the Song Ba Ren bridge is only one phase of a 9th Engineer Bn. project to upgrade and build almost 50 miles of Vietnam's Highway One from Chu Lai to a point just north of the Song Ba Ren.

The 47-mile stretch includes 24 bridges with a combined length of more than 3,000 feet. Present plans call for a 24-foot travelway of 2 1/2-inch asphalt with 4-foot shoulders on all roads and bridges, bringing the total width to 32 feet.

"The bridges and roads we are constructing are vital to the presence of free world forces in this area," said Marine Lt Col. D. V. Davidson (Osage, Iowa) commanding officer of the 9th Engineer Bn. "In addition to their military necessity, the roads and bridges have a profound effect on the local civilian economy. Without them the economy would collapse."

A traffic count on one stretch of the road totaled 2,200 vehicles. Approximately 40 percent of these were American Military, 40 percent Vietnamese civilian and 20 percent Vietnamese military.

On the southern approach to the Song Ba Ren bridge is a small village. Nestled between the houses are the numerous Armor Personnel Carriers of the 713th South Vietnamese Regt. The villagers and Marines have secured a bond of friendship.

"Just about all the villagers know the Marines by their first names," said Hoffman. "They realize the impact the completion of this bridge will have on their community."

The Viet Cong enemy also realizes the impact of the bridge, of course, and will surely try to damage it at least enough to disrupt it as an effective link in communications. However, Hawkins and the other Marine engineers are confident the 713th Vietnamese Regt. which will continue to be charged with its security, will be more determined and successful in defending it than the VC will be in destroying it. After all, Hawkins reasons, the Vietnamese regulars have defended the old Song Ba Ren bridge against repeated VC attempts to destroy the aging structure.

Early this year, more than 20 sampans of North Vietnamese soldiers floated to the bridge in a suicidal attempt to destroy the span. The government troops routed the NVA elements, badly mauling the would-be bridge wreckers. For its heroic action, the 713th was awarded an American unit citation by U.S. infantry elements operating in the area.

"As long as the 713th Regt. is responsible for the security of 'our' bridge," said Hawkins, "we're not going to worry about having to rebuild it."

The bridge has already been used on numerous occasions as a helicopter landing zone for medical evacuation helicopters.

"When Vietnamese soldiers or civilians are wounded or injured, they bring their casualties to the bridge," said Hoffman. "We call in a medevac chopper from LZ Baldy (a U.S. Army position five miles south of the bridge) and the chopper sets down on the bridge to pick up the casualties."

With more than 12,500 man-hours of work expended on the bridge project, there have been no serious accidents. The only injuries have been due to enemy action.

With the bridge completed, the 3rd Platoon will begin construction of a 30-foot observation tower to be used by the bridge security element.

"It's hard to believe just how good we felt after six months of work on the bridge," concluded Hoffman, "and finally being able to walk across the Song Ba Ren on 'our' bridge."

GLOSSARY

AK47. Standard 7.62mm communist assault rifle of NVA.

Amtrac. Marine tracked armored personnel carrier, troops loaded through rear ramp door.

An Hoa. The ancient French fortress that comprised the westernmost logistical base of the Marines. Thirty miles southwest of Da Nang.

AO. Area of Operations.

Arty. Artillery.

ARVN. Army of the Republic of Vietnam (South Vietnam). The term was commonly used to refer to both the individual soldiers and the South Vietnamese army itself. It was pronounced to rhyme with "Marvin."

AWOL. Absent without leave.

Basecamp. A unit's home base.

Basic School. The school attended by all Marine officers once they are commissioned.

Bn. Battalion.

Bush. Any place outside a base where contact with the enemy is a real prospect.

C4. Plastic explosive.

C-130. A large cargo aircraft. Hercules.

CAP. Combined action platoon; joint American Marine/South Vietnamese militia units set up to protect specific villages.

CG. Commanding General.

CG, FMFPac. Commanding General, Fleet Marine Force, Pacific.

Charlie. Slang for "the enemy."

Checkpoint. The exact positions on a topographical map that a Marine patrol must intersect and radio in to headquarters.

Chicom. Chinese Communist (usually refers to enemy hand grenade).

Chinook. CH-47 transport helicopter.

Claymore. Directional, command-detonated, antipersonnel mine.

CLDC-COC. Chu Lai Defense Command — Combat Operations Center.

Comm. Slang for communications.

Concertina. Large rolls of barbed wire used in this configuration.

Corpsman. A medical corpsman is an enlisted sailor who serves with Marines and takes care of their medical needs.

CP. Command post.

C rations, or **C-rats**, or **C's** or **rats**. Combat field meals packed in metal cans.

Da Nang. The giant Marine base and

seaport on the China Sea, thirty miles north of An Hoa at the inception of Highway One.

DI. Marine drill instructors who train boots to be effective Marines.

Dike. A built-up wall with a footpath above a surrounding rice field. Dikes are roads for the rice farmer.

DMZ. Demilitarized Zone. The zone centered on the Ben Hai River and separated North and South Vietnam during the war.

Deuce-and-a-half. A heavy transport truck used for carrying men and supplies.

E-tool. Entrenching tool, military term for a collapsible shovel.

EM club. Enlisted men's club.

Embark. To load aboard.

FAG. 1st Field Artillery Group.

.50 caliber. The standard U.S. heavy machine gun.

Firefight. An engagement of small units employing mainly rifle fire and small arms.

Flak jacket. Properly known as "body armor, upper torso," these were the armored vests worn by U.S. troops.

FO. Forward observer.

.45 caliber. The standard U.S. automatic pistol in Vietnam.

Four holer. Field toilet facility.

Frags. Slang for fragmentation grenades.

G-2. Intelligence division of a Marine divisional staff.

Gook. Derisive, common American nickname for the Vietnamese.

Grunt. Popular nickname for the Marine combat infantryman.

Gunnery Sergeant. This is both a rank, pay grade E-7, and a position, that of the operations NCO of a rifle company. Commonly called "gunny."

H&S Co. Headquarters and Service Company.

Hootch. Any small building; specifically, the straw huts of the peasants.

Huey. Nickname for the UH-1D helicopter.

I Corp Tactical Zone. The northern five provinces of South Vietnam, called "Marineland" by some. I Corp stretched 225 miles from the Demilitarized Zone to the boundary with Binh Dinh province and II Corp Tactical Zone.

Illumination. Night artillery fire used to illuminate an area using a phosphorus filament suspended by parachute.

ISO. Information Services Officer.

ITR. Infantry training regiment. Where all enlisted Marines received advanced infantry skills after they finished recruit training or boot camp.

In-country. To be in Vietnam.

K-bar. A sheath knife.

KIA. Killed in action.

LAAW. U.S. Light Antitank Assault Weapon. A one-shot, throw away weapon used mostly in Vietnam against bunkers.

Land mine. Various types were constructed by the VC, especially utilizing undetonated U.S. bombs.

LST. Landing ship tank. Flat-bottomed naval vessel that could land tanks and other equipment directly across a beach.

GLOSSARY

LZ. Landing zone. Any place where helicopters were called upon to land.

M-14. The standard Marine rifle in Vietnam until early 1967 when it was replaced by the M16.

M-16. The standard rifle in Vietnam from early 1967.

M-26 Fragmentation Hand Grenade. Hand-thrown bomb, which weighs approximately one pound, and contains an explosive charge in a body that shatters into small fragments.

M60 machine gun. Standard U.S. 7.62-mm machine gun.

M79. U.S. shoulder-fired 40-mm grenade launcher.

MACV. Military Assistance Command, Vietnam.

MAG. Marine Aircraft Group.

Medevac. Medical evacuation. Often, but not always, in Vietnam by helicopter.

MIA. Missing in action.

Mike mike. Phonetic pronunciation of mm, i.e., millimeter.

MOS. Military occupational specialty.

NCO. Noncommissioned officer.

NVA. North Vietnamese Army. More properly called the Peoples Army of Vietnam. NVA, like ARVN, its counter part in the south, was popularly used to refer to individual soldiers as well as the army itself.

'Nam. Nickname for Vietnam.

OCS. Officer Candidate School. The commissioning school for Marine officers located at Quantico, Virginia.

Ontos. Tracked vehicle that fired six 106mm recoilless rifles.

OOD. Officer of the Day.

Op. Operation.

Paddy. The rectangular rice fields bordered by dikes and footpaths.

PC. Personnel carrier. A small truck.

PF. Popular Forces.

Phantom. F-4 fighter jet.

Point. Lead Marine in a rifle squad on patrol.

POW. Prisoner of War.

Punji pit. Pit filled with sharpened stakes, placed in camouflaged position on or near trails.

PX. Post exchange. Place where sundry items, tobacco, soap, and the like can be purchased.

Quad fifty truck. 6 × 6 truck with four .50 caliber machine guns mounted on a turntable.

Quantico, Virginia. Training ground for nearly all Marine officers.

R & P Inspection. Rifle & Pistol inspection.

R and R. Rest and recuperation. During Vietnam, it was the only escape from the war afforded the field troops. It lasted five days.

ROKMC. Republic of [South] Korea [pronounced "rock"] Marine Corps.

Rough Riders. The name given the Marine vehicular supply convoys in Vietnam.

RVN. Republic of Vietnam.

S-1. Personnel officer.

S-2. Intelligence section or officer.

S-3. Operations officer.

S-4. Logistics officer.

SA. Small arms fire.

Seabees. Nickname for U.S. Navy construction battalions.

Short. Said of a soldier whose tour in Vietnam is almost over.

Six-by. Two-and-a-half ton or five-ton truck that has six drive wheels.

60 millimeter. Mortar used by both NVA and U.S.

TAD. Tour of Additional Duty.

TAOR. Tactical area of responsibility.

Tet. The Vietnamese lunar new year. Commonly used to refer to the offensive launched by North Vietnam during that holiday in 1968.

3/5. 3rd Battalion, 5th Marine Regiment.

Tiger beer/33 beer. Vietnamese beers.

TKS. 1st Tank Battalion.

Tracer. A bullet with a phosphorous coating designed to burn and provide a visual indication of a bullet's trajectory.

UA. Unauthorized absence.

USA. United States Army.

USAF. United States Air Force.

USMC. United States Marine Corp.

USN. United States Navy.

Utilities. The Marine field uniform. In the army, the same uniform is called "fatigues."

VC. Viet Cong. Communist guerillas.

VCS. Viet Cong suspect.

Ville. Village.

WIA. Wounded in action.

Web-gear. Canvas suspenders and belt used to carry the infantryman's gear.

World, the. Anyplace but Vietnam.

White phosphorus. A very hot incendiary round fired by several types of weapons.

XO. Executive officer. Second in command of a unit.

BIBLIOGRAPHY

The bulk of the material for this book came from several hundred pages of audiotape transcripts, original letters and manuscripts sent at my request by the Engineers of the 9th Engineer Battalion, 1st Marine Division. The following works were also consulted or quoted:

Del Vecchio, John. *The 13th Valley*. New York: Bantam, 1982.

1st Marine Division in Vietnam. New York: M. W. Lads, 1967.

Henderson, Charles. *Marine Sniper*. New York: Berkley, 1986.

Karnow, Stanley. *Vietnam, A History*. New York: Viking, 1983.

Lehrack, Otto J. *No Shining Armor*. Lawrence: University Press of Kansas, 1992.

Moore, Harold G., and Joseph L. Galloway. *We Were Soldiers Once ... and Young*. New York: Random House, 1992.

9th Engineer Battalion, 1st Marine Division (Reinforced), Fleet Marine Force. Command Chronology, 1 June 1966 to 31 December 1966, 1 March 1967 to 31 March 1970 (published monthly; declassified). Fleet Post Office, San Francisco, Calif.

Santoli, Al. *Everything We Had*. New York: Ballantine, 1981.

Summers, Harry G., Jr., *On Strategy: A Critical Analysis of the Vietnam War*. Novato, California: Presidio, 1982.

INDEX

A Shau Valley 94, 101, 103, 104, 107, 108
Abrams, General Creighton 91
Allen, Pete 43, 79, 81, 86
Allon, Peter 3, 93, 129, 164, 176, 191
Althouse, Brian 3, 12, 15, 101, 106, 108, 112, 113, 121, 127, 130, 139, 143, 166, 191
An Tan 44, 45, 47, 57, 64, 68, 77, 78, 94
Austin, Captain 41

Babe, Lt. Colonel 81, 217
Ballard, George E. 3, 8, 145, 147–149, 152, 155, 157, 192
Bastogne 101, 104, 107
Bednar, Michael 208
Binh Son 44, 54, 65, 68
Blumenkrantz, Captain 66
Brooks, Thomas 185
Broomes, John 51
Brown, Fred 51
Brown, Martin L. 3, 12, 16, 17, 25, 116, 122–124, 126, 128, 134, 167, 182, 192
Bryant, Robert 185

Ca Lu 65, 85, 87, 88, 89, 91, 162
Calley, Lt. William 100, 127, 155
Camerow, Jim 77
Camp Carroll 100
Camp Eagle 108
Carras, Thomas P. 3, 25, 153, 157, 158, 159, 168, 193
Carter, Jimmy 174
Casper, Edward L. 3, 14, 22, 83, 84, 99, 164, 175, 193
Chapman, Skip 10
Chappelle, Dickie 49, 52, 64
Chavarie, Norman 135, 151, 188
Clifford, Clark 91
Collier, Jerry L. "Doc" 97, 98, 186
Corson, Terry 187
Coward, Frank 53
Crispin, Lt. Colonel 41, 43, 57
Curtis, Colonel 43

Da Nang 42, 43, 46, 50, 51, 52, 57, 58, 59, 65, 69, 70, 75, 79, 81, 85, 88, 93, 94, 95, 96, 97, 110, 115, 125, 145, 157, 158, 159
Daly, Mike 3, 10, 22, 81, 82, 87, 93, 99, 125, 193
Daniels, MGy Sgt. 41, 78
Dedovitch, John 54, 77
deGaulle, President 27
Dines, Jeffery 185
Diridoni, Can 3, 11, 15, 23, 94, 96, 100, 101–105, 107, 108, 125, 130, 144, 165, 178, 194
DMZ 64, 85
Duc Pho 68, 76
Duncan, Corpsman Kurt 120, 124, 187
Durant, Forbis 187

Eads, John 185
Erdalator 103, 125

5th Marines 78
Floyd, Major Wayne 43
Fording, Sgt. 64
Frank, Jim 62
Friddle, SSgt. Kenneth C. 48, 185

Goins, Robert F. 3, 8, 34, 171, 196
Graham, Dr. Billy 52, 57, 58, 59, 215

Hai Van Pass 97
Handley, Robert 3, 11, 15, 23, 94, 101, 105, 107, 113, 115, 126, 138, 165, 178, 196
Hansen, Wayne 3, 109, 112, 121, 128, 131, 135, 196
Harriman, Averell 107
Hayes, Walter 3, 13, 19, 27, 31, 37, 45, 55, 61, 71, 161, 171, 197
Hedlund, Peter "Swede" 98, 186
Hedren, Tippi 56
Hill 63 65, 109, 135, 162
Hillard, J.L. 51
Hitsman, Jim 83
Hocart, Captain Bill 40
Hoi An 107

Hope, Bob 49, 51, 58, 87, 130, 131, 154
Howell, Larry P. 3, 9, 50, 51, 161, 171, 198
Hue 91, 94, 98, 99, 101, 108

Ia Drang 7

Jackson, Bobby 185
Johnson, President Lyndon 7, 61, 83, 91, 107, 180
Johnson, W.O. Steve 40
Jones, Aaron 185
Jung, William C. 3, 143, 146, 149, 159, 199

Kehoe, Michael J. 62, 185
Kempner, Marion L. 43
Kendle, Randy 139
Kennedy, Bobby 105, 107
Kenney, Eric 1, 3, 23, 165, 177, 200
Kent State University 155
Khe Sanh 83, 87
King, Charles 3, 11, 23, 89, 96, 107, 176, 201
King, Martin Luther 91, 105
Kissinger, Henry 143, 155, 165
Knowlton, Cpl. Bill 49, 65
Kono, Sgt. 41
Kozak, Paul 3, 87, 119, 123, 201
Krulak, Lt. General 64

Laird, Melvin 133
Lanning, David 188
Laos 42, 101
Lavigne, Joseph 186
Leach, Steven 188
Lehrack, Otto 1
Lelansky, Gy Sgt. 41, 48
Le Vesque, Steven 188
Lifset, Major 81
Litwin, Mike 44
Livingston, William 187
Lund, Terry 189

Mabe, Carl 187
McBain, Diane 56
McCan, Rick 84
McGinnis, Wayne 3, 21, 27, 30, 36, 40, 44, 51, 62, 76, 201
McNamara, Robert 75, 91, 100, 180
McNeese, Alon 98, 101, 109
Marble Mountain 65
Massey, Jim 77
Mehaffey, Keith 151, 188
Minh, Ho Chi 143
Mizerak, Lt. 41
Molkentine, Randy W. 138, 188
Molossi, Robert 92, 186
Moore, James 186
Mundy, General Carl 10
My Lai 143, 155

Newman, Charles 188
Nichols, Dave 3, 11, 24, 94, 99, 105, 107, 109, 111, 113, 120, 126, 127, 130, 166, 178, 201
Nixon, Richard 107, 119, 133, 143, 155, 165, 168
Norris, Linza 185

O'Kelley, Jim 3, 9, 13, 21, 39, 41, 43, 45, 47, 54, 57, 59, 63, 64, 65, 67, 71, 76, 77, 79, 81, 83, 85, 162, 201, 215
Operation Pineapple Jungle 87
Operation Rolling Thunder 7
Ortega, Rick 77, 83

Paige, Major Fred 44, 47, 75, 81, 82
Patterson, William 186
Payne, David 77
Perez, Mawny 77
Phu Bai 76, 94, 96, 98, 99, 105, 108, 111, 127
Pierson, Leroy 186
Polyasko, Captain Jerry 54
Powers, Martin 188

Quang Nai 45
Quang Ngai 43, 49, 55

Rainer, Ron 3, 10, 14, 22, 25, 65, 72, 84, 164, 174, 202
Raley, Edwin J. 3, 143, 146, 149, 151, 152, 203
Rathburn, Ted 43, 64
Raye, Martha 49, 50, 51, 52, 55
Ricks, Clyde 3, 12, 25, 147, 150, 151, 152, 156, 158, 167, 182, 203
Rizzo, Reno 115
Roberge, Lawrence Stephen 3, 9, 21, 29, 36, 39, 42, 47, 53, 56, 63, 67, 75, 77, 83, 162, 173, 203
ROKMC 42, 49, 55, 68, 72
Ross, Alan 189

Sablan, Ignacio 186
Savare, Howard L. 83, 100, 187
Schaefer, Robert A. 3, 204
Schaeffer, Arlon Glenn 124, 188
Scheuter, Fred H. 3, 9, 20, 35, 42, 46, 56, 161, 172, 204
Schultz, Elroy 98, 101
Shickel, Sgt. 73
Simmons, James 186
Simonetti, Raymond Joseph 3, 9, 20, 29, 35, 38, 42, 46, 51, 161, 172, 204
Snyder, Donald K. 3, 14, 22, 206
Song Tra Bong River 43, 49
Spadafora, Bill 3, 12, 16, 24, 109–111, 112, 113–115, 122, 126, 131, 133, 135–138, 139, 140, 166, 180, 206
Sperling, Robert Terry 1, 3, 10, 22, 59, 69, 72, 77, 78, 80, 85, 90, 163, 175, 207

Sprague, Steven 83
Stevens, Howard 186
Stuart, John 44
Sullivan, Stephen 187

Tagye, Jim 3, 12, 16, 17, 25, 115, 122–125, 127, 128, 132, 134, 167, 180, 210
Tam Ky 45, 57, 64, 65, 72, 78, 94, 121, 131, 135, 152, 158
Taylor, Ralph 188
Tet 98, 105
Thang Binh 79, 82
Thigpen, Billy T. 77
Tich Tay 68, 76
Trinh, Nguyen Duy 61, 83
Turner, Bill 3, 52, 53, 211

Vasarab, John 3, 11, 15, 23, 67, 70, 72, 77, 78, 81, 85, 88, 90, 177, 211
Virtue, Paul E. 3, 14, 89, 94, 164, 212

Wallick, Bill 83
Watts, Richard 188
Wayne, John 11, 12, 51
Weinstein, Don 62
Welch, Steven Martin 151, 188
Westmoreland, General 7, 61, 83, 91
Wheeler, General Earle 91
Whitaker, Ed 3, 10, 13, 22, 58, 64, 66, 69, 78, 80, 82, 163, 174, 212
Wilkins, William 187
Winn, Richard J. 77
Wood, Fred 83

Yarbrough, George 121, 187
Yates, Charles 187

Zealley, Ted 3, 7, 19, 29, 32, 38, 40, 41, 43, 45, 48, 49, 55, 57, 61, 75, 161, 213

www.ingramcontent.com/pod-product-compliance
Ingram Content Group UK Ltd.
Pitfield, Milton Keynes, MK11 3LW, UK
UKHW050531150426
5217IPUK00026B/1893